CMS Design Using PHP jQuery

Build and improve your in-house PHP CMS by enhancing it with jQuery

Kae Verens

BIRMINGHAM - MUMBAI

CMS Design Using PHP and jQuery

First published: December 2010

Production Reference: 1031210

Published by Packt Publishing Ltd.
32 Lincoln Road
Olton
Birmingham, B27 6PA, UK.

ISBN 978-1-849512-52-7

www.packtpub.com

Cover Image by Asher Wishkerman (a.wishkerman@mpic.de)

Credits

Author

Kae Verens

Reviewers

Tim Nolte

Paul Zabin

Acquisition Editor

Chaitanya Apte

Development Editor

Chaitanya Apte

Technical Editors

Pooja Pande

Aaron Rosario

Indexer

Hemangini Bari

Editorial Team Leader

Aanchal Kumar

Project Team Leader

Ashwin Shetty

Project Coordinators

Zainab Bagasrawala

Poorvi Nair

Proofreader

Lynda Sliwoski

Production Coordinator

Kruthika Bangera

Cover Work

Kruthika Bangera

About the Author

Kae Verens lives in Monaghan, Ireland with his wife Bronwyn and their two kids Jareth and Boann. He has been programming professionally for more than half his life.

Kae started writing in JavaScript in the nineties and started working on server-side languages a few years later. After writing CGI in C and Perl, Kae switched to PHP in 2000, and has worked with it since.

Kae worked for almost ten years with Irish web development company Webworks before branching out to form his own company KV Sites (`http://kvsites.ie/`) a small company which provides CMS and custom software solutions, as well as design, e-mail, and customer support.

Kae wrote the Packt book *jQuery 1.3 with PHP*, which has since become a part of his company's in-house training. Outside of programming, Kae is currently planning a book on budget clavichord design and building, and is the author of the online instructional book *Kae's Guide to Contact Juggling*, available here: `http://tinyurl.com/kae-cj-book`.

Kae is currently the secretary of the Irish PHP Users' Group, `http://php.ie/`, is the owner of the Irish web development company kvsites.ie, `http://kvsites.ie/`, and is the author of popular web-based file manager KFM, `http://kfm.verens.com/`.

This is Kae's second book for Packt, having written *jQuery 1.3 with PHP* in 2009.

In his spare time, Kae plays the guitar and piano, likes to occasionally dust the skateboard off and mess around on it, and is studying Genbukan Ninjutsu.

Acknowledgement

I'd like to thank Packt again, for the great job the reviewers did reining in my ramblings, for their patience when real life intruded and I wasn't always communicative, and for their advice when the book threatened to go on for a few more hundred pages and we had to cut out a few of the planned chapters. Overall, I think we did a good job, and I look forward to seeing what other programmers think of it.

Everything in this book was inspired by having to do it for paying customers. When I started building the CMS this book is based on, it was years ago and the other available OS solutions were simply not what our customers wanted; this allowed me the rare chance to build a CMS all the way up from the beginning, and to overcome each of the hurdles that this presents. I've learned a lot on the way, and I hope you, as readers, can benefit from what I've learned.

My family has had to suffer me being absent for hours every week as I ignored them to concentrate on writing this, so I must thank Bronwyn and my kids Jareth and Boann for their patience!

And I'd like to thank all the reviewers of the previous book—hopefully this one will get as good a reception!

About the Reviewers

Tim Nolte has been involved in web development since 1996. His first website was for Davisco Foods International as a high school student at the Minnesota New Country School in Le Sueur, MN. He has many other interests including music, science fiction, and the outdoors. Tim now lives in the Grand Rapid, Michigan area with his wife and daughter.

Tim began his early web development using a simple text editor. He later moved on to using Dreamweaver and expanding his web development using PHP. Over the years he has had the opportunity to be the developer of many non-profit and business websites. He went on to do web application development in the wireless telecommunications industry at iPCS Wireless, Inc. Today Tim has taken a similar role at Ericsson Services, Inc. where he has expanded his skills and serves customers around the globe.

Recently, Tim has had the opportunity to work with a marketing firm to redesign their website using ExpressionEngine and jQuery, as well as give a hand with the rebuilding of Haiti through the development of the Starfish Haiti website.

In addition to Tim's professional career, he has been able to use his time and talents at Daybreak (www.daybreak.tv). He has volunteered for the role of Online Manager at Daybreak for the past three years, where he continues to help Daybreak with their online presence.

I thank my wife for her support during the time of reviewing this book.

Paul Zabin wrote his first BASIC program back in 1977 and has been hooked ever since. Paul's favorite development platform is a combination jQuery, PHP, and MySQL, which he uses to build Google Gadgets, show off his wife's fine art photography, and to learn the true meaning of a JavaScript closure. Paul contributes back to the development community by publishing Google Spreadsheet templates that track stock portfolios, and occasionally posts articles on LinkedIn on how to get XML stock market data from "the cloud".

Paul lives in Berkeley, California, with his very patient wife Jenna, where they tend to a rare cactus garden. When not programming or watering the plants, he can be found at the local farmers market or newly discovered coffee shop. Paul can be contacted through his public profile at `http://www.linkedin.com/in/ajaxdeveloper/`.

www.PacktPub.com

Support files, eBooks, discount offers and more

You might want to visit www.PacktPub.com for support files and downloads related to your book.

Did you know that Packt offers eBook versions of every book published, with PDF and ePub files available? You can upgrade to the eBook version at www.PacktPub.com and as a print book customer, you are entitled to a discount on the eBook copy. Get in touch with us at service@packtpub.com for more details.

At www.PacktPub.com, you can also read a collection of free technical articles, sign up for a range of free newsletters, and receive exclusive discounts and offers on Packt books and eBooks.

http://PacktLib.PacktPub.com

Do you need instant solutions to your IT questions? PacktLib is Packt's online digital book library. Here, you can access, read, and search across Packt's entire library of books.

Why Subscribe?

- Fully searchable across every book published by Packt
- Copy and paste, print, and bookmark content
- On demand and accessible via web browser

Free Access for Packt account holders

If you have an account with Packt at www.PacktPub.com, you can use this to access PacktLib today and view nine entirely free books. Simply use your login credentials for immediate access.

Table of Contents

Preface	**1**
Chapter 1: CMS Core Design	**7**
The CMS's private and public areas	**8**
The front-end	8
The admin area	10
Plugins	**11**
Files and databases	**12**
Directory structure	12
Database structure	14
The configuration file	15
Hello World	**16**
Setup	16
Front controller	20
Reading page data from the database	23
Summary	**32**
Chapter 2: User Management	**33**
Types of users	**33**
Roles	**34**
Database tables	**36**
Admin area login page	**38**
Logging in	**47**
Logging out	**53**
Forgotten passwords	**55**
User management	**60**
Deleting a user	63
Creating or editing a user	64
Summary	**67**

Chapter 3: Page Management – Part One	**69**
How pages work in a CMS	**69**
Listing pages in the admin area	**70**
Hierarchical viewing of pages	73
Moving and rearranging pages	77
Administration of pages	**78**
Filling the parent selectbox asynchronously	87
Summary	**89**
Chapter 4: Page Management – Part Two	**91**
Dates	**91**
Saving the page	**94**
Creating new top-level pages	**98**
Creating new sub-pages	100
Deleting pages	**101**
Rich-text editing using CKeditor	**103**
File management using KFM	107
Summary	**113**
Chapter 5: Design Templates – Part One	**115**
How do themes and templates work?	**115**
File layout of a theme	118
Setting up Smarty	120
Front-end navigation menu	126
Summary	**132**
Chapter 6: Design Templates – Part Two	**133**
Adding jQuery to the menu	**133**
Preparing the Filament Group Menu	134
Integrating the menu	137
Choosing a theme in the administration area	141
Choosing a page template in the administration area	147
Running Smarty on page content	150
Summary	**152**
Chapter 7: Plugins	**153**
What are plugins?	**153**
Events in the CMS	154
Page types	155
Admin sections	155
Page admin form additions	155
Example plugin configuration	**156**
Enabling plugins	**158**

Handling upgrades and database tables 163
Custom admin area menu 166
Adding an event to the CMS 173
Adding tabs to the page admin 179
Summary 185

Chapter 8: Forms Plugin **187**
How it will work 187
The plugin config 188
Page types in the admin 190
Adding custom content forms to the page admin 194
Defining the form fields 200
Showing the form on the front-end 206
Handling the submission of the form 211
Sending by e-mail 214
Saving in the database 215
Exporting saved data 217
Summary 219

Chapter 9: Image Gallery Plugin **221**
Plugin configuration 222
Page Admin tabs 223
Initial settings 224
Uploading the Images 226
Handling the uploads 228
Adding a kfmget mod_rewrite rule 229
Deleting images 230
Front-end gallery display 232
Settings tab 235
Grid-based gallery 239
Summary 243

Chapter 10: Panels and Widgets – Part One **245**
Creating the panel plugin 245
Registering a panel 248
The panel admin area 251
Showing panels 252
Creating the content snippet plugin 255
Adding widgets to panels 256
Showing widgets 257
Dragging widgets into panels 258
Saving panel contents 261

Showing panels on the front-end	**264**
Summary	**266**
Chapter 11: Panels and Widgets – Part Two	**267**
Widget forms	**267**
Saving the snippet content	274
Renaming widgets	276
Widget header visibility	277
Disabling widgets	279
Disabling a panel	280
Deleting a panel	282
Panel page visibility – admin area code	283
Panel page visibility – front-end code	289
Widget page visibility	289
Summary	**291**
Chapter 12: Building an Installer	**293**
Installing a virtual machine	**294**
Installing VirtualBox	294
Installing the virtual machine	295
Installing the CMS in the VM	300
Creating the installer application	**302**
Core system changes	302
The installer	303
Checking for missing features	**304**
Adding the configuration details	**309**
Summary	**315**
Index	**317**

Preface

PHP and jQuery are two of the most famous open source frameworks used for web development. This book will explain how to leverage their power by building a core CMS which can be used for most projects without needing to be written, and how to add custom plugins that can then be tailored to the individual project.

This book walks you through the creation of a CMS core, including basic page creation and user management, followed by a plugin architecture, and example plugins. Using the methods described in this book, you will find that you can create distinctly different websites and web projects using one codebase, web design templates, and custom-written plugins for any site-specific differences. Example code and explanation is provided for the entire project.

This book describes how to use PHP, MySQL, and jQuery to build an entire CMS from the ground up, complete with plugin architecture, user management, template-driven site design, and an installer. Each chapter walks you through the problems and solutions to various aspects of CMS design, with example code and explanation provided for the chosen solutions. A plugin architecture is explained and built, which allows you to enhance your own CMS by adding site-specific code that doesn't involve "hacking" the core CMS.

By the end of this book, you will have developed a full CMS which can be used to create a large variety of different site designs and capabilities.

What this book covers

Chapter 1, *CMS Core Design*, discusses how a content management system works, and the various ways to administrate it, followed by code which allows a page to be retrieved from a database based on the URL requested.

Chapter 2, User Management, expands on the CMS to build an administration area, with user authentication, and finish with a user management system, including forgotten password management, and captchas.

Chapter 3, Page Management – Part One, discusses how pages are managed in a CMS, and will build the first half of a page management system in the administration area.

Chapter 4, Page Management – Part Two, finishes off the page management system in this chapter, with code for rich-text editing, and file management.

Chapter 5, Design Templates – Part One, focuses on the front-end of the site by discussing how Smarty works. We will start building a templates engine for providing cdesign to the front-end, and a simple navigation menu.

Chapter 6, Design Templates – Part Two, improves on the navigation menu we started in the previous chapter by adding some jQuery to it, and will finish up the templating engine.

Chapter 7, Plugins, discusses how plugins work, and we will demonstrate this by building a plugin to handle page comments.

Chapter 8, Forms Plugin, improves on the plugin architecture by building a forms plugin. The improvements allow entirely new page types to be created using plugins.

Chapter 9, Image Gallery Plugin, an image gallery plugin is created, showing how to manage the uploading and management of images.

Chapter 10, Panels and Widgets – Part One, describes how panels and widgets work. These allow for extremely flexible templates to be created, where non-technical administrators can "design" their own page layouts.

Chapter 11, Panels and Widgets – Part Two, finishes up the panels system by creating a Content Snippet widget, allowing HTML sections to be placed almost anywhere on a page, and even select what pages they appear on.

Chapter 12, Building an Installer, shows how an installer can be created, using virtual machines to help test the installer.

What you need for this book
- PHP 5.2
- jQuery 1.4
- jQuery-UI 1.8.

Most of the code will work exactly in Windows or Mac, but to match perfectly what I've done, I recommend using Linux. In this book, I used Fedora 13 for the creation of the CMS, and CentOS 5.2 for testing in *Chapter 12, Building an Installer*.

Who this book is for

If you want to see jQuery in action with PHP and MySQL code, in the context of a real application, this is the book for you. This book is written for developers who have written multiple scripts or websites, and want to know how to combine them all into one package that can be used to simplify future scripts and sites. The book is aimed at people who understand the basics of PHP and jQuery, and want to know how they can be used effectively to create a large project that is user-friendly and flexible.

Conventions

In this book, you will find a number of styles of text that distinguish between different kinds of information. Here are some examples of these styles, and an explanation of their meaning.

Code words in text are shown as follows: " Create a directory /ww.skins in the CMS webroot."

A block of code is set as follows:

```
<servlet>
    <servlet-name>I18n Servlet</servlet-name>
    <servlet-class>com.liferay.portal.servlet.I18nServlet</servlet
class>
    <load-on-startup>2</load-on-startup>
</servlet>
```

When we wish to draw your attention to a particular part of a code block, the relevant lines or items are set in bold:

```
<portlet>
    <portlet-name>104</portlet-name>
    <icon>/html/icons/update_manager.png</icon>
    <struts-path>update_manager</struts-path>
    <control-panel-entry-category>server</control-panel-entry-
      category>
    <control-panel-entry-weight>4.0</control-panel-entry-weight>
    <control-panel-entry-class> com.liferay.portlet.admin.
```

Any command-line input or output is written as follows:

```
[root@ryuk ~]# yum install VirtualBox
```

New terms and **important words** are shown in bold. Words that you see on the screen, in menus or dialog boxes for example, appear in the text like this: "When we click on the **Users** link in the menu, what we want to see is a list of the existing users".

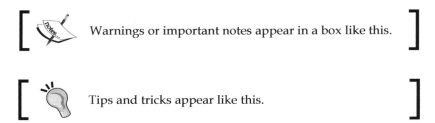

Warnings or important notes appear in a box like this.

Tips and tricks appear like this.

Reader feedback

Feedback from our readers is always welcome. Let us know what you think about this book—what you liked or may have disliked. Reader feedback is important for us to develop titles that you really get the most out of.

To send us general feedback, simply send an e-mail to feedback@packtpub.com, and mention the book title via the subject of your message.

If there is a book that you need and would like to see us publish, please send us a note in the **SUGGEST A TITLE** form on www.packtpub.com or e-mail suggest@packtpub.com.

If there is a topic that you have expertise in and you are interested in either writing or contributing to a book on, see our author guide on www.packtpub.com/authors.

Customer support

Now that you are the proud owner of a Packt book, we have a number of things to help you to get the most from your purchase.

Downloading the example code for this book

You can download the example code files for all Packt books you have purchased from your account at http://www.PacktPub.com. If you purchased this book elsewhere, you can visit http://www.PacktPub.com/support and register to have the files e-mailed directly to you.

Errata

Although we have taken every care to ensure the accuracy of our content, mistakes do happen. If you find a mistake in one of our books—maybe a mistake in the text or the code—we would be grateful if you would report this to us. By doing so, you can save other readers from frustration and help us improve subsequent versions of this book. If you find any errata, please report them by visiting http://www.packtpub. com/support, selecting your book, clicking on the **errata submission form** link, and entering the details of your errata. Once your errata are verified, your submission will be accepted and the errata will be uploaded on our website, or added to any list of existing errata, under the Errata section of that title. Any existing errata can be viewed by selecting your title from http://www.packtpub.com/support.

Piracy

Piracy of copyright material on the Internet is an ongoing problem across all media. At Packt, we take the protection of our copyright and licenses very seriously. If you come across any illegal copies of our works, in any form, on the Internet, please provide us with the location address or website name immediately so that we can pursue a remedy.

Please contact us at copyright@packtpub.com with a link to the suspected pirated material.

We appreciate your help in protecting our authors, and our ability to bring you valuable content.

Questions

You can contact us at questions@packtpub.com if you are having a problem with any aspect of the book, and we will do our best to address it.

1
CMS Core Design

This chapter is an overview of how a CMS is put together.

In the chapter we will discuss topics such as:

- How a CMS's publicly visible part (the "front-end") works
- Various ways that the administration part (the "admin area") can be created
- Discussion of files and database layout
- Overview of how plugins work

We will also build enough of the basics that we can view a "hello world" page, and detect missing pages as well.

This chapter will focus more on discussion than on practical examples, although we'll build a simple practical example at the end.

The "core" of a CMS is its architecture. Just as the motherboard of a computer is its most important component, without which the CPU, screen, RAM, and other parts cannot come together, the CMS core is the "backbone" of the CMS. It's what connects the database, browser interactions, and plugins together.

In this chapter, we will describe the various parts of that core, and over the next few chapters we will build up that core until we have a stable piece of software, upon which we can then start developing extensions (plugins).

If you don't want to type out the code to test it, you can download an archive of the completed project from the Packt website at `http://www.packtpub.com/support`.

This book's CMS is based on a previously written one called **WebME (Website Management Engine)**, which has many more plugins written for it than are described in this book—you can download that version of the project here: `https://code.google.com/p/webworks-webme/`.

The CMS's private and public areas

A CMS consists of the management area (admin area), and the publicly visible area (front-end).

The front-end

One very interesting difference between CMS and non-CMS sites is their treatment of a "web page".

In a non-CMS website, when you request a certain URL from the web server, the web server sees if the requested file exists, and if it does, it returns it. Very simple.

This is because there is a very clear definition of what is a web page, and that is tied explicitly to the URL. `http://example.com/page1.html` and `http://example.com/page2.html` are two distinct web pages, and they correspond to the files `page1.html` and `page2.html` in the websites document root.

In a CMS, the definition might be a bit blurred. Imagine you are in a news section of the site at `http://example.com/news`, and this shows an overview of all news snippets on the website. This might be defined as a page.

Now let's say you "filter" the news. Let's say there are 60 news items, and only 20 are shown on the `/news` page. To view the next 20, you might go to `/news?page=2`.

Is that a different page? In a non-CMS site, certainly it would be, but in a database-backed CMS, the definition of a page can be a little more blurred.

In a CMS, the URLs `/news` and `/news?page=2` may not correspond exactly to two files on the server.

Because a CMS is database-backed, it is not necessary to have a separate physical source file for every page. For example, there is no need to have a `/news` file at all if the content of that page can be served through the root `/index.php` file instead.

When we create a new page in the administration area, there is a choice for the engine to either write a physical file that it corresponds to, or simply save it in the database.

A CMS should only be able to write to files that are in the public webspace under the strictest circumstances.

Instead of creating web pages as files, it is better to use a "controller" to read from a database, based on what the URL was. This reduces the need for the CMS to have write-permissions for the publicly visible part of the site, therefore increasing security.

There is a popular programming pattern called **MVC (Model-View-Controller)**, which is very similar in principle to what a CMS of this type does.

In MVC, a "controller" is sent a request. This request is then parsed by the controller, and any required "model" is initialized and run with any provided data. When the model is finished, the returned data is passed through a "view" to render it in some fashion, which is then returned to the requester.

The CMS version of this is: The website is sent a HTTP request. This request is parsed by the CMS engine, and any required plugins are initialized and run with the HTTP parameters. Then the plugins are finished, they return their results to the CMS, which then renders the results using an HTML template, and sends the result of that back to the browser.

And a real-life example: The CMS is asked for `/news?page=2`. The CMS realizes `/news` uses the "news" plugin and starts that up, passing it the "page=2" parameter. The plugin grabs the information it needs from the database and sends its result back to the CMS. The CMS then creates HTML by passing it all through the template, and sends that back to the browser.

This, in a nutshell, is exactly how the public side (the front-end) of our CMS will work.

So, to rewrite this as an actual process, here is what a CMS does when it receives a request from a browser:

1. The web server sends the request to the CMS.
2. The CMS breaks the request down into its components—the requested page and any parameters.
3. The page is retrieved from the database or a cache.
4. If the page uses any plugins, then those plugins are run, passing them the page content and the request parameters.
5. The resulting data is then rendered into an HTML page through the template.
6. The browser is then sent the HTML.

This will need to be expanded on in order to develop an actual working demonstration. In the final part of this chapter, we will demonstrate the receiving of a request, retrieval of the page from the database, and sending that page to the browser. This will be expanded further in later chapters when we discuss templates and plugins.

The admin area

There are a number of ways that administration of the CMS's database can be done:

1. Pages could be edited "in-place". This means that the admin would log into the public side of the site, and be presented with an only slightly different view than the normal reader. This would allow the admin to add or edit pages, all from the front-end.

2. Administration can be done from an entirely separate domain (`admin.example.com`, for example), to allow the administration to be isolated from the public site.

3. Administration can be done from a directory within the site, protected such that only logged-in users with the right privileges can enter any of the pages.

4. The site can be administrated from a dedicated external program, such as a program running on the desktop of the administrator.

The method most popular CMSs opt for is to administrate the site from a protected directory in the application (option **3** in the previous list).

The choice of which method you use is a personal one. There is no single standard that states you must do it in any particular way. I opt for choice 3 because in my opinion, it has a number of advantages over the others:

1. Upgrading and installing the front-end and admin area are both done as part of one single software upgrade/installation. In options **2** and **4**, the admin area is totally separate from the front-end, and upgrades will need to be coordinated.

2. Keeping the admin area separate from the front-end allows you to have a navigation structure or page layout which is not dependent on the front-end template's design. Option **1** suffers if the template is constrained in any way.

3. Because the admin area is within the directory structure of the site itself, it is accessible from anywhere that the website itself is accessible. This means that you can administrate your website from anywhere that you have Internet access.

In this book, we will discuss how a CMS is built with the administration kept in a directory on the site.

For consistency, even though it is possible to write multiple administrative methods, such as administration remotely through an RPC API as well as locally with the directory-based administration area, it makes sense to concentrate on a single method. This allows you to develop new features quicker, as you don't need to write administrative functions twice or more, and it also removes problems where a change in an API might be corrected in one place but not another.

Plugins

Plugins are the real power behind how a CMS does its thing. Because every site is different, it is not practical to write a single monolithic CMS which would handle absolutely everything, and the administration area of any site using such a CMS would be daunting—you would have extremely complex editing areas for even the most simple sites, to cater for all possible use cases.

Instead, the way we handle differences between sites is by using a very simple core, and extending this with plugins.

The plugins handle anything that the core doesn't handle, and add their own administration forms.

We will discuss how plugins work later on, but for now, let's just take a quick overview.

There are a number of types of plugins that a site can use. The most visible are those which change a page's "type".

A "default" or "normal" page type is one where you enter some text in the admin area, and that is displayed exactly as entered, on the front-end.

An example of how this might be changed with a plugin is if you have a "gallery" plugin, where you choose a directory of images in the admin area, and those images are displayed nicely on the front-end.

In this case, the admin area should look very different from the front end.

How this case is handled in the admin area is that you open up the gallery page, the CMS sees that the page type is "gallery" and knows that the gallery plugin has an admin form which can be used for this page (some plugins don't), and so that form is displayed instead of the normal page form.

On the front-end, similarly, the CMS sees that the page requested is a "gallery" type page, and the gallery plugin has a handler for showing page data a certain way, and so instead of simply printing the normal body text, the CMS asks the plugin what to do and does that instead (which then displays a nice gallery of images).

A less obvious plugin might be something like a logger. In this case, the log plugin would have a number of "triggers", each of which runs a function in the log plugin's included files. For example, the `onstart` trigger might take a note of the start time of the page load, and the `onfinish` trigger might then record data such as how long it took to load the page (on the server-side), how much memory was used, how large the page's HTML was, and so on.

Another word for **trigger** is **event**. The words are interchangeable. An event is a well-established word in JavaScript. It is equivalent to the idea of triggers in database terminology. I chose to use the word trigger in this book, but they are essentially the same.

With this in mind, we know that the 6-point page load flow that we looked at in the *The front-end* section is simplistic—in truth, it's full of little trigger-checks to see when or if plugins should be called.

Files and databases

In this section, we will discuss how the CMS files and database tables should be laid out and named.

Directory structure

Earlier in the chapter, I gave an example URL for a news page, `http://example.com/news`. One thing to note about this is that there is no "dot" in it. The non-CMS examples all ended in `.html`, but there's no "**.whatever**" in this one.

One reason this is very good is that it is human-readable. Saying *"www dot my site dot com slash news slash the space book"* is a lot easier than saying something like *"www dot my site dot com slash index dot p h p question-mark page equals 437"*.

It's also useful, in that if you decide to change your site in a few years to use a totally different CMS or even programming language, it's easier to reconcile `/news` on the old system with `/news` on the new one than to reconcile `/index.php?id=437` with `/default.asp?pageid=437`—especially if there are external sites that link to the old page URL.

In the CMS we are building, we have two file reference types:

1. References such as `/news` or `/my/page` are references to pages, and will be displayed through the CMS's front controller. They do not exist as actual files on the system, but as entries in the database.

2. Anything with a dot in it is a reference to an actual real file, and will not be passed to the front controller. For example, something like `/f/images/test.jpg` or `/j/the-script.js`.

This is managed by using a web server module called `mod_rewrite` to take all HTTP requests and parse them before they're sent to the PHP engine.

In our CMS, we will keep the admin area in a directory called /ww.admin. The reason for this is that the dot in the directory name indicates to the web server that everything in that directory is to be referenced as an actual file, and not to be passed to the front controller. The "ww" stands for "Webworks WebME", the name of the original CMS that this book's project is based on. You could change this to whatever you want. WordPress' admin area, for example, is at /wp-admin.

If the directory was just called /admin and you had a page in your CMS also called "admin", then this would cause ambiguity that we really don't want.

Similarly, if you have a page called "about-applicationname-3.0", this would cause a problem because the application would believe you are looking for a file.

The simplest solution is to ban all page names that have dots in them, and to ensure that any files specific to your CMS all have dots in them. This keeps the two strictly apart.

Another strategy is to not allow page names which are three characters or less in length. This then allows you to use short names for your own purposes. For example, using "/j/" to hold all your JavaScript files. Single-letter directories can be considered bad-practice, as it can be hard to remember their purpose when there is more than one or two of them, so whether you use /j and /f, or /ww.javascript and /ww.files is up to you.

So, application-specific root directories in the CMS should have a dot in the name, or should be three characters or less in length, so they are easily distinguishable from page names.

The directory structure that I use from the web root is as follows:

```
/                 # web root
/.private         # configuration directory
/ww.admin         # admin area
/ww.cache         # CMS caches
/f                # admin-uploaded file resources
/i                # CMS images
/ww.incs          # CMS function libraries
/j                # CMS JavaScript files
/ww.php_classes   # CMS PHP class files
/ww.plugins       # CMS plugins
/ww.skins         # templates
```

There are only two files kept in the web root. All others are kept in whichever directory makes the most sense for them.

The two files in the web root are:

- `index.php` — this file is the front-end controller. All page requests are passed through this file, and it then loads up libraries, plugins, and so on, as needed.
- `.htaccess` — this file contains the `mod_rewrite` rules that tell the web server how to parse HTTP requests, redirecting through `index.php` (or other controllers, as we'll see later) or directly to the web server, depending on the request.

The reason I chose to use short names for /f, /i, and /j, is historical — up until recently, broadband was not widely available. Every byte counted. Therefore, it made sense to use short names for things whenever possible. It's a very minor optimization. The savings may seem tiny, but when you consider that "smartphones" are becoming popular, and their bandwidth tends to be Edge or 3G, which is much slower than standard broadband, it still makes sense to have a habit of being concise in your directory naming schemes.

Database structure

The database structure of a simple CMS core contains only a few tables.

You need to record information about the pages of the website, and information about users such as administrators.

If any plugins require tables, they will install those tables themselves, but the core of a CMS should only have a few tables.

Here's what we will use for our initial table list:

- pages — this table holds information about each page, such as name, id, creation date, and so on.
- user_accounts — data about users, such as e-mail address, password, and so on.
- groups — the groups that users can be assigned to. The only one that we will absolutely need is "_administrator", but there are uses for this which we'll discuss later.

For optimization purposes, we should try to make as few database queries as possible. This will become obvious when we discuss site navigation in *Chapter 3, Page Management – Part One*, where there are quite a lot of queries needed for complex menus.

Some CMSes record their active plugins and other settings in the database, but it is a waste to use a database to retrieve a setting that is not likely to change very often at all, and yet is needed on every page.

Instead, we will record details of active plugins in the config file.

The configuration file

A **configuration file** (**config file**) is needed so that the CMS knows how to connect to the database, where the site resources are kept, and other little snippets of information needed to "bootstrap" the site.

The config file also keeps track of little bits of information which need to be used on every page, such as what plugins are active, what the site theme is, and other info that is rarely changed (if ever) and yet is referred to a lot.

The config file in our CMS is kept in a directory named /.private, which has a .htaccess file in it preventing the web server from allowing any access to it from a browser.

The reason the directory has a dot at the front, instead of the usual "ww." prefix, is that we don't want people (even developers!) editing anything in it by hand, and files with a dot at the front are usually hidden from normal viewing by FTP clients, terminal views, and so on.

It's really more of a deterrent than anything else, and if you really feel the need to edit it, you can just go right in and do that (if you have access rights, and so on).

There are two ways a configuration file can be written:

- **Parse-able format**. In this form, the configuration file is opened, and any configuration variables are extracted from it by running a script which reads it.
- **Executable format**. In this form, the configuration file is an actual PHP script, and is loaded using include() or require().

Using a parseable file, the CMS will be able to read the file and if there is something wrong with it, will be able to display an error on-screen. It has the disadvantage that it will be re-parsed every time it is loaded, whereas the executable PHP form can be compiled and cached by an engine such as Zend, or any other accelerator you might have installed..

The second form, executable, needs to be written correctly or the engine will break, but it has the advantages that it doesn't need to be parsed every time, if an accelerator is used, and also it allows for alternative configuration settings to be chosen based on arbitrary conditions (for example, setting the theme to a test one if you add `?theme=test` to the URL).

Hello World

We've discussed the basics behind how a CMS's core works. Now let's build a simple example.

We will not bother with the admin area yet. Instead, let's quickly build up a visible example of the front-end.

I'm not going to go very in-depth into how to create a test site—as a developer, you've probably done it many times, so this is just a quick reminder.

Setup

First, create a database. In my example, I will use the name "cmsdb" for the database, with the username "cmsuser" and the password "cmspass".

You can use phpMyAdmin or some other similar tool to create the database. I prefer to do it using the MySQL console itself.

```
mysql> create database cmsdb;
Query OK, 1 row affected (0.00 sec)
mysql> grant all on cmsdb.* to cmsuser@localhost identified by
'cmspass';
Query OK, 0 rows affected (0.00 sec)
mysql> flush privileges;
Query OK, 0 rows affected (0.00 sec)
```

Now, let's set up the web environment.

Create a directory where your CMS will live. In my case, I'm using a Linux machine, and the directory that I'm using is `/home/kae/websites/cms/`. In your case, it could be `/Users/~yourname/httpd/site` or `D:/wwwroot/cms/`, or whatever you end up using. In any case, create the directory. We'll call that directory the "web root" when referencing it in the future.

Add the site to your Apache server's `httpd.conf` file. In my case, I use virtual hosts so that I can have a number of sites on the same machine. I'm naming this one "cms":

```
<VirtualHost *:80>
    ServerName cms
    DocumentRoot /home/kae/websites/cms
</VirtualHost>
```

Restart the web server after adding the domain.

Note that we will be adding to the `httpd.conf` later in this chapter. I prefer to show things in pieces, as it is easier to explain them as they are shown.

And now, make sure that your machine knows how to reach the domain. This is easy if you're using a proper full domain like "myexample.cms.com", but for test sites, I generally use one-word domain names and then tell the machine that the domain is located on the machine itself.

To do this in Linux, simply add the following line to the `/etc/hosts` file on your laptop or desktop machine:

```
127.0.0.1 cms
```

Note that this will only work if the test server is running on the machine you are testing from (for example, I run my test server on my laptop, therefore `127.0.0.1` is correct). If your test server is not the machine you are browsing on, you need to change `127.0.0.1` to whatever the machine's IP address is.

To test this, create an `index.html` file in the web root, and view it in your browser:

```
<html>
  <body>
    <em>it worked<em>
  </body>
</html>
```

And here is how it looks:

If you have all of this done, then it's time to create the Hello World example.

We'll discuss writing an installer in the final chapter. This chapter is more about "bootstrapping" your first CMS. In the meantime, we will do all of this manually.

In your web root, create a directory and call it .private. This directory will hold the config file.

Create the file .private/config.php and add a basic config (tailored to your own settings):

```php
<?php
$DBVARS=array(
   'username'=>'cmsuser',
   'password '=>'cmspass',
   'hostname'=>'localhost',
   'db_name' =>'cmsdb'
);
```

This will be expanded throughout the book as we add new capabilities to the system. For now, we only need database access.

Note that I didn't put a closing ?> in that file. A common problem with PHP (and other server-side web languages) happens if you accidentally output empty space to the browser before you are finished outputting the headers. As we are building a templated CMS, all output should happen right at the end of the PHP script, when we're sure we're done compiling the output.

If you place ?> terminators at the ends of your files, it's easy to accidentally also place invisible break-lines (\n, \r) as well. Removing the ?> removes that problem as well. There is no right or wrong here. PHP is perfectly happy with files that end or don't end with ?>, so it is up to you whether you do so.

We don't want people looking into the .private directory at all, so we will add a file, .private/.htaccess, to deny read-access to everyone:

```
order allow,deny
deny from all
```

Note that in order for .htaccess files to work, you must enable them in your web-server's configuration.

The simplest way to do this is to set AllowOverride to all in your Apache configuration file for the web directory, then restart the server.

An example using my own setup is as follows:

```
<Directory "/home/kae/websites">
    Options All
    AllowOverride All
    Order allow,deny
    Allow from all
</Directory>
```

You can tune this to your own needs by reading the Apache manual online.

After doing this and restarting your web server, you will find that you can load up `http://cms/` but you can't load up `http://cms/.private/config.php`.

Next, let's start on the front controller.

Front controller

If you remember from what we discussed earlier, when a page is requested from the CMS, it will go through the front-end controller, which will figure out what kind of page it is, and render the appropriate HTML to the browser.

Note that although we are using a front controller, we are not using true MVC. True MVC is very strict about the separation of the content, the model, and the view.

This is easy enough to manage in small coding segments, but when combining HTML, JavaScript, PHP, and CSS, it's a lot more tricky.

Throughout the book, we will try to keep the various parts separate, but given the choice between complex or verbose code and simple or short code, we will opt for the simple or short route.

Some CMSes prefer to use URLs such as `http://cms/index.php?page=432`, but that's ugly and unreadable to the casual viewer.

We will do something similar, but disguise it such that the end-user doesn't realize that's basically what's happening.

First off, delete the test `index.html`, and create this file as `index.php`:

```php
<?php
header('Content-type: text/plain');

echo "POST:\n";
var_dump($_POST);

echo "\n\nGET:\n";
var_dump($_GET);
```

That displays any details that are sent to the server through POST or GET:

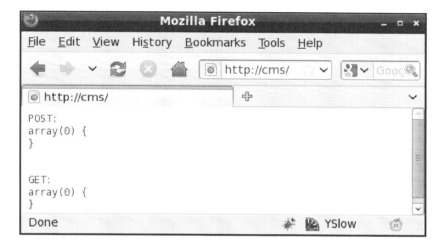

Now, let's do the redirect magic.

Create a `.htaccess` file in the web root:

```
<IfModule mod_deflate.c>
  SetOutputFilter DEFLATE
</IfModule>

php_flag magic_quotes_gpc off

RewriteEngine on
RewriteRule ^([^./]{3}[^.]*)$ /index.php?page=$1 [QSA,L]
```

The `mod_deflate` bit compresses data as it is sent (if `mod_deflate` is installed).

We turn off "magic quotes" if they're enabled. Magic quotes are an old deprecated trick used by early PHP versions to allow HTTP data to be used in strings on the server without needing to properly escape them. This causes more problems than it solves, so it is being removed from later PHP versions.

The rewrite section takes any page name requests which are three or more characters in length and do not contain dots, and redirects those to index.php. The QSA part tells Apache to also forward any query-string parts, and the L tells Apache that if this rule matches, then don't process any more.

You can test that now.

Open your browser and go to http://cms/test, and you should see the following output:

Notice the GET array now has the page name, which we can use in the next section to retrieve data from the database.

And if you put in a dot, you should get a standard **404** message:

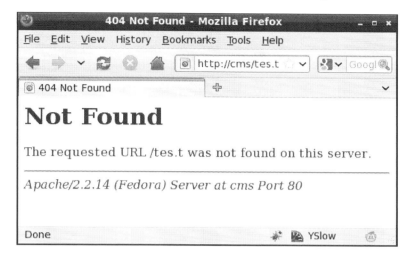

We will discuss proper handling of 404 pages in *Chapter 3, Page Management – Part One*.

Reading page data from the database

Okay—now that we can tell the CMS what page we're looking for, we need to write code that will use that information and retrieve the right data from the database.

First, let's create the "pages" table in the database. Use your MySQL console or phpMyAdmin to run the following:

```
CREATE TABLE `pages` (
  `id` int(11) NOT NULL auto_increment,
  `name` text,
  `body` mediumtext,
  `parent` int(11) default '0',
  `ord` int(11) NOT NULL default '0',
  `cdate` datetime default NULL ,
  `special` bigint(20) default NULL,
  `edate` datetime default NULL,
  `title` text,
  `template` text,
  `type` varchar(64) default NULL,
  `keywords` text,
  `description` text,
  `associated_date` date default NULL,
```

```
    `vars` text,
    PRIMARY KEY   (`id`)
  )  DEFAULT CHARSET=utf8;
```

This is the most important table of the database. The various parts of it are:

Name	Description
id	The ID of the page in the database. Must be unique. This is an internal reference.
name	When a URL http://cms/page_name is called, 'page_name' is what's searched for in the database.
body	This is the main HTML of the page.
parent	In a hierarchical site, this references the 'parent' of the page. For example, in the URL http://cms/deep/page, the 'page' entry's parent field will be equal to the 'deep' entry's ID.
ord	When pages are listed, in what position of the list will this page be shown.
cdate	Date that the page was created on.
special	This is used to indicate various 'special' aspects about a page—such as whether the page is the site's home page, or is a site map, or is a 404 handler, and so on. These are details that are important enough that they should be built into the core instead of as a plugin.
edate	Date that the page was last edited on.
title	This is shown in the browser's window header. When you search online and find pages titled "Untitled Document", it's because the author didn't bother changing this.
template	Which template (of the site skin) should this page use. We'll see how this is used in a later chapter.
type	Type of page is this. For now, we won't use this, but it becomes important once we start using plugins.
keywords	This is used by search engines.
description	Again, used by search engines.
associated_date	Pages sometimes need to have a date associated with them. An example is a news page, where the associated date may not be the created or last-edited date.
vars	This is a 'miscellaneous' field, where plugins that need to add values to the page can add them as a JSON object.

We'll discuss these further throughout the book. For now, we are more concerned with simply installing a single page.

Insert two rows into the database:

```
mysql> insert into pages (name,body,special,type)
  values('Home','<p>Hello World</p>',1,0);
Query OK, 1 row affected (0.00 sec)

mysql> insert into pages (name,body,special,type)
  values('Second Page','<p>A Second Page</p>',0,0);
Query OK, 1 row affected (0.00 sec)
```

For the purposes of this test, we install two pages. The first one, "Home", has its `special` field set to 1, which means "this is the home page". This means that if the website is called without any particular page requested, then this page will be used (in other words, we want `http://cms/` to equate to `http://cms/Home`).

In both cases, we set the `type` field to 0, meaning "normal". When we add plugins later, this field will become important.

There are four files involved in displaying the pages.

- `/index.php`: This is the front-end controller. It receives the request, loads up any required files, and then displays the result.
- `/ww.incs/common.php`: This is a list of common functions for displaying pages. For this demo, all it will do is load `basics.php`.
- `/ww.incs/basics.php`: A list of functions common to all CMS actions. Includes database access and the setting up of basic variables.
- `/ww.php_classes/Page.php`: The `Page` class loads up page data from the database.

The process flow is as follows:

1. `index.php` is called by the `mod_rewrite` script.
2. `index.php` then loads up `common.php` which also loads `basics.php`.
3. `index.php` initializes the page, causing `Page.php` to be loaded.
4. `index.php` then displays the body of the loaded page.

Create this file as `index.php` in the web root:

```php
<?php
// { common variables and functions
include_once('ww.incs/common.php');
$page=isset($_REQUEST['page'])?$_REQUEST['page']:'';
$id=isset($_REQUEST['id'])?(int)$_REQUEST['id']:0;
// }
```

```php
// { get current page id
if(!$id){
  if($page){ // load by name
    $r=Page::getInstanceByName($page);
    if($r && isset($r->id))$id=$r->id;
    unset($r);
  }
  if(!$id){ // else load by special
    $special=1;
    if(!$page){
      $r=Page::getInstanceBySpecial($special);
      if($r && isset($r->id))$id=$r->id;
      unset($r);
    }
  }
}
// }
// { load page data
if($id){
  $PAGEDATA=(isset($r) && $r)? $r : Page::getInstance($id);
}
else{
  echo '404 thing goes here';
  exit;
}
// }

echo $PAGEDATA->body;
```

This is a simplified version of what we'll have later on. Basically, we check to see if the page ID is mentioned in the URL. If not, we load up the page using its name (through the Page object) to figure out the ID.

When we have the page data imported into the $PAGEDATA variable, we simply render it to the screen.

The ww.incs/common.php file is pretty bare at the moment:

```php
<?php
require dirname(__FILE__).'/basics.php';
```

That will include common functions to do with page display. For now, all it does is load up the ww.incs/basics.php file:

```php
<?php
session_start();
```

```php
function __autoload($name) {
  require $name . '.php';
}
function dbInit(){
  if(isset($GLOBALS['db']))return $GLOBALS['db'];
  global $DBVARS;
  $db=new PDO('mysql:host='.$DBVARS['hostname']
    .';dbname='.$DBVARS['db_name'],
    $DBVARS['username'],
    $DBVARS['password']
  );
  $db->query('SET NAMES utf8');
  $db->num_queries=0;
  $GLOBALS['db']=$db;
  return $db;
}
function dbQuery($query){
  $db=dbInit();
  $q=$db->query($query);
  $db->num_queries++;
  return $q;
}
function dbRow($query) {
  $q = dbQuery($query);
  return $q->fetch(PDO::FETCH_ASSOC);
}
define('SCRIPTBASE', $_SERVER['DOCUMENT_ROOT'] . '/');
require SCRIPTBASE . '.private/config.php';
if(!defined('CONFIG_FILE'))
  define('CONFIG_FILE',SCRIPTBASE.'.private/config.php');
set_include_path(SCRIPTBASE.'ww.php_classes'
  .PATH_SEPARATOR.get_include_path());
```

First, we start off a session to record any data which may need to be passed from page to page.

Next, we set an auto-load function so that we can use objects without explicitly needing to require() their files. You can see that in action in the index.php where we used the Page object despite it not being explicitly included.

Next, we have three helper functions for databases. Because connecting to a database takes up precious resources, it is a waste of time to connect to the database upon every single request to the server. And so we connect only when the first database request is called, and cache that connection for the rest of the script.

Next, we define a few constants:

- SCRIPTBASE: This is the directory that the CMS is located in
- CONFIG_FILE: This is the location of the configuration file

There will be a few more constants later when we get to themes and uploadable files.

Finally, we have the ww.php_classes/Page.php class file:

```php
<?php
class Page{
  static $instances        = array();
  static $instancesByName  = array();
  static $instancesBySpecial= array();
  function __construct($v,$byField=0,$fromRow=0,$pvq=0){
    # byField: 0=ID; 1=Name; 3=special
    if (!$byField && is_numeric($v)){ // by ID
      $r=$fromRow?
        $fromRow:
        ($v?
          dbRow("select * from pages where id=$v limit 1"):
          array()
        );
    }
    else if ($byField == 1){ // by name
      $name=strtolower(str_replace('-','_',$v));
      $fname='page_by_name_'.md5($name);
      $r=dbRow("select * from pages where name like '"
        .addslashes($name)."' limit 1");
    }
    else if ($byField == 3 && is_numeric($v)){ // by special
      $fname='page_by_special_'.$v;
      $r=dbRow(
        "select * from pages where special&$v limit 1");
    }
    else return false;
    if(!count($r || !is_array($r))return false;
    if(!isset($r['id']))$r['id']=0;
    if(!isset($r['type']))$r['type']=0;
    if(!isset($r['special']))$r['special']=0;
    if(!isset($r['name']))$r['name']='NO NAME SUPPLIED';
    foreach ($r as $k=>$v) $this->{$k}=$v;
    $this->urlname=$r['name'];
    $this->dbVals=$r;
    self::$instances[$this->id] =& $this;
```

```
    self::$instancesByName[preg_replace(
      '/[^a-z0-9]/','-',strtolower($this->urlname)
    )] =& $this;
    self::$instancesBySpecial[$this->special] =& $this;
    if(!$this->vars)$this->vars='{}';
    $this->vars=json_decode($this->vars);
  }
  function getInstance($id=0,$fromRow=false,$pvq=false){
    if (!is_numeric($id)) return false;
    if (!@array_key_exists($id,self::$instances))
      self::$instances[$id]=new Page($id,0,$fromRow,$pvq);
    return self::$instances[$id];
  }
  function getInstanceByName($name=''){
    $name=strtolower($name);
    $nameIndex=preg_replace('#[^a-z0-9/]#','-',$name);
    if(@array_key_exists($nameIndex,self::$instancesByName))
      return self::$instancesByName[$nameIndex];
    self::$instancesByName[$nameIndex]=new Page($name,1);
    return self::$instancesByName[$nameIndex];
  }
  function getInstanceBySpecial($sp=0){
    if (!is_numeric($sp)) return false;
    if (!@array_key_exists($sp,$instancesBySpecial))
      $instancesBySpecial[$sp]=new Page($sp,3);
    return $instancesBySpecial[$sp];
  }
}
```

This may look complex at first glance, but it's not all that bad.

There are three methods, getInstance, getInstanceByName, and getInstanceBySpecial, each of which finds the requested page using its own method:

- getInstance is used if you know the ID of the page.

- getInstanceByName is used if you know the name of the page. We'll expand this later to include hierarchical names such as "/sub/page/one".

- getInstanceBySpecial is used if there's no particular page requested, but it's a special case. For example, the front page has the value 1. This is recorded as a bit mask, so for example, if a page is both the front page and a sitemap (shown later), then it would be recorded as 3, which is 1 plus 2 (values of Home Page and Sitemap respectively).

With this code in place, you can now load up pages. Here's an example using the page name "Home", as seen in the next screenshot:

Notice that the request uses the lower-case **home** instead of the upper-case "Home". Because MySQL is case-insensitive by default, and humans tend to not care whether something is upper-case or lower-case, it makes sense to allow any case to be used at all in the page name, as seen in the next screenshot:

And in the case that no page name is given at all, the `index.php` file will load up using the special "home page" case:

And finally, in the case that a page simply doesn't exist at all, we are able to trap that, as seen in the next screenshot:

Because we can trap this 404, we can do some interesting things such as show a list of possible matches that the reader can then choose from. This won't be handled in this book, but feel free to either redirect to the root or a search page, or any other solution you want.

Summary

In this chapter, we looked at how a CMS works, and built enough of the basics that we could then view a "Hello World" page, in a few different ways, with 404s trapped as well.

In the next chapter, we will discuss how users and groups work, to allow granular permissions, and we will build a login script, including forgotten password functionality and captchas.

2
User Management

User management is one of the core functions of a CMS—the engine needs to know who is allowed to edit documents, and needs a way to manage those users.

In this chapter, we will discuss the following points:

- Overview of user management
- What "roles" are, and how they work
- Storage of user data in a database
- Creation of a login system
- Using the ReCaptcha tool
- Forgotten-password management
- Create a user-management system

We will cover the basics of role-management, but will not go in-depth into it, as none of the features in the project CMS we are building will require it.

Types of users

As applications evolve from simple scripts to complex systems, developers tend to add code and ideas as they occur and are needed.

In the beginning, when creating simple CMSs, this means that user access is confined to administrator logins, as user logins are not usually necessary for simple systems like news reporting, or image galleries.

So, the developer creates a table of administrators.

Later on, as the system evolves, it becomes necessary to create front-end users, so that people can log in and contribute comments or content, or purchase items with a user-based discount.

Again, because the system is slowly evolving, the developer now adds a table of front-end users.

But things then get complex — what if we want administrators to correspond with commenters, or someone who uses the system as a normal user but is also an admin?

One solution to this is to have one table of users, and a flag which states whether the user is a normal user or an admin.

But then, we have another problem — what if you want some users to be admins, but you want them to have access only to certain parts of the backend area? For example, let's say the user is in charge of uploading news stories — that user needs access to the admin area, but should not have access to, say, the user management areas.

Roles

The solution is not to use flags, but to use "roles" (also called "groups").

A role is a group of permissions which you can assign to a user. I will use the words "role" and "group" interchangeably in the book — they essentially mean the same thing when speaking of user rights.

For example, you might have a role such as "page editor", which includes the following permissions:

- Can create pages
- Can delete pages
- Can edit pages

You might have a user who is allowed to edit pages and also to edit online store products, in which case you need to either have a single group which covers all those permissions, or two groups ("page editor" and "online store editor"), and the user is a member of both.

The latter case, multiple groups, is much easier to manage, and is in fact necessary; as the number of possible combinations of permissions grows exponentially, more roles are created.

Another important question is, where do these role names come from? Does an administrator create them?

It's an interesting question, because the answer is both "yes" and "no".

If in order to create roles, you need to be a member of the "administrator" role, then who creates the "administrator" role? What if the role is deleted?

So we have a case where a role should not be created by an administrator.

On the other hand, we might have an online store, and want to assign a 5% discount to all users who are members of the role "favored customers". Who creates that role? It makes sense that the administrator should be allowed to create as many custom roles as is needed. And it is impossible for a sensible application to be created which predicts all the roles that will be required by a user-defined system.

So, we have a case where a role should be created by an administrator.

In these cases, it is okay if the admin deletes the "favored customers" role, but not if the "administrator" role is deleted.

How do we get around this?

One solution, which we'll use in this book, is to prefix system-generated role names with '_', and to disallow administrators from editing or creating role names that use that scheme.

We will define two starter roles:

- _administrators: This role gives a user permission to enter the admin part of a system
- _superadministrators: This role is a special one, which gives a user total access

We will not build a role management system in this book, because none of the other chapters will require it. We are discussing it here because it is better to prepare for a future need than to stumble across the need and have to rewrite a lot of hardcoded behavior.

Database tables

To record the users in the database, we need to create the `user_accounts` table, and the groups table to record the roles (groups).

First, here is the `user_accounts` table. Enter it using phpMyAdmin, or the console:

```
CREATE TABLE `user_accounts` (
  `id` int(11) UNSIGNED NOT NULL AUTO_INCREMENT ,
  `email` text,
  `password` char(32) DEFAULT NULL,
  `active` tinyint DEFAULT '0',
  `groups` text,
  `activation_key` varchar(32) DEFAULT NULL,
  `extras` text,
  PRIMARY KEY (`id`)
) DEFAULT CHARSET=utf8;
```

Name	Description
id	This is the primary key of the table. It's used when a reference to the user needs to be recorded.
email	You can never tell how large an e-mail address should be, so this is recorded as a text field.
password	This will always by 32 characters long, because it is recorded as an MD5 string.
active	This should be a Boolean (true/false), but there is no Boolean field in MySQL. This field says whether the user is active or disabled. If disabled, then the user cannot log in.
groups	This is a text field, again, because we cannot tell how long it should be. This will contain a JSON-encoded list of group names that the user belongs to.
activation_ key	If the user forgets his/her password, or is registering for the first time, then an activation key will be sent out to the user's e-mail address. This is a random string which we generate using MD5.
extras	When registering a user, it is frequently desired that a list of extra custom fields such as name, address, phone number (and so on) also be recorded. This field will record all of those using JSON. If you prefer, you could call this "usermeta", and adjust your copy of the code accordingly.

Note the usage of JSON for the groups field (or "column", if you prefer that word). Deciding whether to fully normalize a database, or whether to combine some values for the sake of speed, is a decision that often needs to be made.

In this table, I've decided to combine the groups into one field for the sake of speed, as the alternative is to use three table (the `user_accounts` table, the `groups` table, and a linking table), which would be slower than what we have here.

If in the future, it becomes necessary to separate this out into a fully normalized database, a simple upgrade script can be used to do this.

For now, populate the table with one entry for yourself, so we can test a login. Remember that the password needs to be MD5-encoded.

Note that MD5, SHA1, and other hashing functions are all vulnerable to collision-testing. If a hacker was to somehow get a copy of your database, it would be possible to eventually find working passwords for each MD5 or SHA1 hash. Of course, for this to happen, the hacker must first break into your database, in which case you have a bigger problem.

Whether you use SHA1, MD5, bcrypt, scrypt, or any of the other hashing functions is a compromise between your need for security (bcrypt being more secure), or speed (MD5 and SHA1 being fast).

Here's an example insert line:

```
insert into user_accounts
  (email,password,active,groups)
  values(
    'kae@verens.com',
    md5('kae@verens.com|my password'),
    1,
    '["_superadministrators"]'
  )
;
```

Notice that the groups field uses JSON.

If we used a comma-delimited text field, then that would make it impossible to have a group name with a comma in it. The same is true of other character delimiters.

Also, if we used integer primary key references (to the groups table) then it would require a table join, which takes time.

By putting the actual name of the group in the field instead of a reference to an external table row, we are saving time and resources.

The password field is also very important to take note of.

We encrypt the password in the database using MD5. This is so that no one knows any user's password, even the database administrator.

However, simply encrypting the password with MD5 is not enough. For example, the MD5 of the word password is 5f4dcc3b5aa765d61d8327deb882cf99. This may look secure, but when I run a search for that MD5 string in a search engine, I get 28,300 results!

This is because there are vast databases online with the MD5s of all the common passwords.

So, we "salt" the MD5 by adding the user's e-mail address to it, which causes the passwords to be encrypted differently for each user, even if they all use the same password.

This gets around the problem of users using simple passwords that are easily cracked by looking up the MD5. It will not stop a determined hacker who is willing to devote vast resources to the effort, but as I said earlier, if someone has managed to get at the database in the first place, you probably have bigger problems.

Now, let's put this table to use by creating the login form and the login mechanism.

Admin area login page

In *Chapter 1, CMS Core Design*, we discussed a number of different systems used by CMSs to allow administrators to log in. Some have the administrator log in using the same form as a normal user would log in with, some have totally separate domains dedicated to administration, and some even have dedicated desktop programs.

We will use a defined directory within the CMS structure, /ww.admin. This is how CMSs such as Joomla! or WordPress manage administration. In Joomla!, administrators log into /administrator, and in WordPress, administrators log into /wp-admin.

How the administration pages will work is that whenever a page is loaded, it checks first to see if you are logged in as an admin, and if not, you are shown a login page.

So, create the directory ww.admin in your web root, and let's create a page called index.php in that directory:

```php
<?php
require 'admin_libs.php';
echo 'you are logged in!';
```

The file `/ww.admin/admin_libs.php` will be included by every page in the admin area. Create that now:

```php
<?php
require $_SERVER['DOCUMENT_ROOT'].'/ww.incs/basics.php';
function is_admin(){
  if(!isset($_SESSION['userdata']))return false;
  return (
    isset(
      $_SESSION['userdata']['groups']['_administrators']
    ) ||
    isset(
      $_SESSION['userdata']['groups']['_superadministrators']
    )
  );
}
if(!is_admin()){
  require SCRIPTBASE.'ww.admin/login/login.php';
  exit;
}
```

So what happens here is that each time the `admin_libs.php` file is loaded, it checks first that a `userdata` session variable has been created and that it contains either the group `_administrators` or `_superadministrators`. Remember, `_administrators` have access to the admin area, and `_superadministrators` have total access—there is not much of a difference in this book's project, but the difference is important enough that we should "future-proof" the system by using this difference now.

If the function `is_admin()` returns `false`, then the browser is sent a login page, which we'll create next.

Create a directory `/ww.admin/login`, and create the file `login.php` in it:

```html
<html>
 <head>
  <title>Login</title>
  <link rel="stylesheet" type="text/css"
    href="/ww.admin/login/login.css" />
 </head>
 <body>
  <div id="header"></div>
  <div class="tabs">,
   <ul>
     <li><a href="#tab1">Login</a></li>
     <li><a href="#tab2">Forgotten Password</a></li>
```

```
    </ul>
    <div id="tab1">
     <form method="post"
       action="/ww.incs/login.php?redirect=<?php
       echo $_SERVER['PHP_SELF'];
       ?>">
      <table>
       <tr><th>email</th><td>
        <input id="email" name="email" type="email" />
       </td></tr>
       <tr><th>password</th><td>
        <input type="password" name="password" />
       </td></tr>
       <tr><th colspan="2" align="right">
        <input name="action" type="submit"
          value="login" class="login" />
       </th></tr>
      </table>
     </form>
    </div>
    <div id="tab2">
     <form method="post"
       action="/ww.incs/forgotten-password.php?redirect=<?php
       echo $_SERVER['PHP_SELF'];
       ?>">
      <table>
       <tr><th>email</th><td>
        <input id="email" type="text" name="email" />
       </td></tr>
       <tr><th colspan="2" align="right">
        <input name="action" type="submit"
          value="resend my password" class="login" />
       </th></tr>
      </table>
     </form>
    </div>
   </div>
  </body>
</html>
```

A login.css file is referenced in that source. The contents of it are not important to what we're doing, so we won't bother repeating it here. The CSS and images are available to download from Packt's website along with all source code from this project.

There are two forms in there; the first is for logging in, and the second is for reminding the user of the password, if the password has been forgotten.

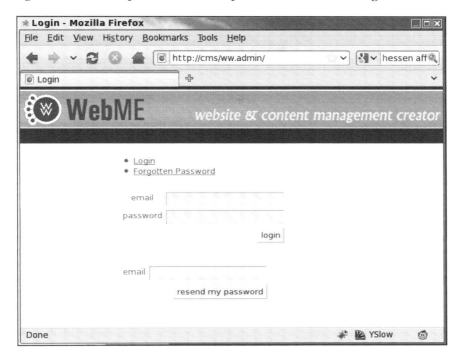

Notice that we ask for the e-mail address of the user, and not a username.

When people choose usernames, if there are a lot of users in the system, it is likely that the username that the person wants in the first place is already taken. For example, I like to log in everywhere as "kae". Unfortunately, in very large systems, that username can be already taken. This would be a bigger problem for people named "James" or "John", and so on.

E-mails, though, are unique. You cannot have two people logged in who have the same e-mail address.

Another reason is that e-mail addresses tend not to be forgotten. People generally have only one or two e-mail addresses that they use. If it's not one, it's the other.

Yet another reason is that if you have forgotten your password, then a reminder service can be used to send a "reset" URL to the registrant's e-mail account.

If you go a very long time without forgetting the password, then it is possible that by the time you need the reminder, you will no longer have access to the e-mail account you used to create the account–you may have changed company, or some other reason.

But, if you're using your e-mail address as the account name, and realize you are about to lose access to it, then the very act of logging in will remind you that you need to change the user account details before you forget the password.

Another thing to note about the HTML is the target of the forms.

We have a single login point, /ww.incs/login.php, which can be used by both administrators and normal users. The redirect parameter is used to tell the server where the browser should be sent after the login is done.

We're not quite done yet with that file. The screen is a little bit bland. We can use our first piece of jQuery to liven it up a bit using tabs.

Change the header by adding these highlighted lines:

```
<title>Login</title>
<script src="http://ajax.googleapis.com/ajax/libs/jquery/1.4.2/
jquery.min.js"></script>
<script src="http://ajax.googleapis.com/ajax/libs/jqueryui/1.8.0/
jquery-ui.min.js"></script>
<link rel="stylesheet" type="text/css" href="http://ajax.
googleapis.com/ajax/libs/jqueryui/1.8.0/themes/south-street/jquery-ui.
css" />
<script src="/ww.admin/login/login.js"></script>
<link rel="stylesheet" type="text/css"
  href="/ww.admin/login/login.css" />
```

The first three highlighted lines load up jQuery and jQuery UI from Google's **Content Delivery Network (CDN)**, and load up a jQuery UI stylesheet as well.

Some people don't like to use Google's CDN, so you may want to download the jQuery and jQuery UI files and link to them on your local server. I've never had a problem using Google's CDN.

Linking to a CDN has some advantages, such as quicker access in cases where the browser is far from the site (the CDN copy may be physically closer to the browser, thus causing less network lag), less bandwidth usage for your own site, and less files to maintain on your own system.

When building a large application, there's a lot of "widget" functionality (tabs, auto completes, sliders, drag/drop, and so on) which may be used in various places. The jQuery UI project provides a lot of these, and is extremely simple to use.

The last line is a link to a local script, which we'll use to set up the tabs. Create the file /ww.admin/login/login.js:

```
$(function(){
  $('.tabs').tabs();
});
```

This small piece of code tells jQuery: "When the page is finished loading, run the function .tabs() against all elements with the class tabs".

 Wrapping a function inside $() is equivalent to running $(document). ready() with the function as a parameter.

After the browser runs that tiny piece of code, the **Login** page now looks like this:

And if the **Forgotten Password** tab is clicked, then it appears as follows:

For a full explanation of how tabs work, see the jQuery UI website—`http://jqueryui.com/demos/tabs/`.

There is one more thing that is needed before the login form is complete.

In order to stop malicious robot programs from trying to log in using brute force to guess the password, and also to stop similar robots from sending out reminder e-mails to you and resetting your password, we will use a "captcha" to verify that whoever is filling in the form is human.

A captcha is a picture of some text. It is obscured slightly by deforming the image or adding static, and so on, so that it is not easy for a robot to decipher it using an optical character recognition program.

Generating captchas is not difficult—there are many scripts online that do it for you. However, if you use a script that you are not constantly tweaking, then it is possible that someone will eventually find a way to decipher the captcha automatically.

A good solution is to use the **reCAPTCHA** library (`http://recaptcha.net/`). This is a well-known captcha program which generates images based on photographs of old books. It also provides alternative audio from old radio shows in case the user cannot see clearly.

Download the latest `recaptcha-php` script from `http://code.google.com/p/` `recaptcha/`—at the time of writing, this is `recaptcha-php-1.10.zip`—and unzip it in `/ww.incs` so you have a directory called `/ww.incs/recaptcha-php-1.10`. If you found a newer one, replace `-1.10` with whatever is appropriate.

You will also need to get an API key. This is a string of characters which identifies you to the reCAPTCHA engine when it's used. Do this by creating a user account at `http://recaptcha.net/`. If you plan on using your CMS on more than one domain, then make sure to tick the **Enable this key on all domains** check-box while registering.

After registering, you will be given a "public key" and a "private key".

We will record the keys in a file named `/ww.incs/recaptcha.php`:

```php
<?php
require SCRIPTBASE
  .'ww.incs/recaptcha-php-1.10/recaptchalib.php';

define('RECAPTCHA_PRIVATE',''); // place private key here
define('RECAPTCHA_PUBLIC','');  // place public key here
```

Replace the second parameters of these lines with your keys We've placed this file in the `/ww.incs/` directory so that it can be accessed by any code that needs it, whether it's in the admin section or the public section. Also, as the file is named `captcha.php` and doesn't mention the version number of the library, installing a new copy of the reCAPTCHA library involves simply unzipping it in the `/ww.incs` directory and changing the given `require` line to match it.

At the top of the `/ww.admin/login/login.php` page, add these highlighted lines:

```php
<?php
  require SCRIPTBASE.'ww.incs/recaptcha.php';
  $captcha=recaptcha_get_html(RECAPTCHA_PUBLIC);
?>
<html>
  <head>
```

And in the login form's table, add this just before the submit button's row:

```html
<tr id="captcha">
  <th>captcha</th>
  <td><?php echo $captcha; ?></td>
</tr>
```

When the given code is rendered, the captcha writes some HTML which imports an external JavaScript file, and if no JavaScript is available to the browser, then it also shows an `iframe` with alternative HTML in it.

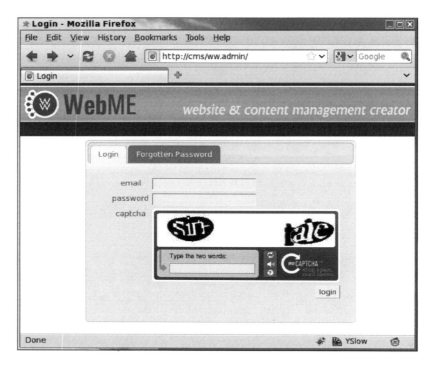

Because we have two forms on the page, we should logically want two captchas as well. Unfortunately, you cannot have two captchas on the same page, as each image will be different (they're never cached), and each new captcha invalidates the old one. So, if you had two, only one of them would work.

So, what we will do is add a little bit of jQuery that moves the captcha whenever a tab is clicked.

To do this, rewrite the `/ww.admin/login/login.js` file completely:

```
$(function(){
  // remove the captcha's script element
  $('#captcha script').remove();
  // set up tabs
  $('.tabs').tabs({
    show:function(event,ui){
      // if the captcha is already here, return
      if($('#captcha',ui.panel).length)return;
      // move the captcha into this panel
```

```
        $('table tr:last',ui.panel).before($('#captcha'));
      }
    });
  });
```

When the page is loaded, the given script runs.

First, it removes the captcha's `<script>` element. Otherwise, when it is moved, the script will run again, breaking the captcha.

Then, we add some code which tells jQuery UI that whenever a tab panel is shown, we want to check it for the captcha row. If the row doesn't exist, then move it from where it is, to the present panel.

The highlighted line handles the moving.

Okay! We are finally finished with the login forms. Now, let's handle the actual login.

Logging in

It is tempting to have a separate login script for the admin and normal users, but this can cause problems in the future if you ever change how logins work.

In the form that we created, we set the action to /ww.incs/login.php, with an added parameter named "redirect".

What's involved with a login is as follows:

- Verify that the submitted captcha is correct (we don't want robots logging in!)
- Verify there is an entry in user_accounts where the submitted e-mail address and password are matched
- If all is well, set a session variable named userdata which holds the user's information (saves looking it up in the database all the time)
- Send the browser to wherever the redirect link pointed it, or to the root of the site if none is provided, or if the provided one is invalid
- If anything goes wrong, still send the browser on to the redirect page, but also give an error message as an added parameter

Some of the code for the login will also be needed for other aspects of logins, such as logouts and forgotten passwords, so we'll start this by creating /ww.incs/login-libs.php:

```php
<?php
require 'basics.php';

$url='/';
$err=0;

function login_redirect($url,$msg='success'){
  if($msg)$url.='?login_msg='.$msg;
  header('Location: '.$url);
  echo '<a href="'.htmlspecialchars($url).'">redirect</a>';
  exit;
}
// set up the redirect
if(isset($_REQUEST['redirect'])){
  $url=preg_replace('/[\?\&].*/','',$_REQUEST['redirect']);
  if($url=='')$url='/';
}
```

All of the login functions will require a redirect after the action, so this creates a function for handling the redirect, and does some simple validation on the requested redirect_url, such as removing any query string parameters.

If the parameters were not removed, it is possible an admin on your CMS might be fooled into going to a link such as http://cms/ww.admin/?delete-all-pages, and after the login, they might be redirected back to that (fake, just an example) URL which would then proceed and delete all pages.

So, we neutralize this problem by removing anything past a ? or &.

Create a file, /ww.incs/login.php, containing the following code:

```php
<?php
require 'login-libs.php';

login_check_is_email_provided();

// check that the password is provided
if(!isset($_REQUEST['password']) || $_REQUEST['password']==''){
  login_redirect($url,'nopassword');
}
login_check_is_captcha_provided();
login_check_is_captcha_valid();
```

```
// check that the email/password combination matches a row in the user
table
$password=md5($_REQUEST['email'].'|'.$_REQUEST['password']);
$r=dbRow('select * from user_accounts where
  email="'.addslashes($_REQUEST['email']).'" and
  password="'.$password.'" and active'
);
if($r==false){
  login_redirect($url,'loginfailed');
}

// success! set the session variable, then redirect
$_SESSION['userdata']=$r;
$groups=json_decode($r['groups']);
$_SESSION['userdata']['groups']=array();
foreach($groups as $g)$_SESSION['userdata']['groups'][$g]=true;
if($r['extras']=='')$r['extras']='[]';
$_SESSION['userdata']['extras']=json_decode($r['extras']);

login_redirect($url);
```

This checks all inputs, sets a session variable if the login is valid, and in all cases
does a redirect to send the browser where it was going. The $_REQUEST super-global
variable is generated by merging the $_POST and $_GET variables.

There are a number of functions referenced in there that are not defined. We define
those in /ww.incs/login-libs.php so they can be reused by the other login scripts
(add the functions to the end of the file):

```
// check that the email address is provided and valid
function login_check_is_email_provided(){
  if(
    !isset($_REQUEST['email']) || $_REQUEST['email']==''
    || !filter_var($_REQUEST['email'], FILTER_VALIDATE_EMAIL)
  ){
    login_redirect($GLOBALS['url'],'noemail');
  }
}

// check that the captcha is provided
function login_check_is_captcha_provided(){
  if(
    !isset($_REQUEST["recaptcha_challenge_field"]) || $_
REQUEST["recaptcha_challenge_field"]==''
    || !isset($_REQUEST["recaptcha_response_field"]) || $_
REQUEST["recaptcha_response_field"]==''
  ){
```

```php
      login_redirect($GLOBALS['url'],'nocaptcha');
    }
  }
  // check that the captcha is valid
  function login_check_is_captcha_valid(){
    require 'recaptcha.php';
    $resp=recaptcha_check_answer(
      RECAPTCHA_PRIVATE,
      $_SERVER["REMOTE_ADDR"],
      $_REQUEST["recaptcha_challenge_field"],
      $_REQUEST["recaptcha_response_field"]
    );
    if(!$resp->is_valid){
      login_redirect($GLOBALS['url'],'invalidcaptcha');
    }
  }
```

You'll also have noticed that the `login_redirect()` function has two parameters; the first is the URL to redirect to, and the second is a text code which designates a message to be shown.

Now let's make use of that message code.

First create a file `/ww.incs/login-codes.php`:

```php
  <?php
  $login_msg_codes=array(
    'success'=>'login successful.',
    'noemail'=>'no email address provided, or the email'
      .' address was invalid.',
    'nopassword'=>'no password provided.',
    'nocaptcha'=>'no captcha provided.',
    'invalidcaptcha'=>'captcha invalid.',
    'loginfailed'=>'login incorrect. if you\'ve forgotten'
      .' your password, please use the Forgotten Password form.',
    'permissiondenied'=>'your user account does not have'
      .' permission for this area.'
  );
```

These correspond to the `$msg` codes in the login script.

I've added two, for those cases where a person has logged in as a normal user but doesn't have access permission for the admin area (or another area where the user doesn't have the required role).

Let's use the codes. Edit the `/ww.admin/login/login.php` file and add the following highlighted lines:

```
    <div id="header"></div>
<?php
if(isset($_REQUEST['login_msg'])){
  require SCRIPTBASE.'ww.incs/login-codes.php';
  $login_msg=(int)$_REQUEST['login_msg'];
  if(isset($login_msg_codes[$login_msg])){
    echo '<script>$(function(){$("<strong>'
      .htmlspecialchars($login_msg_codes[$login_msg])
      .'</strong>").dialog({modal:true});});</script>';
  }
}
?>
    <div class="tabs">
```

We first check that a valid message code was sent, then display it as a modal dialog using jQuery UI's `.dialog` plugin.

A visitor could simply change the URL's `login_msg` value to make the various messages appear, but it would be pointless of them to do that as it would not affect their user status.

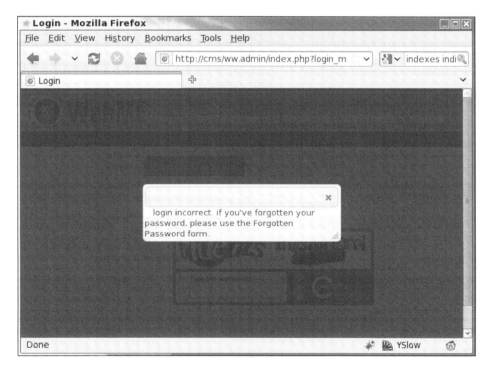

You can change the dialog content so it has some prettier HTML if you wish.

Now, what if a user is logged in, but doesn't have admin rights?

We'll start testing this one by adding a user to the database with no groups:

```
mysql> insert into user_accounts
    (email,password,active,groups)
    values('user@verens.com',
      md5('user@verens.com|userpass'),1,'[]');
Query OK, 1 row affected (0.03 sec)
```

Now, we will change the /ww.admin/admin_libs.php file—remember that it has a function in it called is_admin(). Change that function to this:

```
function is_admin(){
   if(!isset($_SESSION['userdata']))return false;
   if(
     isset($_SESSION['userdata']['groups']['_administrators']) ||
     isset(
     $_SESSION['userdata']['groups']['_superadministrators'])
   )return true;
   if(!isset($_REQUEST['login_msg'])) $_REQUEST['login_
msg']='permissiondenied';
   return false;
}
```

So in this case, we know that the user is logged in, and doesn't have admin rights, so we set the $_REQUEST['login_msg'] to 'permissiondenied' if there is not already another message set.

We avoid overwriting an existing message because that existing message has priority. For example, a logged-in user trying to log in as an admin user would not find the "permission denied" message very useful when the actual problem is that they got the password wrong.

Okay — so now do the login and use your proper admin details, filling in the captcha correctly.

As bland as that appears, this little message means you've successfully written a login script, which verifies your e-mail and password, with a captcha, and verifies that you are either an administrator or superadministrator.

We are now in the admin area properly!

So, what do we need next? We have not written the forgotten password reminder, and we also need to provide a method of logging out.

Let's do the logout first.

Logging out

Logging out is much simpler than logging in. All we need to do is to remove the `userdata` session variable that we created when logging in.

First off, let's edit `/ww.admin/index.php` to add in some design, and the start of the admin menu, including the logout link:

```php
<?php
require 'header.php';
echo 'you are logged in!';
require 'footer.php';
```

The footer will simply close off the HTML of the design, so here's `/ww.admin/footer.php`:

```
    </div>
   </body>
 </html>
```

And here's the header— /ww.admin/header.php:

```php
<?php
header('Content-type: text/html; Charset=utf-8');
require 'admin_libs.php';
?>
<html>
  <head>
    <script src="http://ajax.googleapis.com/ajax/
      libs/jquery/1.4.2/jquery.min.js"></script>
    <script src="http://ajax.googleapis.com/ajax/
      libs/jqueryui/1.8.0/jquery-ui.min.js"></script>
    <link rel="stylesheet" href="/ww.admin/theme/admin.css"
      type="text/css" />
    <link rel="stylesheet" href="http://ajax.googleapis.com/
      ajax/libs/jqueryui/1.8.0/themes/south-street/
      jquery-ui.css" type="text/css" />
  </head>
  <body>
    <div id="header">
      <div id="menu-top">
        <ul>
          <li><a
            href="/ww.incs/logout.php?redirect=/ww.admin/">
            Log Out</a></li>
        </ul>
      </div>
    </div>
    <div id="wrapper">
```

We will be using jQuery and jQuery UI in all parts of the admin area, so they are included by default.

Again, I've linked to a CSS file which I won't go through in this book. You can download it with the rest of the files from Packt.

Here's the admin index page now with the design and **Log Out** link included:

Now, let's create /ww.incs/logout.php:

```php
<?php
$url='/';
session_start();
// set up the redirect
if(isset($_REQUEST['redirect'])){
  $url=preg_replace('/[\?\&].*/','',$_REQUEST['redirect']);
  if($url=='')$url='/';
}
unset($_SESSION['userdata']);
header('Location: '.$url);
echo '<a href="'.htmlspecialchars($url).'">redirect</a>';
```

In this case, it's not necessary to include any libraries (the /ww.incs/basics.php file, for example). All we need to do is unset $_SESSION['userdata'] and redirect the browser. And so, we don't need to include login-libs.php.

Now, let's work on the forgotten password section.

Forgotten passwords

There are many ways that CMSs handle missing passwords. In some cases, a new password is sent out through e-mail, in some cases, a security question lets the site verify that the user is who he or she claims to be, and in some cases, a validation e-mail is sent to verify the requester is the owner of the e-mail address.

In this section, I'll mention a few security concerns. I must add that in most cases, it is very unlikely that they will ever happen. But, as a developer of software, you should be aware of those things that can go wrong and do your best to make sure they don't happen in the first place.

If you give the option of resetting the password when a user fills in their e-mail address in the forgotten password form, there are some problems to beware of:

1. You may have just allowed an anonymous person to invalidate someone's account just because they knew the e-mail address of the valid user. If this is done repeatedly, it can really annoy that user, who may have to use a different password every time they log in.
2. E-mail is insecure. Because it is sent through plain text in most cases (yes, PGP e-mail is possible, but it is rarely used by normal users), you are sending passwords that can be potentially read by the e-mail hosters, or anyone that "taps the line".

If you give the option of changing a password by verifying the identity of the user using a "security question", there are also some problems. Some sites make the user pick from a set list of questions, none of which are secure:

1. It is easy to figure out someone's mother's maiden name. There are many genealogy websites online where that information is readily available.
2. Asking who the user's first teacher was is silly. Personally, I barely remember who I met two years ago; let alone 30 years ago!
3. Asking the name of the user's pet assumes that there is a pet in the first place, and that there is only one pet (I have three cats at the moment). Also, all of your friends probably know that pet's name. My cats are Buffy, Thurston, and Tweedo.
4. Car's license number. Again, there is an assumption. I don't drive, and have never owned a car.

Allowing the user to pick a security question is also silly. In most cases, the question will be obvious. As an example, I was chatting with a friend once about this very problem, and demonstrated it by opening up his Hotmail account—as his security question, he'd written something silly like "wibble", and I guessed correctly that if his security question was as much rubbish as that, then his answer would also be rubbish. I entered "wibble" again and was in.

There is possibly no real correct solution to the problem of verifying someone's identity over the Internet, so it's best to choose the "least worst" of the methods.

I mentioned a third possibility—sending out a validation e-mail. E-mail is a very personal form of identification. It is rare these days that you will find anyone online that doesn't have one, and usually, they've had the same e-mail address for years on end—people get attached to their e-mail addresses. The validation e-mail method involves some simple steps:

1. In the validation e-mail method, the user has forgotten their password, and goes to the forgotten password form and enters their e-mail address.

2. An e-mail is sent to the e-mail address with a link embedded in it. This link has a validation code attached which is recorded in the database.

3. When the user clicks on the link, this verifies the person's identity and logs the person into the site.

4. The verification code is then removed from the database. This way the login links only work one single time.

It's not even necessary that the user reset the password as long as they're happy enough to generate a fresh validation link each time—on some sites I use very infrequently, I tend to have "moved on" to a new password and keep forgetting the password I used for those infrequent visits, so for those sites, I'm always using a validation link to log in!

Anyway—enough musing. Let's create the file /ww.incs/password-reminder.php:

```php
<?php
require 'login-libs.php';

login_check_is_email_provided();

login_check_is_captcha_provided();
login_check_is_captcha_valid();

// check that the email matches a row in the user table
$r=dbRow('select email from user_accounts where
    email="'.addslashes($_REQUEST['email']).'" and active'
);
if($r==false){
    login_redirect($url,'nosuchemail');
}

// success! generate a validation email, then redirect
$validation_code=md5(time().'|'.$r['email']);
$email_domain=preg_replace('/^www\./','',$_SERVER['HTTP_HOST']);
dbQuery('update user_accounts set activation_key="'.$validation_
code.'"
    where email="'.addslashes($r['email']).'"');
```

```
$validation_url='http://'.$_SERVER['HTTP_HOST'].'/ww.incs/forgotten-
password-validate.php?verification_code='.$validation_code.'&email='.$
r['email'].'&redirect_url='.$url;
mail(
    $r['email'],
    "[$email_domain] forgotten password",
    "Hello!\n\nThe forgotten password form at http://".$_SERVER['HTTP_
HOST']."/ was submitted. If you did not do this, you can safely
discard this email.\n\nTo log into your account, please use the link
below, and then reset your password.\n\n$validation_url",
    "From: no-reply@$email_domain\nReply-to: no-reply@$email_domain"
);

login_redirect($url,'validationsent');
```

This script is very similar to the login script, but all references to the `password` field in the database and `$_REQUEST` have been removed, and we add in the validation link generator.

Notice that we have added two message codes. Amend `/ww.incs/login-codes.php` and add them:

```
'permissiondenied'=>'your user account does not have'
    .' permission for this area.',
'nosuchemail'=>'that email address does not exist in the'
    .' user accounts database',
'validationsent'=>'a validation message has been sent to'
    .' your email address. please check your email.'
);
```

The e-mail's content, when it arrives, will look something like this:

```
Hello!

The forgotten password form at http://cms/ was submitted. If you did
not do this, you can safely discard this email.

To log into your account, please use the link below, and then reset
your password.

http://cms/ww.incs/forgotten-password-verification.php?verification_co
de=97e5daf0d6b96c1945ed450d29c63a42&email=kae@verens.com &redirect_
url=/ww.admin/index.php
```

You should feel free to amend the validation code generator to write whatever message you want into it.

Now, we need to write the validation script, /ww.incs/forgotten-password-verification.php:

```php
<?php
require 'login-libs.php';
login_check_is_email_provided();
// check that a verification code was provided
if( !isset($_REQUEST['verification_code'])
  || $_REQUEST['verification_code']==''
){
  login_redirect($url,'novalidation');
}
// check that the email/verification code combination matches a row in
the user table
$password=md5($_REQUEST['email'].'|'.$_REQUEST['password']);
$r=dbRow('select * from user_accounts where
  email="'.addslashes($_REQUEST['email']).'" and
  verification_code="'.$_REQUEST['verification_code'].'" and active'
);
if($r==false){
  login_redirect($url,'validationfailed');
}
// success! set the session variable, clear the code from the
// db, then redirect
dbQuery('update user_accounts set verification_code="" where
  email="'.addslashes($_REQUEST['email']).'"');
$_SESSION['userdata']=$r;
$groups=json_decode($r['groups']);
$_SESSION['userdata']['groups']=array();
foreach($groups as $g)$_SESSION['userdata']['groups'][$g]=true;
if($r['extras']=='')$r['extras']='[]';
$_SESSION['userdata']['extras']=json_decode($r['extras']);
login_redirect($url,'verified');
```

In this one, we verify the e-mail address and validation code, and if they both are correct, then we do a login, and send a message reminding the user to reset their password.

Add these new message codes to /ww.incs/login-codes.php:

```
    'validationsent'=>'a validation message has been sent to your email
address. please check your email.',
    'novalidation'=>'no validation code provided.',
    'validationfailed'=>'that email and validation code combination does
not exist. maybe it has already been used. please use the Forgotten
Password to resend the validation email.',
    'verified'=>'you have verified your email address and we have logged
you in. please remember to reset your password.'
);
```

And that is our login system completed.

In the next section, we will create a user management area in the admin area.

User management

Okay! We now have the admin area login working, so let's build the first admin page. This will be the user management page, which allows us to create, delete, and edit users.

So first, we need to edit the /ww.admin/header.php to add in a link to the user management page. In the next chapter, we will rewrite the menu to make it easier to add items to it. For now, the links will be hardcoded as top-level menu items.

Change the menu list to this:

```
<ul>
  <li><a href="/ww.admin/users.php">Users</a></li>
  <li><a href="/ww.incs/logout.php?redirect=/ww.admin/">
    Log Out</a></li>
</ul>
```

Next, we will create /ww.admin/users.php:

```php
<?php
require 'header.php';
echo '<h1>User Management</h1>';
echo '<div class="left-menu">';
echo '<a href="/ww.admin/users.php">Users</a>';
echo '</div>';
echo '<div class="has-left-menu">';
echo '<h2>User Management</h2>';
if(isset($_REQUEST['action']))require 'users/actions.php';
if(isset($_REQUEST['id']))require 'users/form.php';
```

```
require 'users/list.php';
echo '</div>';

echo '<script src="/ww.admin/users/users.js"></script>';
require 'footer.php';
```

Because management involves multiple separate functions—displaying lists of items and details of specific items, editing items, deleting and creating, if you do all this in one single file, the file gets huge and unmanageable.

Similarly, if you separate all these functions into separate files and keep all those files in one directory, it makes it difficult for a developer to find the right file to edit (see the root directory of a Mantis BT 1.2.0rc2 installation for an example: 219 files!).

To make it easier to figure out what's going on, I like to place grouped files into their own directories. Hence the login files are in /ww.admin/login/, the user management files are in /ww.admin/users/, and we'll see more examples as the book goes on.

Anyway... when we click on the **Users** link in the menu, what we want to see is a list of existing users.

Add this to /ww.incs/basics.php to give us a dbAll() function:

```
function dbAll($query,$key='') {
  $q = dbQuery($query);
  $results=array();
  while($r=$q->fetch(PDO::FETCH_ASSOC))$results[]=$r;
  if(!$key)return $results;
  $arr=array();
  foreach($results as $r)$arr[$r[$key]]=$r;
  return $arr;
}
```

What that does is, given an SQL query, it will build an array of results and return that.

I haven't commented on it yet, but the db* functions we are writing here use the PDO library to connect to the database.

One reason for using dbAll, dbQuery, and so on, instead of accessing the database directly through PDO, mysql[i]_connect, or any other method, is that it's easier to port the engine to another database or database library if all DB methods are encapsulated in a small number of wrapper functions.

If given a second parameter (for example, 'id'), then the returned array will be indexed using that parameter's value from each result row.

We'll also need a function for returning a single value. Add this to the same file:

```
function dbOne($query, $field='') {
  $r = dbRow($query);
  return $r[$field];
}
function dbLastInsertId() {
  return dbOne('select last_insert_id() as id','id');
}
```

Now that we have that, let's write /ww.incs/users/list.php:

```
<?php
$users=dbAll('select id,email,groups from user_accounts
  order by email');
echo '<table style="min-width:50%">
  <tr><th>User</th><th>Groups</th><th>Actions</th></tr>';
foreach($users as $user){
  echo '<tr><th><a href="users.php?id='.$user['id']
    .'">'.htmlspecialchars($user['email']).'</a></th>';
  echo '<td>'.join(', ',json_decode($user['groups'])).'</td>';
  echo '<td><a href="users.php?id='.$user['id'].'">edit</a>';
  echo ' <a href="users.php?id='.$user['id']
    .'&amp;action=delete" onclick="return confirm(\'are you
    sure you want to delete this user?\')">[x]</a></td></tr>';
}
echo '</table>';
echo '<a class="button" href="users.php?id=-1">
  Create User</a>';
```

That gives me the following result:

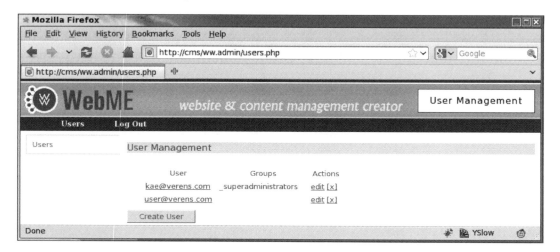

We can now see the existing users, as well as the groups that they belong to.

 The code I wrote here generates and echoes HTML directly to the HTTP stream. This is a "down and dirty" method of very quickly generating some code and displaying it. A more appropriate method would be to use a templating engine such as Smarty. Feel free to enhance the code after we've looked at Smarty later in the book.

Before talking about editing and creating, we will look at the delete action.

Deleting a user

In the previous screenshot, you can see an **[x]** beside both users. The link is intentionally small and obscure, because we really don't want to accidentally delete a user by clicking the wrong link. So, we make the delete link more difficult to click.

We also add a JavaScript confirm() so that if an admin does click it, they are given the chance to say "No, I did not intend to click this".

Now we can write the code to do the deletion.

Create the file /ww.admin/users/actions.php:

```php
<?php
$id=(int)$_REQUEST['id'];
if($_REQUEST['action']=='delete'){
  dbQuery("delete from user_accounts where id=$id");
  unset($_REQUEST['id']);
}
```

What happens with this is that the delete link is clicked, the user is deleted, then the /ww.admin/users.php page displays the users list again.

Creating or editing a user

Creating and editing can both be done from the same form.

Basically, what happens is that you select to create or edit a user, which sends the user's ID to the server.

The server then uses that ID to get the user's data from the database. If the data doesn't exist, the result will obviously be blank.

The result is then used to fill in the user form.

When submitted, if the user ID is not valid, then the submission is used to create a new user.

For this form, we will need to create the groups database table, and populate it with _administrator and _superadministrator:

```
CREATE TABLE `groups` (
  `id` int(11) NOT NULL AUTO_INCREMENT,
  `name` text,
  PRIMARY KEY (`id`)
) DEFAULT CHARSET=utf8;
insert into groups values(1,"_superadministrators");
insert into groups values(2,"_administrators");
```

And now, create /ww.admin/users/form.php:

```
<?php
$id=(int)$_REQUEST['id'];
$groups=array();
$r=dbRow("select * from user_accounts where id=$id");
if(!is_array($r) || !count($r)){
  $r=array('id'=>-1,'email'=>'','active'=>0);
}
echo '<form action="users.php?id='.$id.'" method="post">'
        .'<input type="hidden" name="id" value="'.$id.'" /><table>'
        .'<tr><th>Email</th>
          <td><input name="email" value="'.htmlspecialchars($r['ema
il']).'" /></td>
        </tr>'
        .'<tr><th>Password</th>
          <td><input name="password" type="password" /></td>
```

```
        </tr>'
        .'<tr><th>(repeat)</th>
          <td><input name="password2" type="password" /></td>
        </tr>'
        .'<tr><th>Groups</th><td class="groups">';
$grs=dbAll('select id,name from groups');
$gms=array();
foreach($grs as $g){   $groups[$g['id']]=$g['name'];
}
$grs=json_decode($r['groups']);
foreach($groups as $k=>$g){
  echo '<input type="checkbox" name="groups['.$k.']"';
  if(in_array($g,$grs))echo ' checked="checked"';
  echo ' />',htmlspecialchars($g),'<br />';
}
echo '</td></tr>';
// }
echo '<tr><th>Active</th><td><select name="active">
  <option value="0">No</option>
  <option value="1"'.($r['active']?'
  selected="selected"':'').'>Yes</option></select></td></tr>';
echo '</table>';
echo '<input type="submit" name="action" value="Save" />';
echo '</form>';
```

After clicking on the **kae@verens.com** link, we get this form:

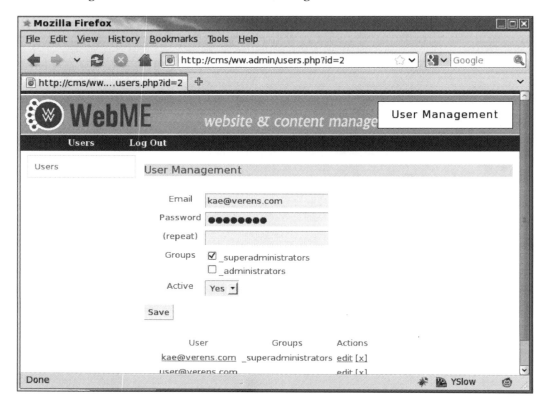

Next, we just need to save the updated data.

We can do this by adding this code to the end of the /ww.admin/users/actions. php file:

```
if($_REQUEST['action']=='Save'){
  $groups=$_REQUEST['groups'];
  if(!count($groups))$groups=array(0);
  $grs=dbAll('select name from groups where id in ('
    .addslashes(join(',',array_keys($groups)))
    .') order by name');
  $groups=array();
  foreach($grs as $r)$groups[]=$r['name'];
  $sql='set email="'.addslashes($_REQUEST['email']).'",
    active="'.(int)$_REQUEST['active'].'",
    groups="'.addslashes(json_encode($groups)).'"';
  if(
```

```
    isset($_REQUEST['password']) &&
    $_REQUEST['password']!=''
){
  if($_REQUEST['password']!==$_REQUEST['password2'])
    echo '<em>Password not updated. Must be entered
      the same twice.</em>';
  else $sql.=',password=md5("'.addslashes(
    $_REQUEST['email'].'|'.$_REQUEST['password']
  ).'")';
}
if($id==-1){
  dbQuery('insert into user_accounts '.$sql);
  $_REQUEST['id']=dbLastInsertId();
}
else{
  dbQuery('update user_accounts '.$sql.' where id='.$id);
}
echo '<em>users updated</em>';
}
```

That script will handle both the creation and editing of users.

We will discuss the creation and editing of groups later in the book.

Summary

In this chapter, we created the login system, including captcha management and forgotten password management.

We also created a user management system for creating and editing users.

In the next chapter, we will start building the page management system.

3
Page Management – Part One

In this chapter, we will create the forms for page management, and will build a system for moving the pages around using drag-and-drop.

We will discuss the following topics:

- How pages are requested and generated
- Listing the pages in the admin area
- Administration of pages

Page management will be concluded in the next chapter, where we will discuss saving the pages, and integrate a rich-text editor and a file manager.

How pages work in a CMS

As we discussed in *Chapter 1*, *CMS Core Design*, a "page" is simply the main content which should be shown when a certain URL is requested.

In a non-CMS website, this is easy to see, as a single URL returns a distinct HTML file. In a CMS though, the page is generated dynamically, and may include features such as plugins, different views depending on whether the reader was searching for something, whether pagination is used, and other little complexities.

In most websites, a page is easily identified as the large content area in the middle (this is an over-simplification). In others, it's harder to tell, as the onscreen page may be composed of content snippets from other parts of the site.

We handle these differences by using page "types", each of which can be rendered differently on the front-end. Examples of types include gallery pages, forms, news contents, search results, and so on.

In this chapter, we will create the simplest type, which we will call "normal". This consists of a content-entry textarea in the admin area, and direct output of that content on the front-end. You could call this "default" if you want, but since a CMS is not always used by people from a technical background, it makes sense to use a word that they are more likely to recognize. I have been asked before by clients what "default" means, but I've never been asked what "normal" means.

If you remember from the first chapter, we discussed what should go in the core, and what should be a plugin.

At the very least, a CMS needs some way to create the simplest of web pages. This is why the "normal" type is not a plugin, but is built into the core.

Listing pages in the admin area

To begin, we will add Pages to the admin menu. Edit /ww.admin/header.php and add the following highlighted line:

```
<ul>
    <li><a href="/ww.admin/pages.php">Pages</a></li>
    <li><a href="/ww.admin/users.php">Users</a></li>
```

And one more thing—when we log into the administration part of the CMS, it makes sense to have the "front page" of the admin area be the Pages section. After all, most of the work in a CMS is done in the Pages section.

So, we change /ww.admin/index.php so it is a synonym for /ww.admin/pages.php. Replace the /ww.admin/index.php file with this:

```
<?php
require 'pages.php';
```

Next, let's get started on the Pages section.

First, we will create /ww.admin/pages.php:

```
<?php
require 'header.php';
echo '<h1>Pages</h1>';
// { load menu
echo '<div class="left-menu">';
require 'pages/menu.php';
echo '</div>';
// }
// { load main page
echo '<div class="has-left-menu">';
require 'pages/forms.php';
```

```
echo '</div>';
// }
echo '<style type="text/css">
  @import "pages/css.css";</style>';
require 'footer.php';
```

Notice how I've commented blocks of code, using // { to open the comment at the beginning of the block, and // } at the end of the block.

This is done because a number of text editors have a feature called "**folding**", which allows blocks enclosed within delimiters such as { and } to be hidden from view, with just the first line showing.

For instance, the previous code example looks like this in my Vim editor:

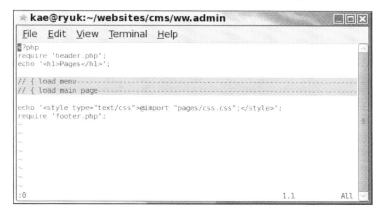

What the page.php does is to load the headers, load the menu and page form, and then load the footers. There will be more added later in this chapter.

For now, create the directory /ww.admin/pages and create a file in it called / ww.admin/pages/forms.php:

```
<h2>FORM GOES HERE</h2>
```

And now we can create the page menu. Use the following code to create the file / ww.admin/pages/menu.php:

```
<?php
echo '<div id="pages-wrapper">';
$rs=dbAll('select id,type,name,parent from pages order by ord,name');
$pages=array();
foreach($rs as $r){
  if(!isset($pages[$r['parent']]))$pages[$r['parent']]=array();
  $pages[$r['parent']][]=$r;
}
```

```
function show_pages($id,$pages){
  if(!isset($pages[$id]))return;
  echo '<ul>';
  foreach($pages[$id] as $page){
    echo '<li id="page_'.$page['id'].'">'
      .'<a href="pages.php?id='.$page['id'].'">'
      .'<ins> </ins>'.htmlspecialchars($page['name'])
      .'</a>';
    show_pages($page['id'],$pages);
    echo '</li>';
  }
  echo '</ul>';
}
show_pages(0,$pages);
echo '</div>';
```

That will build up a `<ul>` tree of pages.

Note the use of the "parent" field in there. Most websites follow a hierarchical "parent-child" method of arranging pages, with all pages being a child of either another page, or the "root" of the site. The parent field is filled with the ID of the page within which it is situated.

There are two main ways to indicate which page is the "front" page (that is, what page is shown when someone loads up `http://cms/` with no page name indicated).

1. You can have one single page in the database which has a parent of 0, meaning that it has no parent—this page is what is looked for when `http://cms/` is called. In this scheme, pages such as `http://cms/pagename` have their parent field set to the ID of the one page which has a parent of 0.

2. You can have many pages which have 0 as their parent, and each of these is said to be a "top-level" page. One page in the database has a flag set in the `special` field which indicates that this is the front page. In this scheme, pages named like `http://cms/pagename` all have a parent of 0, and the page corresponding to `http://cms/` can be located anywhere at all in the database.

Case 1 has a disadvantage, in that if you want to change what page is the front page, you need to move the current page under another one (or delete it), then move all the current page's child-pages so they have the new front page's ID as a parent, and this can get messy if the new front-page already had some sub-pages—especially if there are any with the same names.

Case 2 is a much better choice because you can change the front page whenever you want, and it doesn't cause any problems at all.

When you view the site in your browser now, it looks like this (based on the pages we created manually back in *Chapter 1, CMS Core Design*):

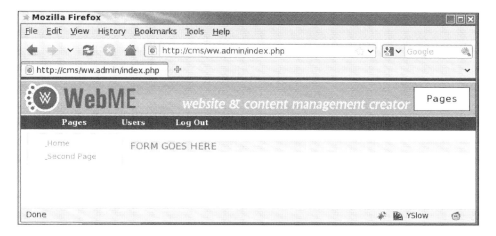

Hierarchical viewing of pages

Let's update the database slightly so that we can see the hierarchy of the site pages visually.

Go to your MySQL console, and change the Second Page so that its parent field is the ID of the Home page:

```
mysql> select id,name,parent from pages;
+----+-------------+--------+
| id | name        | parent |
+----+-------------+--------+
| 24 | Home        |      0 |
| 25 | Second Page |      0 |
+----+-------------+--------+
2 rows in set (0.00 sec)
mysql> update pages set parent=24 where id=25;
Query OK, 1 row affected (0.00 sec)
Rows matched: 1  Changed: 1  Warnings: 0
```

After the update, we refresh the site in the browser:

You can see the **Second Page** has indented slightly because it is now a child page of **Home**, and is contained in a sub-`<ul>` in the HTML.

We can improve on this vastly, though.

There is a jQuery plugin called `jstree` which re-draws `<ul>` trees in a way that is more familiar to users of visual file managers.

It also has the added features that you can drag the tree nodes around, and attach events to clicks on the nodes.

We will use these features later in the chapter to allow creation and deletion of pages, and changing of page parents through drag-and-drop.

Create the directory `/j/` in the root of the website.

Remember that we indicated in the first chapter that the CMS directories would all include dots in them, unless they were less than three characters long.

One of the reasons we name this directory `/j/` instead of `/ww.javascript/`, is that it is short, thus saving a few bytes of bandwidth for the end-user, who may be using something bandwidth-light such as a smartphone.

This may not be a big deal, but if we got into the habit of making small shortcuts like this whenever possible, then the small shortcuts would eventually add up to a second or two of extra speed.

Every unnoticeable optimization can help to make a noticeable one when combined with many more.

Anyway—create the `/j/` directory, and download the `jstree` script from `http://jstree.com/` such that when extracted, the `jquery.tree.js` file is located at `/j/jquery.jstree/jquery.tree.js`.

I have used version `0.9.9a` in the CMS described in this book.

Now edit `/ww.admin/pages/menu.php` and add the following highlighted lines before the first line:

```
<script src="/j/jquery.jstree/jquery.tree.js"></script>
<script src="/ww.admin/pages/menu.js"></script>
<?php
```

And create the file `/ww.admin/pages/menu.js`:

```
$(function(){
  $('#pages-wrapper').tree();
});
```

And immediately, we have a beautified hierarchical tree, as seen in the following screenshot:

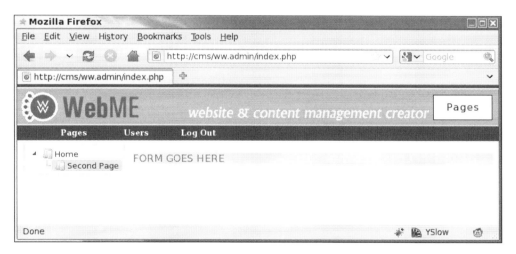

If you try, you'll see that you can drag those page names around, with little icons and signs indicating where a page can be dropped, as shown in the next two screenshots:

Before we get into the actual editing of pages, let's improve on this menu one last time. We will add a button to indicate we want to create a new top-level page, and we will also record drag-and-drop events so that they actually do move the pages around.

Change the /ww.admin/pages/menu.js file to this:

```
$(function(){
  $('#pages-wrapper').tree({
    callback:{
      onchange:function(node,tree){
        document.location='pages.php?action=edit&id='
          +node.id.replace(/.*_/,'');
      },
      onmove:function(node){
        var p=$.tree.focused().parent(node);
        var new_order=[],nodes=node.parentNode.childNodes;
        for(var i=0;i<nodes.length;++i)
          new_order.push(nodes[i].id.replace(/.*_/,''));
        $.getJSON('/ww.admin/pages/move_page.php?id='
          +node.id.replace(/.*_/,'')+'&parent_id='
          +(p==-1?0:p[0].id.replace(/.*_/,''))
          +'&order='+new_order);
      }
    }
  });
  var div=$(
    '<div><i>right-click for options</i><br /><br /></div>');
  $('<button>add main page</button>')
    .click(pages_add_main_page)
    .appendTo(div);
  div.appendTo('#pages-wrapper');
});
function pages_add_main_page(){}
```

We've added a few pieces of functionality to the tree here.

First, we have the onchange callback.

When a tree node (a page name) is clicked, the browser is redirected to pages. php?edit= with the page's ID at the end-note that when creating the <ul> tree, we added an ID to every <li>, such that a page with the ID 24 would have an <li> with the ID page_24.

So, all we need to do when a node (the <li>) is clicked, is to remove the page_ part, and use that to open up page.php for editing that page.

Second, we added an onmove callback. This is called after a drag-and-drop event has completed.

What we do in this is slightly more complex—we get the new parent's ID, and we make an array which records the IDs of all its direct descendant child pages. We then send all that data to /ww.admin/pages/move_page.php, which we'll create in just a moment.

Finally, we've added a message to right-click on the tree for further functionality, which we'll detail later in the chapter, and a button to create a new top-level page, which we'll also detail later in the chapter. A dummy function needs to be added so this code will run without error. We'll replace it with a real one later.

Moving and rearranging pages

Now when you drag a page name to a different place on the tree, an Ajax call is made to /ww.admin/pages/move_page.php, with some details included in the call.

Here's a screenshot showing (using Firebug) what is sent in a sample drag:

We are sending the page ID (25), the new parent ID (0), and the new page order of pages which have the parent ID 0 (25, 24).

So, let's create /ww.admin/pages/move_page.php:

```php
<?php
require '../admin_libs.php';

$id=(int)$_REQUEST['id'];
$to=(int)$_REQUEST['parent_id'];
$order=explode(',',$_REQUEST['order']);
dbQuery('update pages set parent='.$to.' where id='.$id  );
for($i=0;$i<count($order);++$i){
  $pid=(int)$order[$i];
  dbQuery("update pages set ord=$i where id=$pid");
  echo "update pages set ord=$i where id=$pid\n";
}
```

Simple! It records exactly what it was sent.

Administration of pages

Okay—we now have a list of the existing pages. Let's add some functionality to edit them.

The form for creating a page is a bit long, so what we'll do is to build it up a bit at a time, explaining as we go. Replace the file /ww.admin/pages/forms.php with the following:

```php
<?php
if(isset($_REQUEST['id']))$id=(int)$_REQUEST['id'];
else $id=0;
if($id){ // check that page id exists
  $page=dbRow("SELECT * FROM pages WHERE id=$id");
  if($page!==false){
    $page_vars=json_decode($page['vars'],true);
    $edit=true;
  }
}
if(!isset($edit)){
  $parent=isset($_REQUEST['parent'])?
    (int)$_REQUEST['parent']:0;
  $special=0;
  if(isset($_REQUEST['hidden']))$special+=2;
  $page=array('parent'=>$parent,'type'=>'0','body'=>'',
```

```
        'name'=>'','title'=>'','ord'=>0,'description'=>'',
        'id'=>0,'keywords'=>'','special'=>$special,
        'template'=>'');
    $page_vars=array();
    $id=0;
    $edit=false;
}
```

What the given code does is to initialize an array named $page for the main page details, and another named page_vars for any custom details that are not part of the main page table—for example, data recorded as part of a plugin.

If an ID is passed as part of the URL, then that page's data is loaded.

As an example, if I add the line var_dump($page); and then load up /ww.admin/pages.php?action=edit&id=25 in my browser (a page which exists in my database), this is what's shown:

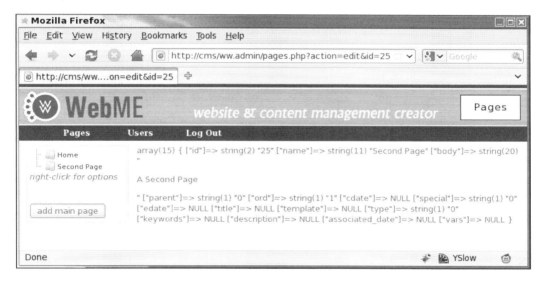

This shows all the data about that page available in the database table.

If the ID passed in the URL is 0, or any other ID which does not correspond to an existing page ID, then we still initialize $page but with empty values:

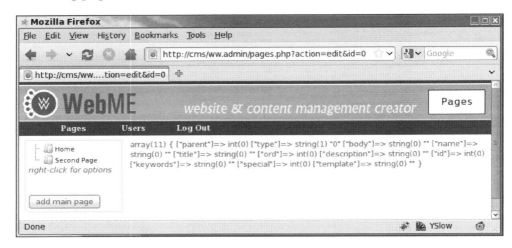

Because pages can get quite complex, especially when we add in different page types using plugins later in the book, we break the page form into different tabs.

For the "normal" page type, we will have two tabs—common details, and advanced options.

The common details tab will contain options that are changed very often, such as page name, page content, and so on.

The advanced options tab will contain more rarely-changed options such as meta tags, templates, and so on. We call it "advanced", but that's only because "rarely changed options" doesn't sound as concise, and also because most website administrators will not know what to do with some of these options.

So, let's add the tab menu to /ww.admin/pages/forms.php:

```
// { if page is hidden from navigation, show a message saying that
if($page['special']&2)
   echo '<em>NOTE: this page is currently hidden from the
        front-end navigation. Use the "Advanced Options" to
        un-hide it.</em>';
// }
echo '<form id="pages_form" method="post">';
echo '<input type="hidden" name="id" value="',$id,'" />'
    ,'<div class="tabs"><ul>'
    ,'<li><a href="#tabs-common-details">Common Details</a></li>'
    ,'<li><a href="#tabs-advanced-options">Advanced Options</a></li>'
```

```
    ;
// add plugin tabs here
echo '</ul>';
```

Above the page form, we display a small message if the page we're viewing is currently not visible in the navigation menu on the front-end of the site—if the `special` field has its 2 bit flagged, then that means that the page is not shown in the navigation menu.

Bitmasks are useful for when you have "yes/no" values and don't want to take up a whole database field for each value.

After this, we open the form.

Note that an action parameter is not provided in my code. Although the W3C HTML 4.01 specification says that the action is required, no browsers actually enforce this. If a browser comes across a form which has no action, then it defaults to the same page.

This is also true of `<style>`, where type defaults to `text/css`, and `<script>`, where type defaults to `javascript`.

Next we display the tab menu, which is the list of tabs to be shown.

Note the second-last line, which is a comment about plugin tabs. When we get to plugins in a later chapter, some of them may have enough extra options that they need a new tab on the page form. We'll handle that when we get to it.

Next, let's add the common details tab to the same file:

```
// { Common Details
echo '<div id="tabs-common-details"><table
    style="clear:right;width:100%;"><%;"< tr>`;
// { name
echo '<th width="5%">name</th><td width="23%">
  <input
    id="name" name="name"
    value="',htmlspecialchars($page['name']),'" /></td>';
// }
// { title
echo '<th width="10%">title</th><td width="23%">
  <input
    name="title"
    value="',htmlspecialchars($page['title']),'" /></td>';
// }
// { url
echo '<th colspan="2">';
```

```
if($edit){
  $u='/'.str_replace(' ','-',$page['name']);
  echo '<a style="font-weight:bold;color:red" href="',$u
    ,'" target="_blank">VIEW PAGE</a>';
}
else echo ' ';
echo '</th>';
// }
echo '</tr><tr>';
// { type
echo '<th>type</th><td><select name="type"><option
    value="0">normal</option>';
// insert plugin page types here
echo '</select></td>';
// }
// { parent
echo '<th>parent</th><td><select name="parent">';
if($page['parent']){
  $parent=Page::getInstance($page['parent']);
  echo '<option value="',$parent->id,'">'
    ,htmlspecialchars($parent->name),'</option>';
}
else echo '<option value="0"> -- ','none',' -- </option>';
echo '</select>',"\n\n",'</td>';
// }
if(!isset($page['associated_date']) || !preg_match(
  '/^[0-9]{4}-[0-9]{2}-[0-9]{2}$/',$page['associated_date']
  ) || $page['associated_date']=='0000-00-00'
    $page['associated_date']=date('Y-m-d');
echo '<th>Associated Date</th><td><input
    name="associated_date" class="date-human" value="',
    $page['associated_date'],'" /></td>';
echo '</tr>';
// }
// { page-type-specific data
echo '<tr><th>body</th><td colspan="5">';
echo '<textarea name="body">',
    htmlspecialchars($page['body']),'</textarea>';
echo '</td></tr>';
// }
echo '</table></div>';
// }
```

The given code shows the commonly changed details of the page database table. They include:

- `name`
- `title`
- `type`
- `parent`
- `associated_date`
- `body`

We'll enhance a few of those after we've finished the form. For now, a few things should be noted about the form and its options.

- **URL**: When you are editing a page, it's good to view it in another window or tab. To do this, we provide a link to the front-end page. Clicking on the link opens a new tab or window.

- **Type**: The page type by default is "normal", and in the select-box we built previously, that is the only option. We will enhance that when we get to plugins in a later chapter.

- **Parent**: This is the page which the currently edited page is contained within. In the earlier form, we display only the current parent, and don't provide any other options. There's a reason for that which we'll explain after we finish the main form HTML.

- **Associated date**: There are a number of dates associated with a page. We record the created and last-edited date internally (useful for plugins or logging), but sometimes the admin wants to record a date specific to the page. For example, if the page is part of a news system, we will enhance this date input box after the form is completed.

- **Body**: This is the content which will be shown on the front-end. It's plain HTML. Of course, writing HTML for content is not a task you should push on the average administrator, so we will enhance that.

Here's a screenshot of the first tab (I've temporarily completed the jQuery tabs to get this shot—we'll do it in the chapter later on):

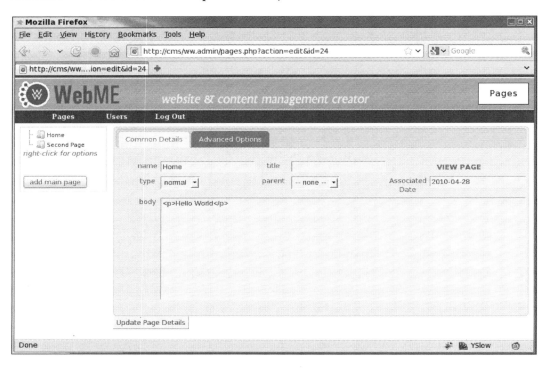

You can see that the date input box is quite large. There's a reason for that, which we'll see in the next chapter.

The second tab will be a bit shorter. Let's add that now. Add the following code to the /ww.admin/pages/forms.php file:

```
// { Advanced Options
echo '<div id="tabs-advanced-options">';
echo '<table><tr><td>';
// { metadata
echo '<h4>MetaData</h4><table>';
echo '<tr><th>keywords</th><td>
  <input name="keywords"
    value="',htmlspecialchars($page['keywords']),'"
  /></td></tr>';
echo '<tr><th>description</th><td>
  <input name="description"
    value="',htmlspecialchars($page['description']),'"
  /></td></tr>';
```

```php
// { template
// we'll add this in the next chapter
// }
echo '</table>';
// }
echo '</td><td>';
// { special
echo '<h4>Special</h4>';
$specials=array('Is Home Page',
    'Does not appear in navigation');
for($i=0;$i<count($specials);++$i){
  if($specials[$i]!=''){
    echo '<input type="checkbox" name="special[',$i,']"';
    if($page['special']&pow(2,$i))echo ' checked="checked"';
    echo ' />',$specials[$i],'<br />';
  }
}
// }
// { other
echo '<h4>Other</h4>';
echo '<table>';
// { order of sub-pages
echo '<tr><th>Order of sub-pages</th><td><select name="page_
vars[order_of_sub_pages]">';
$arr=array('as shown in admin menu','alphabetically',
    'by associated date');
foreach($arr as $k=>$v){
  echo '<option value="',$k,'"';
  if(isset($page_vars['order_of_sub_pages']) &&
      $page_vars['order_of_sub_pages']==$k)
      echo ' selected="selected"';
  echo '>',$v,'</option>';
}
echo '</select>';
echo '<select name="page_vars[order_of_sub_pages_dir]">
    <option value="0">ascending (a-z, 0-9)</option>';
echo '<option value="1"';
if(isset($page_vars['order_of_sub_pages_dir']) &&
    $page_vars['order_of_sub_pages_dir']=='1')
    echo ' selected="selected"';
echo '>descending (z-a, 9-0)</option></select></td></tr>';
// }
echo '</table>';
// }
echo '</td></tr></table></div>';
// }
```

There's not a lot to explain here. There are some extra "advanced" options which I've not added here, which are useful for the system when it's been more completed (plugins added, themes or templates completed, and so on).

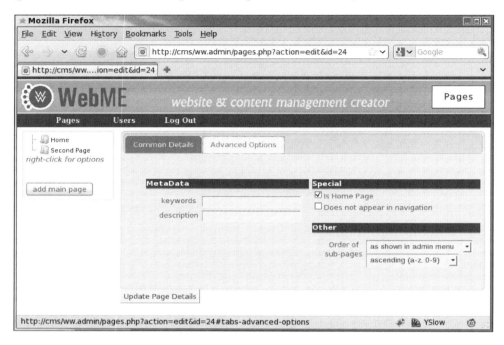

First, we add inputs for **keywords** and **description** meta-data. Most people appear to leave these alone, which is why it's not on the front tab.

We will add templates and themes in the next chapter. For now, I've added a commented placeholder.

After this, we show a list of "specials". I've included just two here—a marker to say whether the current page is the home page, and another marker to indicate that the page should not appear in front-end navigation.

Finally (for now), we show two drop-down boxes, to let the administrator decide what order the current page's sub-pages should be shown in the front-end navigation. For example, you might want a list of authors to be alphabetical or new items to appear by date descending, but in most cases you will want the pages to appear in the same order as they appear in the admin area (which you can change by dragging page names in the navigation menu on the left-hand side).

Okay—now let's complete the form and add in the tabs code.

There is one more section which we could add—some plugins might want to add tabs to this form. We'll get to that later in the book.

Add this code to the file /ww.admin/pages/forms.php:

```
echo '</div><input type="submit" name="action" value="',
    ($edit?'Update Page Details':'Insert Page Details')
    ,'" /></form>';
echo '<script>window.currentpageid='.$id.';</script>';
echo '<script src="/ww.admin/pages/pages.js"></script>';
```

And let's create the file /ww.admin/pages/pages.js:

```
$(function(){
  $('.tabs').tabs();
});
```

The window.currentpageid variable will be used in the next section.

That completes the basics of the form.

Next, let's look at those inputs we highlighted earlier as needing some enhancements.

Filling the parent selectbox asynchronously

In very large websites, it can sometimes be very slow to load up the Page form, because of the "parents" drop-down. This select-box tells the server what page the current page is located under.

If you fill that at the time of loading the form, then the size of the downloaded HTML can be quite large.

A solution for this problem was developed for my previous book (*jQuery 1.3 with PHP*), and as part of that book, the solution was packaged into a jQuery plugin which solves the problem here.

Download the remoteselectoptions plugin from http://plugins.jquery.com/project/remoteselectoptions and unzip it in your /j/ directory.

What this plugin does, is that in the initial load of your page's HTML, you enter just one option in the select-box, and it will get the rest of the options only when it becomes necessary (that is, when the select-box is clicked).

To get this to work with the **parents** select-box, change the `/ww.admin/pages/pages.js` file to this:

```
$(function(){
  $('.tabs').tabs();
  $('#pages_form select[name=parent]').remoteselectoptions({
    url:'/ww.admin/pages/get_parents.php',
    other_GET_params:currentpageid
  });
});
```

And because this plugin is useful for quite a few places in the admin, let's add it to `/ww.admin/header.php` (the highlighted line):

```
<script src="http://ajax.googleapis.com/ajax/libs
    /jqueryui/1.8.0/jquery-ui.min.js"></script>
<script src="/j/jquery.remoteselectoptions
    /jquery.remoteselectoptions.js"></script>
<link rel="stylesheet" href="http://ajax.googleapis.com/ajax
    /libs/jqueryui/1.8.0/themes/south-street/jquery-ui.css"
    type="text/css" />
```

And you can see from the `pages.js` file that another file is required to build up the actual list of page names. Create this as `/ww.admin/pages/get_parents.php`:

```
<?php
require '../admin_libs.php';
function page_show_pagenames($i=0,$n=1,$s=0,$id=0){
  $q=dbAll('select name,id from pages where parent="'
      .$i.'" and id!="'.$id.'" order by ord,name');
  if(count($q)<1)return;
  foreach($q as $r){
    if($r['id']!=''){
      echo '<option value="'.$r['id'].'" title="'
          .htmlspecialchars($r['name']).'"';
      echo($s==$r['id'])?' selected="selected">':'>';
      for($j=0;$j<$n;$j++)echo ' ';
      $name=$r['name'];
      if(strlen($name)>20)$name=substr($name,0,17).'...';
      echo htmlspecialchars($name).'</option>';
      page_show_pagenames($r['id'],$n+1,$s,$id);
    }
  }
}
$selected=isset($_REQUEST['selected'])
```

```
    ?$_REQUEST['selected']:0;
$id=isset($_REQUEST['other_GET_params'])
    ?(int)$_REQUEST['other_GET_params']:-1;
echo '<option value="0"> --  none  -- </option>';
page_show_pagenames(0,0,$selected,$id);
```

The `remoteselectoptions` plugin sends a query to this page, with two parameters—the currently selected parent's ID, and the current page ID.

The previous code builds up an option list, taking care to not allow the admin to choose to place a page within itself, or within any page which is contained hierarchically under itself. That would make the page disappear from all navigation, including the admin navigation.

For the current example, that means that the only options available are either **none** (that is, the page is a top-level one), or **Second Page**, as in our example, there are currently only two pages, and obviously you can't place **Home** under **Home**.

Okay—we've done enough now that you can take a break before we start on the next chapter, where we'll finish off page creation.

Summary

In this chapter, we built the basics of page management, including creation of the form for page management, and a few jQuery tools for making page location management easy and improving the selection of large select-boxes.

In the next chapter, we will complete the page management section, and build a simple menu system for the front-end so we can navigate between pages.

4
Page Management – Part Two

In this chapter, we will complete the page-management section, and will build a simple navigation menu for the front-end.

We will discuss the following topics:

- How to make human-readable dates
- Rich-text editing
- File management for images and files

At the end of this chapter, we will have a completed page management system.

Dates

Dates are annoying. The scheme I prefer is to enter dates the same way MySQL accepts them — `yyyy-mm-dd hh:mm:ss`. From left to right, each subsequent element is smaller than the previous. It's logical, and can be sorted sensibly using a simple numeric sorter.

Unfortunately, most people don't read or write dates in that format. They'd prefer something like `08/07/06`.

Dates in that format do not make sense. Is it the 8th day of the 7th month of 2006, or the 7th day of the 8th month of 2006, or even the 6th day of the 7th month of 2008? Date formats are different all around the world.

Therefore, you cannot trust human administrators to enter the dates manually.

A very quick solution is to use the jQuery UI's `datepicker` plugin.

Temporarily (we'll remove it in a minute) add the highlighted lines to `/ww.admin/pages/pages.js`:

```
    other_GET_params:currentpageid
  });
  $('.date-human').datepicker({
    'dateFormat':'yy-mm-dd'
  });
});
```

When the date field is clicked, this appears:

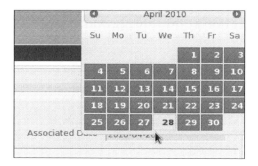

It's a great calendar, but there's still a flaw: Before you click on the date field, and even after you select the date, the field is still in `yyyy-mm-dd` format.

While MySQL will thank you for entering the date in a sane format, you will have people asking you why the date is not shown in a humanly readable way.

We can't simply change the date format to accept something more reasonable such as "May 23rd, 2010", because we would then need to ensure that we can understand this on the server-side, which might take more work than we really want to do.

So we need to do something else.

The `datepicker` plugin has an option which lets you update two fields at the same time. This is the solution—we will display a dummy field which is humanly readable, and when that's clicked, the calendar will appear and you will be able to choose a date, which will then be set in the human-readable field and in the real form field.

Don't forget to remove that temporary code from `/ww.admin/pages/pages.js`.

Because this is a very useful feature, which we will use throughout the admin area whenever a date is needed, we will add a global JavaScript file which will run on all pages.

Edit `/ww.admin/header.php` and add the following highlighted line:

```
<script src="/j/jquery.remoteselectoptions
    /jquery.remoteselectoptions.js"></script>
<script src="/ww.admin/j/admin.js"></script>
<link rel="stylesheet" href="http://ajax.googleapis.com
    /ajax/libs/jqueryui/1.8.0/themes/south-street
    /jquery-ui.css" type="text/css" />
```

And then we'll create the `/ww.admin/j/` directory and a file named `/ww.admin/j/admin.js`:

```javascript
function convert_date_to_human_readable(){
  var $this=$(this);
  var id='date-input-'+Math.random().toString()
    .replace(/\./,'');
  var dparts=$this.val().split(/-/);
  $this
    .datepicker({
      dateFormat:'yy-mm-dd',
      modal:true,
      altField:'#'+id,
      altFormat:'DD, d MM, yy',
      onSelect:function(dateText,inst){
        this.value=dateText;
      }
    });
  var $wrapper=$this.wrap(
    '<div style="position:relative" />');
  var $input=$('<input id="'+id+'" class="date-human-readable"
    value="'+date_m2h($this.val())+'" />');
  $input.insertAfter($this);
  $this.css({
    'position':'absolute',
    'opacity':0
  });
  $this
    .datepicker(
      'setDate', new Date(dparts[0],dparts[1]-1,dparts[2])
    );
}
$(function(){
  $('input.date-human').each(convert_date_to_human_readable);
});
```

This takes the computer-readable date input and creates a copy of it, but in a human-readable format.

The original date input box is then made invisible and laid across the new one. When it is clicked, the date is updated on both of them, but only the human-readable one is shown.

Much better. Easy for a human to read, and also usable by the server.

Saving the page

We created the form, and except for making the body textarea more user-friendly, it's just about finished. Let's do that now.

When you click on the **Insert Page Details** button (or **Update Page Details**, if an ID was provided), the form data is posted to the server.

We need to perform these actions before the page menu is displayed, so it is up-to-date.

Edit /ww.admin/pages.php, and add the following highlighted lines before the load menu section:

```
echo '<h1>Pages</h1>';
// { perform any actions
if(isset($_REQUEST['action'])){
  if($_REQUEST['action']=='Update Page Details'
    || $_REQUEST['action']=='Insert Page Details'){
    require 'pages/action.edit.php';
  }
  else if($_REQUEST['action']=='delete'){
    'pages/action.delete.php';
  }
}
// }
// { load menu
```

If an action parameter is sent to the server, then the server will use this block to decide whether you want to edit or delete the page. We'll handle deletes later in the chapter.

Notice that we are handling inserts and updates with the same file, `action.edit.php`—in the database, there is almost no difference between the two when using MySQL.

So, let's create that file now. We'll do it a bit at a time, like how we did the form, as it's a bit long.

Create `/ww.admin/pages/action.edit.php` with this code:

```php
<?php
function pages_setup_name($id,$pid){
  $name=trim($_REQUEST['name']);
  if(dbOne('select id from pages where
      name="'.addslashes($name).'" and parent='.$pid.'
      and id!='.$id,'id')){
    $i=2;
    while(dbOne('select id from pages where
        name="'.addslashes($name.$i).'" and parent='.$pid.'
        and id!='.$id,'id'))$i++;
    echo '<em>A page named "'.htmlspecialchars($name).'"
        already exists. Page name amended to "'
        .htmlspecialchars($name.$i).'".</em>';
    $name=$name.$i;
  }
  return $name;
}
```

The first piece is a function which tests the submitted page name. If that name is the same as another page which has the same parent, then a number is added to the end and a message is shown explaining this.

Here's an example, creating a page named "Home" in the top level (we already have a page named "Home"):

Next we'll create a function for testing the inputted `special` variable. Add this to the same file:

```
function pages_setup_specials($id=0){
  $special=0;
  $specials=isset($_REQUEST['special'])
      ?$_REQUEST['special']:array();
  foreach($specials as $a=>$b)
      $special+=pow(2,$a);
  $homes=dbOne("SELECT COUNT(id) AS ids FROM pages
      WHERE (special&1) AND id!=$id",'ids');
  if($special&1){ // there can be only one homepage
    if($homes!=0){
      dbQuery("UPDATE pages SET special=special-1
          WHERE special&1");
    }
  }
  else{
    if($homes==0){
      $special+=1;
      echo '<em>This page has been marked as the site\'s
        Home Page, because there must always be one.</em>';
    }
  }
  return $special;
}
```

In this function, we build up the `special` variable, which is a bit field.

A **bit** field is a number which uses binary math to combine a few "yes/no" answers into one single value. It's good for saving space and fields in the database.

Each value has a value assigned to it which is a power of two. The interesting thing to note about powers of two is that in binary, they're always represented as a 1 with some 0s after it. For example, 1 is represented as 00000001, 2 is 00000010, 4 is 00000100, and so on.

When you have a bit field such as 00000011 (each number here is a bit), it's easy to see that this is composed of the values 1 and 2 combined, which are 2^0 and 2^1 respectively.

The `&` operator lets us check quickly if a certain bit is turned on (is 1) or not. For example, 00010011 & 16 is true, and 00010011 & 32 is false, because the 16 bit is on and the 32 bit is off.

In the database, we set a bit for the homepage, which we say has a value of 1. In the previous function, we need to make sure that after inserting or updating a page, there is always exactly one homepage.

The only other one we've set so far is "does not appear in navigation menu", which we've given the value 2. If we added a third bitflag ("is a 404 handler", for example), it would have the value 4, then 8, and so on.

Okay—now we will set up our variables. Add this to the same file:

```
// { set up common variables
$id               =(int)$_REQUEST['id'];
$pid              =(int)$_REQUEST['parent'];
$keywords         =$_REQUEST['keywords'];
$description      =$_REQUEST['description'];
$associated_date  =$_REQUEST['associated_date'];
$title            =$_REQUEST['title'];
$name             =pages_setup_name($id,$pid);
$body             =$_REQUEST['body'];
$special          =pages_setup_specials($id);
if(isset($_REQUEST['page_vars']))
    $vars=json_encode($_REQUEST['page_vars']);
else $vars='[]';
// }
```

Then we will add the main body of the page update SQL to the same file:

```
// { create SQL
$q='edate=now(),type="'.addslashes($_REQUEST['type']).'",
    associated_date="'.addslashes($associated_date).'",
    keywords="'.addslashes($keywords).'",
    description="'.addslashes($description).'",
    name="'.addslashes($name).'",
    title="'.addslashes($title).'",
    body="'.addslashes($body).'",parent='.$pid.',
    special='.$special.',vars="'.addslashes($vars).'"';
// }
```

This is SQL which is common to both creating and updating a page.

Finally we run the actual query and perform the action. Add this to the same file:

```
// { run the query
if($_REQUEST['action']=='Update Page Details'){
  $q="update pages set $q where id=$id";
  dbQuery($q);
}
```

```
else{
  $q="insert into pages set cdate=now(),$q";
  dbQuery($q);
  $_REQUEST['id']=dbLastInsertId();
}
// }
echo '<em>Page Saved</em>';
```

In the first case, we simply run an update.

In the second, we run an `insert`, adding the creation date to the query, and then setting `$_REQUEST['id']` to the ID of the entry that we just created.

Creating new top-level pages

If you've been trying all this, you'll have noticed that you can create a top-level page simply by clicking on the admin area's **Pages** link in the top menu, and then you're shown an empty **Insert Page Details** form.

It makes sense, though, to also have it available from the pagelist on the left-hand side.

So, let's make that **add main page** button useful.

If you remember, we created a `pages_add_main_page` function in the `menu.js` file, just as a placeholder until we got everything else done.

Open up that file now, `/ww.admin/pages/menu.js`, and replace that function with the following two new functions:

```
function pages_add_main_page(){
  pages_new(0);
}
function pages_new(p){
  $('<form id="newpage_dialog" action="/ww.admin/pages.php"
      method="post">
    <input type="hidden" name="action"
        value="Insert Page Details" />
    <input type="hidden" name="special[1]"
        value="1" />
    <input type="hidden" name="parent" value="'+p+'" />
    <table>
      <tr><th>Name</th><td><input name="name" /></td></tr>
      <tr><th>Page Type</th><td><select name="type">
          <option value="0">normal</option>
          </select></td></tr>
```

```
    <tr><th>Associated Date</th><td>
        <input name="associated_date" class="date-human"
        id="newpage_date" /></td></tr>
    </table>
   </form>')
 .dialog({
  modal:true,
  buttons:{
    'Create Page': function() {
      $('#newpage_dialog').submit();
    },
    'Cancel': function() {
      $(this).dialog('destroy');
      $(this).remove();
    }
  }
 });
 $('#newpage_date').each(convert_date_to_human_readable);
 return false;
}
```

When the **add main page** button is clicked, a dialog box is created asking some basic
information about the page to create:

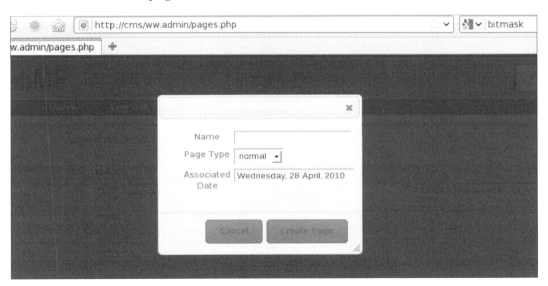

We include a few hidden inputs.

- `action`: To tell the server this is an **Insert Page Details** action.

- `special`: When **Create Page** is clicked, the page will be saved in the database, but we should hide it initially so that front-end readers don't see a half-finished page. So, the `special[1]` flag is set ($2^1 == 2$, which is the value for hiding a page).

- `parent`: Note that this is a variable. We can use the same dialog to create sub-pages.

When the dialog has been created, the date input box is converted to human-readable, the same as we did earlier.

Creating new sub-pages

We will add sub-pages by using context menus on the page list. Note that we have a message saying **right-click for options** under the list.

First, add this function to the `/ww.admin/pages/menu.js` file:

```
function pages_add_subpage(node,tree){
  var p=node[0].id.replace(/.*_/,'');
  pages_new(p);
}
```

We will now need to activate the context menu. This is done by adding a `contextmenu` plugin to the `jstree` plugin. Luckily, it comes with the download, so you've already installed it. Add it to the page by editing `/ww.admin/pages/menu.php` and add this highlighted line:

```
<script src="/j/jquery.jstree/jquery.tree.js"></script>
<script src=
    "/j/jquery.jstree/plugins/jquery.tree.contextmenu.js">
</script>
<script src="/ww.admin/pages/menu.js"></script>
```

And now, we edit the `.tree()` call in `/ww.admin/menu.js` to tell it what to do:

```
$('#pages-wrapper').tree({
  callback:{
// SKIPPED FOR BREVITY - DO NOT DELETE THESE LINES
  },
  plugins:{
    'contextmenu':{
      'items':{
```

```
            'create' : {
              'label' : "Create Page",
              'icon'   : "create",
              'visible' : function (NODE, TREE_OBJ) {
                if(NODE.length != 1) return 0;
                return TREE_OBJ.check("creatable", NODE);
              },
              'action':pages_add_subpage,
              'separator_after' : true
            },
            'rename':false,
            'remove':false
          }
        }
      }
    });
```

By default, the contextmenu has three links: create, rename, and remove. You need to turn off any you're not currently using by setting them to false.

Now if you right-click on any page name in the pagelist, you will have a choice to create a sub-page under it.

Deleting pages

We will add deletions in the same way, using the context menu.

Edit the same file, and this time in the contextmenu code, replace the remove: false line with these:

```
            'remove' : {
              'label' : "Delete Page",
              'icon'   : "remove",
              'visible' : function (NODE, TREE_OBJ) {
                if(NODE.length != 1) return 0;
                return TREE_OBJ.check("deletable", NODE);
              },
              'action':pages_delete,
              'separator_after' : true
            }
```

And add the `pages_delete` function to the same file:

```
function pages_delete(node,tree){
  if(!confirm(
      "Are you sure you want to delete this page?"))return;
  $.getJSON('/ww.admin/pages/delete.php?id='
      +node[0].id.replace(/.*_/,''),function(){
    document.location=document.location.toString();
  });
}
```

One thing to always keep in mind is whenever creating any code that deletes something in your CMS, you must ask the administrator if he/she is sure, just to make sure it wasn't an accidental click. If the administrator confirms that the click was intentional, then it's not your fault if something important was deleted.

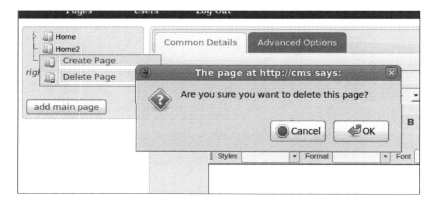

So, the `pages_delete` function first checks for this, and then calls the server to remove the file. The page is then refreshed because this may significantly change the page list tree, as we'll see now.

Create the `/ww.admin/pages/delete.php` file:

```
<?php
require '../admin_libs.php';
$id=(int)$_REQUEST['id'];
if(!$id)exit;
$r=dbRow("SELECT COUNT(id) AS pagecount FROM pages");
if($r['pagecount']<2){
  die('cannot delete - there must always be one page');
}
else{
  $pid=dbOne("select parent from pages
```

```
         where id=$id",'parent');
    dbQuery("delete from pages where id=$id");
    dbQuery("update pages set parent=$pid where parent=$id");
  }
  echo 1;
```

First, we ensure that there is always at least one page in the database. If deleting this page would empty the table, then we refuse to do it. There is no need to add an alert explaining this, as it should be clear to anyone that deleting the last remaining page in a website leaves the website with no content at all. Simply refusing the deletion should be enough.

Next, we delete the page.

Finally, any pages which were contained within that page (pages which had this one as their parent), are moved up in the tree so they are contained in the deleted page's old parent.

For example, if you had a page, page1>page2>page3 (where > indicates the hierarchy), and you removed page2, then page3 would then be in the position page1>page3.

This can cause a large difference in the treestructure if there were quite a few pages contained under the deleted one, so the page needs to be refreshed.

Rich-text editing using CKeditor

Anything entered into the body textarea will be displayed directly on the front-end. We've used a plain textarea for now, but this is not ideal.

It's not a good idea to assume that the administrator knows HTML. Most of them will not.

For a long time, the only reasonable solution for this was to use a text markup language such as Textism or BBCode, which allow you to enter text such as this _is_ a *word*, which will be converted to this is a word.

While that's a good compromise, in the last few years it has become possible to use "what you see is what you get"-style editors, where you can type into the textarea and use buttons or key combinations to style the text and see it right there.

These editors are known as **Rich-text Editors** (RTEs). When describing them to clients, though, I find it's easier to describe them as small Word-like editors. In fact, they're usually designed very similar to the wordprocessor packages that people use in their normal office work.

The first one I used was HTMLarea, but that project eventually was discontinued, and I moved onto FCKeditor. Recently, that project has been rewritten and is now available as CKeditor from `http://ckeditor.com/`.

While it is interesting to offer a choice of RTE or plaintext editing to the administrator (WordPress offers the choice, for example), I've never had a client which asked for plain text. After all, the point of a CMS is to ease the editing of websites and their pages and content, so why ruin this by then writing HTML instead of using an RTE?

Apart from CKeditor, the only other very popular RTE is TinyMCE. There are many other editors, but when you read about them, they are usually compared against CKeditor or TinyMCE.

So, let's start by downloading CKeditor from `http://ckeditor.com/download`—I'm using version 3.2.1. Download it and extract to `/j/`. It will create a directory called `/j/ckeditor/`.

CKeditor is useful enough that we will use it a lot in the admin area. So, we will add it as a plugin that's loaded on all pages. Edit `/ww.admin/header.php` and add the highlighted line:

```
<script src="/ww.admin/j/admin.js"></script>
<script src="/j/ckeditor/ckeditor.js"></script>
<link rel="stylesheet" href="http://ajax.googleapis.com/
    ajax/libs/jqueryui/1.8.0/themes/south-street/
    jquery-ui.css" type="text/css" />
```

To display CKeditor, the method I prefer to use is to create a textarea, and convert it to an editor afterwards using some JavaScript.

The code to do this is repetitive enough that it makes sense to create a small function for it. Add this to `/ww.admin/admin_libs.php`:

```
function ckeditor($name,$value='',$height=250){
  return '<textarea style="width:100%;height:'.$height.'px"
      name="'.addslashes($name).'">'.htmlspecialchars($value)
      .'</textarea><script>$(function(){
          CKEDITOR.replace("'.addslashes($name).'",{
          });
      });</script>';
}
```

The second parameter for the `CKEDITOR.replace` function call is to supply options to CKeditor. We'll get to that in a minute.

Now, let's use it. In `/ww.admin/pages/forms.php,` change the `page-type-specific data` block to the following:

```
// { page-type-specific data
echo '<tr><th>body</th><td colspan="5">';
echo ckeditor('body',$page['body']);
echo '</td></tr>';
// }
```

Now when you load up the page admin, you'll see we have the RTE embedded:

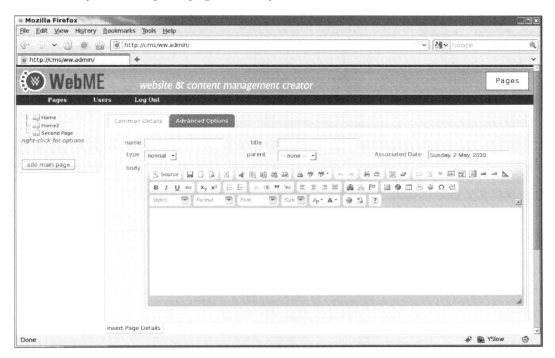

That toolbar is much too full though. The first time an administrator sees that, they would be terrified! Most things an admin will want to do in a web page are really simple—make something bold, insert an image or table, and so on.

I prefer to give the admin a much smaller toolbar.

You can do this by editing the `/j/ckeditor/config.js` file. Here's what I have:

```
CKEDITOR.editorConfig = function( config )
{
  config.skin="v2";
  config.toolbar="WebME";
```

```
config.toolbar_WebME=[
    ['Maximize','Source','Cut','Copy','Paste','PasteText'],
    ['Undo','Redo','RemoveFormat','Bold','Italic',
        'Underline','Subscript','Superscript'],
    ['NumberedList','BulletedList','Outdent','Indent'],
    ['JustifyLeft','JustifyCenter','JustifyRight'],
    ['Link','Unlink','Anchor','Image','Flash','Table',
        'SpecialChar'],
    ['TextColor','BGColor'],
    ['Styles','Format','Font','FontSize']
    ];
};
```

First, I've set the CKeditor skin to `"v2"`, which looks a bit more like what people are used to (Open Office Writer or MS Word). There are others in `/j/ckeditor/skins/` if you prefer to use a different one.

Next we set the editor to use the `"WebME"` set of buttons, and finally, we define those buttons.

Each sub-array is a group of buttons which are similar in purpose. If you resize the editor (notice that the bottom right-hand side of the editor is CMS Design With PHP and jQuery) then each of those groups of buttons will be kept together.

You can compare the default toolbar and the custom toolbar in the following screenshot, the new one is at the bottom:

You can see the custom toolbar is more compact, allowing more room in the textarea to see what is written, and is more like what you would find in the default toolbar of a word processor.

An administrator can use this editor as easily as they would use any word processor—you can copy or paste from sources such as websites or word processor documents and the formats will be mostly retained.

In fact, you can even copy from websites and any images in the copied text will also be copied! The `src` parameter of the image will be the original source, so you should not do this on websites which are not yours. Embedding an image on your site and yet linking to the original site can be seen as rude (it's called **inline linking**, but is also known as **leeching** and **hot-linking**) as you are using someone else's bandwidth to supply the image.

File management using KFM

So, let's say you want to upload your own images or files and link to them through the RTE?

When FCKeditor was the main RTE on the Internet, it had a file manager built in. This file manager allowed you to do some very basic things such as create directories or upload files.

That was about the limit of its capabilities though—if you wanted to rename a file, move it, delete it, and so on, there was simply no way to do it.

The file manager was limited for a number of reasons.

It was designed to work with several separate server-side languages, such as PHP, ASP, Java, and Perl, and adding any one feature meant writing the server-side implementation for it several times over. Concentrating on one single language was not acceptable to the development team, as they wanted it to appeal to all users of the RTE.

There is also that the team was developing a commercial file manager add-on for CKeditor called CKfinder, so enhancing the free file manager was a conflict of interest.

Luckily, the CKeditor plugin system is not hard to work with, so in 2006 I started building my own file manager specifically for use in a CMS with FCKeditor/CKeditor, which I called **KFM** (**Kae's File Manager**).

I started developing KFM with MooTools, but it soon became obvious that jQuery was much better for it, so it was converted to use jQuery. Using jQuery meant less code for me (and my co-developer Benjamin) to write, and also, the more jQuery I used the less I had to maintain myself, because there is a large community out there catering to jQuery.

Download a copy of KFM from `http://kfm.verens.com/`. You can use either the latest stable copy (1.4.5 at the time of writing this book), or the Nightly version, which is compiled each night from subversions. I will use the Nightly version, which you can get by clicking on **nightly** on the front page.

Extract it in /j/. It will create a directory called trunk. Rename that to kfm.

Now delete the /j/kfm/admin/ directory. We will handle administration through the configuration files, and will not allow configuration on-the-fly by administrators.

How KFM works is that you tell it what directory it is to maintain (/f/ in our case) and what database to use to manage the files. There are many other configuration settings, but those are the most important.

For the database, you can use PostGres, MySQL, or SQLite. I prefer to use SQLite, because it is stored as a single file, which you can actually save within the /f/ directory itself (KFM creates a hidden directory called /f/.files and saves its data in there).

This makes it easy for you to back up the entire file storage system and move it to another server if you want, including the database as well. With MySQL or PostGres, you'd have to export the data to a file, move the files, then import the data on the far end.

KFM does a lot of image manipulation, in order to provide thumbnails, and so on. To do this, your PHP server needs to either have GD compiled (this is usually true), or to have ImageMagick installed.

I prefer to use ImageMagick, because it is quicker than GD, and less resource-hungry.

If you are building your CMS on a Windows server, you may have to use GD.

Configuration is managed by creating a file /j/kfm/configuration.php:

```php
<?php
$kfm_userfiles_address=$_SERVER['DOCUMENT_ROOT'].'/f/';
$kfm_userfiles_output='/f/';
$kfm_dont_send_metrics=1;
```

You can see the full list of configuration settings in /j/kfm/configuration.dist. php. KFM loads the dist file first, and then your own file, so you only need to enter the options that you want to change.

In the previous code snippet, we set $kfm_userfiles_address to the full local address of the website's /f/ directory (as if you were on the machine from a console and wanted to navigate to it).

We also set the $kfm_userfiles_output setting to '/f/', to tell KFM where in the website's online-accessible directories the files are kept.

Finally, we set `$kfm_dont_send_metrics` to 1. By default, when KFM is loaded up for the first time every day, it "phones home" to tell the KFM server how many people are using it, and what version is being used—this is so the developers have a reasonable idea what versions of KFM they should support and what can be safely decided to be obsolete. Setting this option to 1 tells KFM not to bother doing this (as the main developer of KFM, I am usually using the most up-to-date version).

Now, create the directory `/f/`, and make sure it is writable by the web server.

In Linux, you can accomplish this in a number of different ways. The simplest is to change the permissions on the directory to "0777" (which means read/write/execute for everyone). This is not advisable on servers where other people may have user accounts, such as virtual host accounts.

A better method is to use suPHP (`http://www.suphp.org/`), which runs PHP scripts using your own username instead of the webserver's. This means that you can secure the files so that they are only accessible or editable by you, and yet the webserver can still work with them.

Setup of suPHP is outside the scope of this book. Feel free to use whichever you want.

For the sake of simplicity, I will assume you are on your own server and no other person has an account on it (this is becoming much more popular lately, thanks to server virtualization), and so you can use the "0777" method.

You should now have an installed copy of KFM.

Test it by going to /j/kfm/ in your browser. You should see something similar to the following screenshot (I've uploaded a few images through the **File Upload** section to test it):

If your installation fails, ask for help on the kfm.verens.com forum.

Okay—you should now have KFM installed. Now, let's connect it to CKeditor.

Hooking the two together is easy—in /ww.admin/admin_libs.php, add the following highlighted line to the CKEDITOR function:

```
CKEDITOR.replace("'.addslashes($name).'",{
    filebrowserBrowseUrl:"/j/kfm/"
});
```

Now when you click on the image icon or link icon in CKeditor, the pop-up window will have a **Browse Server** button:-

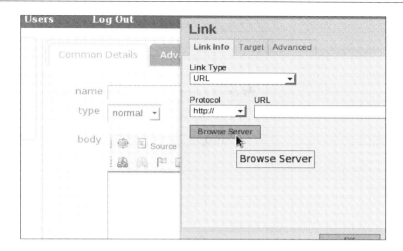

Clicking on that will pop up a new window with KFM in it to let you select the file you want:

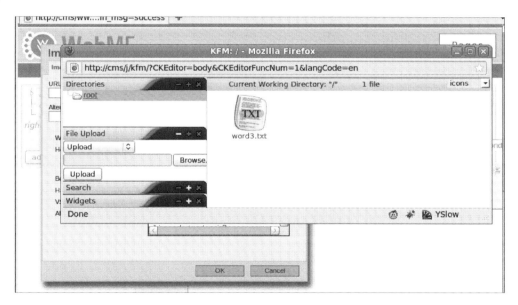

We are almost finished.

We now need to make sure that only authorized users can log into KFM.

After KFM has loaded its configuration, it then loads up another file if it exists, /j/kfm/api/config.php, which is there for developers, in case they want to integrate their CMSes with KFM.

By default this file does not exist in the usual distribution.

Create it and add this content:

```php
<?php
if($_SERVER['PHP_SELF']=='/j/kfm/get.php' ||
   (isset($kfm_api_auth_override) && $kfm_api_auth_override))
      $inc='/ww.incs/basics.php';
else $inc='/ww.admin/admin_libs.php';
include_once $_SERVER['DOCUMENT_ROOT'].$inc;

$kfm_userfiles_address=$_SERVER['DOCUMENT_ROOT'].'/f/';
if(!session_id()){
  if(isset($_GET['cms_session']))
      session_id($_GET['cms_session']);
  session_start();
}
if($_SERVER['PHP_SELF']=='/j/kfm/get.php'){
  $kfm_do_not_save_session=true;
}
$kfm_api_auth_override=true;
$kfm->defaultSetting('file_handler','return');
$kfm->defaultSetting('file_url','filename');
$kfm->defaultSetting('return_file_id_to_cms',false);
```

The first few lines are the most important.

When a file is retrieved through KFM, it always comes through /j/kfm/get.php. Within the KFM interface, for example, the thumbnails are retrieved through that script, and if a file is downloaded, it is downloaded through that script.

So, if that file is loaded in a browser, it needs to be allowed.

Later in the book, we will see plugins which will use KFM's functions to accomplish some things, such as the gallery plugin. To allow those plugins to use KFM, we need to set a variable in the plugin to true ($kfm_api_auth_override). If KFM loads and that variable is set, then permission is granted.

Otherwise, the browser must be logged in as an administrator.

The rest of the lines are additional configuration options which are generally done through the KFM admin area (which we've deleted), and some optimization settings as well.

One final thing needs to be done.

KFM uses an __autoload function to load its classes. WebME also uses an __autoload function. You can only have one of these.

So, we'll rewrite the __autoload function in /ww.incs/basics.php to only get set if no other function of that name exists. Add the following highlighted lines:

```
if(!function_exists('__autoload')){
  function __autoload($name) {
    require $name . '.php';
  }
}
```

And that's it! Now if you log out of the admin area, and try go to /j/kfm/, you will see that you are asked to log in again.

Summary

In this chapter, we finished the page management system.

This included the display and management of page data in the admin area, embedding a rich-text editor, and adding a filemanagement package as well.

In the next chapter, we will look at theme management, and displaying pages and page navigation menus on the front-end.

5
Design Templates – Part One

This chapter will demonstrate how the content of the website can be embedded in a design template.

The design of a site is also known as the "theme" or "skin". I will use these words interchangeably. They both refer to the same thing.

A theme is composed of one or more page templates. The page template is used to define a layout of a specific page (for example, a "splash page" vs. a content page), while the theme says overall what the website looks like—colors, images, and so on. Designers call this the "look and feel" of the website.

In this chapter, we will discuss:

- How themes and templates work
- Smarty templating engine
- Creation of a theme
- Front-end navigation

We will continue with these topics into the next chapter, which will improve on the navigation using jQuery, and then we'll build a theme management system.

How do themes and templates work?

A "theme" is a term which describes the overall look and feel of a website. It describes what the various elements look like—headers, links, tables, lists, and so on. It defines the colors that are used, and any common background images such as gradients or logos. The theme contains one or more templates, and any images or other resources that will be required by those templates.

A "template" is basically an HTML snippet which defines the layout of a page — where on the page the menu is located, are there panels, is there a header and footer. It uses the theme's design, so that other templates in the same site have a similar feel to them.

In the CMS we are building, a template uses a few codes to define where the various elements go on a page.

As an example, here is a very simple template, using code designed to work with the Smarty templating engine:

```
<!doctype html>
<html>
  <head>
    {{$METADATA}}
  </head>
  <body>
    {{MENU direction="horizontal"}}
    {{$PAGECONTENT}}
  </body>
</html>
```

The three highlighted lines are template codes which show where the CMS should place various HTML snippets that it generates.

PHP is itself described as a templating engine, as you can mix it in with HTML simply enough (and in fact, that's how it was originally designed).

You might ask, why bother using an external engine such as Smarty at all when PHP is one itself?

Here is the above template written as PHP:

```
<!doctype html>
<html>
  <head>
    <?php
    require 'common.php';
    echo $METADATA;
    ?>
  </head>
  <body>
    <?php
    MENU (array('direction'=>'horizontal'));
    echo $PAGECONTENT;
    ?>
  </body>
</html>
```

The difference here is not huge, but the first example is easier for a non-PHP user (such as a designer) to use, whereas the second one requires a bit of knowledge of PHP.

Also, notice in the second one, the require line is used to set up the variables $METADATA and $PAGECONTENT. A non-PHP programmer might be confused if they forgot to include that and there were empty spaces in the resulting HTML.

Another very important reason is that PHP files tend to be tied to specific URLs, such as http://cms/page1.php. If you have a number of different pages, and the designer wants to adjust the design, the designer needs to change all of those existing pages.

If the template is kept in an external page and interpreted through an engine, you get a number of advantages:

- Designers don't and can't write PHP in the template files. This makes the engine more robust, allowing the designers to do what they want without risking breakage.
- Programmers don't mess with template files. This means that there is no overlap between what the programmers and designers are doing, making the end product more stable than if they were constantly tweaking each others' code.
- Because the templates are external, you can swap designs by moving the theme directories around.

I think the most important aspect of this is the separation of concerns. The programmer (you) handles programming, the designer handles design, and the only time the work collides is when the design is being interpreted by the templating engine.

Writing your own templating engine is not hard. For a few years, I used my own, which was based on code similar to the previous examples.

One problem with home-grown templating engines is that they do not always have the robustness and speed of the more established engines.

Smarty speeds up its parsing by compiling the template into a PHP script, and then caching that script in a directory set aside for that purpose.

If you use an accelerator such as APC, ionCube, Zend, and so on, then that compiled script will then be cached in-memory by the accelerator, speeding it up even further.

There are other templating engines out there—Twig, FastTemplate, PHAML, and others. They all do basically the same thing, so which you use is perhaps a personal choice. For me, Smarty works and I've no reason to choose another. It's simple to use, and fast.

File layout of a theme

We've discussed how a templating engine works. Now let's look at a more concrete example.

1. Create a directory /ww.skins in the CMS webroot.

2. Within that directory, each theme has its own directory. We will create a very simple theme called "basic".

3. Create a directory /ww.skins/basic, and in that, create the following directories:

/ww.skins/basic/h	This will hold the HTML template files.
/ww.skins/basic/c	This will hold any CSS files.
/ww.skins/basic/i	This will hold images.

Usually, that will be enough for any theme. The only necessary directory there is /h. The others are simply to keep things neat.

If I wanted to add JavaScript specific to that theme, then I would add it to a /ww.skins/basic/j directory. You can see how it all works.

In this basic theme, we will have two templates. One with a menu across the top (horizontal), and one with a menu on the left-hand side (vertical). We will then assign these templates to different pages in the admin area.

In the admin area, the templates will be displayed in alphabetical order.

If there is one template that you prefer to be the default one used by new pages, then the template should be named _default.html. After sorting alphabetically, the underscore causes this file to be top of the list, versus other filenames which begin with letters.

.html is used as the extension for the template so that the designer can easily view the file in a browser to check that it looks okay.

Let's create a default template then, with a menu on the left-hand side. Create this file as /ww.skins/basic/h/_default.html:

```
<!doctype html>
<html>
  <head>
    {{$METADATA} }
    <link rel="stylesheet"
        href="/ww.skins/basic/c/style.css"/>
  </head>
```

```
<body>
  <div id="menu-wrapper">{{MENU
      direction="horizontal"}}</div>
  <div id="page-wrapper">{{$PAGECONTENT}}</div>
</body>
</html>
```

The reason that {{ is used instead of {, is that it if the designer used the brace character ({) for anything in the HTML, or the admin used it in the page content, then it would very likely cause the templating engine to crash — it would become confused because it could not tell whether you meant to just display the character, or use it as part of a code.

By doubling the braces {{ ... }}, we reduce the chance of this happening immensely. Doubled braces very rarely (I've never seen it at all) come up in normal page text.

The reason we use braces at all, and not something more obviously programmatic such as "<!--{ ... }-->", is that it is readable. It is easier to read "insert {{$pagename}} here" than to read "insert <!--{$pagename}--> here".

I've introduced two variables and a function in the template:

{{$METADATA}}	This variable is an automatically generated string consisting of <head> child elements such as <title> and <script> tags to load jQuery, and so on.
{{$PAGECONTENT}}	This variable is the page body text.
{{MENU}}	This is a function which builds up a menu. It can have a number of options attached. You've seen "direction" in the template example code. We'll discuss this later in the chapter.

The template includes a hardcoded reference to the stylesheet.

We could insist that the stylesheet always be named /ww.skins/themename/c/styles.css, and that would allow us to include it automatically in the {{$METADATA}} variable, but we can't do this — different templates may need different styles that cause problems if they are within the one stylesheet.

Another reason is that if the stylesheet is in the template code, then the designer can work on the design without needing to load it through the CMS.

Setting up Smarty

Okay—we have a simple template. Let's display it on the front-end.

To do this, we first edit /ww.incs/basics.php to have it figure out where the theme is. Add this code to the end of the file:

```
// { theme variables
if(isset($DBVARS['theme_dir']))
    define('THEME_DIR',$DBVARS['theme_dir']);
else define('THEME_DIR',SCRIPTBASE.'ww.skins');
if(isset($DBVARS['theme']) && $DBVARS['theme'])
    define('THEME',$DBVARS['theme']);
else{
  $dir=new DirectoryIterator(THEME_DIR);
  $DBVARS['theme']='.default';
  foreach($dir as $file){
    if($file->isDot())continue;
    $DBVARS['theme']=$file->getFileName();
    break;
  }
  define('THEME',$DBVARS['theme']);
}
// }
```

In this, we set two constants:

THEME_DIR	This is the directory which holds the themes repository. Note that we leave the option open for it to be located somewhere other than /ww.skins if we want to move it.
THEME	The name of the selected theme. This is the name of the directory which holds the theme files.

The $DBVARS array, from /.private/config.php, was originally intended to only hold information on database access, but as I added to the CMS, I found this was the simplest place to put information which we need to load in every page of the website.

Instead of creating a second array, for non-database stuff, it made sense to have one single array of site-wide configuration options. Logically, it should be renamed to something like $SITE_OPTIONS, but it doesn't really matter. I only use it directly in one or two places. Everywhere else, it's the resulting defined constants that are used.

After setting up THEME_DIR, defaulting to /ww.skins if we don't explicitly set it to something else, we then set up THEME.

If no $DBVARS['theme']$ variable has been explicitly set, then THEME is set to the first directory found in THEME_DIR. In our example case, that will be the /ww.skins/basic directory.

Now we need to install Smarty.

To do this, go to http://www.smarty.net/download.php and download it. I am using version 2.6.26.

Unzip it in your /ww.incs directory, so there is then a /ww.incs/Smarty-2.6.26 directory.

We do not need to use Smarty absolutely everywhere. For example, we don't use it in the admin area, as there is no real need to do templating there.

For this reason, we don't put the Smarty setup code in /ww.incs/basics.php.

Open up /ww.incs/common.php, and add this to the end of it:

```
require_once SCRIPTBASE
    . 'ww.incs/Smarty-2.6.26/libs/Smarty.class.php';
function smarty_setup($cdir){
  $smarty = new Smarty;
  if(!file_exists(SCRIPTBASE.'ww.cache/'.$cdir)){
    if(!mkdir(SCRIPTBASE.'ww.cache/'.$cdir)){
      die(SCRIPTBASE.'ww.cache/'.$cdir.' not created.<br />
          please make sure that '.USERBASE.'ww.cache is
          writable by the web-server');
    }
  }
  $smarty->compile_dir=SCRIPTBASE.'ww.cache/'.$cdir;
  $smarty->left_delimiter = '{{';
  $smarty->right_delimiter = '}}';
  $smarty->register_function('MENU', 'menu_show_fg');
  return $smarty;
}
```

As we'll see shortly, Smarty will not only be used in the theme's templates. It can be used in other places as well. To reduce repetition, we create a smarty_setup() function where common initializations are placed, and common functions are set up.

First, we make sure that the compile directory exists. If not, we create it (or die() trying).

We change the delimiters next to {{ and }}.

Also note the MENU function (you'll remember from the template code) is registered here. If Smarty encounters a MENU call in a template, it will call the menu_show_fg() function, which we'll define later in this chapter.

We do not define $METADATA or $PAGECONTENT here because they are explicitly tied to the page template.

Remove the last line (the echo $PAGEDATA->body; line) from /index.php.

We discussed how pages can have different "types". The $PAGECONTENT variable may need to be set up in different ways depending on the type, so we add a switch to the index.php to generate it:

```
// { set up pagecontent
switch($PAGEDATA->type){
  case '0': // { normal page
    $pagecontent=$PAGEDATA->body;
    break;
  // }
  // other cases will be handled here later
}
// }
```

That gets the page body and sets $pagecontent with it (we'll add it to Smarty shortly).

Next, we need to define the $METADATA variable. For that, we'll add the following code to the same file (/index.php):

```
// { set up metadata
  // { page title
  $title=($PAGEDATA->title!='')?
    $PAGEDATA->title:
    str_replace('www.','',$_SERVER['HTTP_HOST']).' > '
      .$PAGEDATA->name;
  $metadata='<title>'.htmlspecialchars($title).'</title>';
  // }
  // { show stylesheet and javascript links
  $metadata.='<script src="http://ajax.googleapis.com/ajax/
    libs/jquery/1.4.2/jquery.min.js"></script>'
    .'<script src="http://ajax.googleapis.com/ajax/libs/
    jqueryui/1.8.1/jquery-ui.min.js"></script>' ;
  // }
  // { meta tags
  $metadata.='<meta http-equiv="Content-Type"
    content="text/html; charset=UTF-8" />';
  if($PAGEDATA->keywords)
```

```
    $metadata.='<meta http-equiv="keywords" content="'
        .htmlspecialchars($PAGEDATA->keywords).'" />';
    if($PAGEDATA->description)$metadata.='<meta
        http-equiv="description"
        content="'.htmlspecialchars($PAGEDATA->description).'"
        />';
    // }
    // }
```

If a page title was not provided, then the title is set up as the server's hostname plus the page name.

We include the jQuery and jQuery-UI libraries on every page.

The Content-Type metadata is included because even if we send it as a header, sometimes someone may save a web page to their hard drive. When a page is loaded from a hard drive without using a server, there is no Content-Type header sent so the file itself needs to contain the hint.

Finally, we add keywords and descriptions if they are needed.

Note that we added jQuery-UI, but did not choose one of the jQuery-UI themes. We'll talk about that later in this chapter, when building the page menu.

Next, we need to choose which template to show. Remember that we discussed how site designs may have multiple templates, and each page needs to select one or another.

We haven't yet added the admin part for choosing a template, so what we'll do is, similar to the THEME setup, we will simply look in the theme directory and choose the first template we find (in alphabetical order, so _default.html would naturally be first).

Edit index.php and add this code:

```
// { set up template
if(file_exists(THEME_DIR.'/'.THEME.'/h/'
    .$PAGEDATA->template.'.html')){
  $template=THEME_DIR.'/'.THEME.'/h/'
      .$PAGEDATA->template.'.html';
}
else if(file_exists(THEME_DIR.'/'.THEME.'/h/_default.html')){
  $template=THEME_DIR.'/'.THEME.'/h/_default.html';
}
else{
  $d=array();
```

```
    $dir=new DirectoryIterator(THEME_DIR.'/'.THEME.'/h/');
    foreach($dir as $f){
      if($f->isDot())continue;
      $n=$f->getFilename();
      if(preg_match('/^inc\./',$n))continue;
      if(preg_match('/\.html$/',$n))
          $d[]=preg_replace('/\.html$/','',$n);
    }
    asort($d);
    $template=THEME_DIR.'/'.THEME.'/h/'.$d[0].'.html';
  }
  if($template=='')die('no template created.
     please create a template first');
  // }
```

So, the order here is:

1. Use the database-defined template if it is defined and exists.
2. Use `_default.html` if it exists.
3. Use whatever is alphabetically first in the directory.
4. `die()`!

The reason we check for `_default.html` explicitly is that it saves time. We have set the convention so when creating a theme the designer should name the default template `_default.html`, so it is a waste of resources to search and sort when it can simply be set.

Note that we are ignoring any templates which begin with `"inc."`. Smarty can include files external to the template, so some people like to save the HTML for common headers and footers in external files, then include them in the template. If we simply add another convention that all included files must start with `"inc."` (for example, `inc.footer.html`), then using this code, we will only ever select a full template, and not accidentally use a partial file.

For full instructions on what Smarty can do, you should refer to the online documentation at `http://www.smarty.net/`.

Finally, we set up Smarty and tell it to render the template.

Add this to the end of the same file:

```
$smarty=smarty_setup('pages');
$smarty->template_dir=THEME_DIR.'/'.THEME.'/h/';
// { some straight replaces
$smarty->assign('PAGECONTENT',$pagecontent);
```

```
$smarty->assign('PAGEDATA',$PAGEDATA);
$smarty->assign('METADATA',$metadata);
// }
// { display the document
header('Content-type: text/html; Charset=utf-8');
$smarty->display($template);
// }
```

This section first sets up Smarty, telling it to use the /ww.cache/pages directory for caching compiled versions of the template.

Then the $pagecontent and $metadata variables are assigned to it.

We also assign the $PAGEDATA object to it, which lets us expose the page object to Smarty, in case the designer wants to use some aspect of it directly in the design. For example, the page name can be displayed with {{$PAGEDATA->name|escape}}, or the last edited date can be shown with {{$PAGEDATA->edate|date_format}}.

Before viewing this in a browser, edit the /ww.skins/basics/_default.html file, and change the double braces around the MENU call to single braces. We haven't yet defined that function, so we don't want Smarty to fail when it encounters it.

When viewed in a browser, we now have this screenshot:

It is very similar to the one from *Chapter 1, CMS Core Design*, except that we now have the page title set correctly.

Viewing the source, we see that the template has correctly been wrapped around the page content:

```
Source of: http://cms/ - Mozilla Firefox
File  Edit  View  Help

<!doctype html>
<html>
        <head>
                <title>Kae's home page</title><script
src="http://ajax.googleapis.com/ajax/libs/jquery/1.4.2/jquery.min.js"></script>
<script src="http://ajax.googleapis.com/ajax/libs/jqueryui/1.8.1/jquery-ui.min.js">
</script><meta http-equiv="Content-Type" content="text/html; charset=UTF-8"
/><meta http-equiv="keywords" content="webme,cms,jquery,php" /><meta
http-equiv="description" content="an example website" />
                <style src="/ww.skins/basic/c/style.css"></style>
        </head>
        <body>
                <div id="menu-wrapper">{MENU direction="vertical"}</div>
                <div id="page-wrapper"><p>Hello World</p></div>
        </body>
</html>

Line 6, Col 9
```

Okay—we can now see that the templating engine works for simple variable substitution. Now let's add in functions, and get the menu working.

Before going onto the next section, edit the template again and fix the braces so they're double again.

Front-end navigation menu

The easiest way to create a navigation menu is simply to list all the pages on the site. However, that does not give a contextual feel for where everything is in relation to everything else.

In the admin area, we created a hierarchical `<ul>` list. This is probably the easiest menu which gives a good feel. And, using jQuery, we can provide that `<ul>` list in all cases and transform it to whatever we want.

Let's start by creating the templating engine's MENU function with a `<ul>` tree, and we'll expand on that afterwards.

We've already registered MENU to run the function `show_menu_fg()`, so let's create that function.

We will add it to `/ww.incs/common.php`, where most page-specific functions go:

```
function menu_show_fg($opts){
  $c='';
  $options=array(
```

```
        'direction' => 0,   // 0: horizontal, 1: vertical
        'parent'    => 0,   // top-level
        'background'=> '',  // sub-menu background colour
        'columns'   => 1,   // for wide drop-down sub-menus
        'opacity'   => 0    // opacity of the sub-menu
    );
    foreach($opts as $k=>$v){
        if(isset($options[$k]))$options[$k]=$v;
    }
    if(!is_numeric($options['parent'])){
        $r=Page::getInstanceByName($options['parent']);
        if($r)$options['parent']=$r->id;
    }
    if(is_numeric($options['direction'])){
        if($options['direction']=='0')
            $options['direction']='horizontal';
        else $options['direction']='vertical';
    }
    $menuid=$GLOBALS['fg_menus']++;
    $c.='<div class="menu-fg menu-fg-'.$options['direction']
        .'" id="menu-fg-'.$menuid.'">'
        .menu_build_fg($options['parent'],0,$options)
        .'</div>';
    return $c;
}
$fg_menus=0;
```

menu_show_fg() is called with an array of options as its only parameter. The first few lines of the function override any default values with values that were specified in the array (inspired by how jQuery plugins handle options).

Next, we set up some variables, such as getting details about the menu's parent page if there is one, and convert the direction to use words instead of numbers if a number was given.

Then, we generate an ID for the menu, to distinguish it from any others that might be on the page. This is stored in a global variable. In a more structured system, this might be stored in a static variable in a class (such as how Page instances are cached in the /ww.php_classes/Page.php file), but the emphasis here is on speed, and it's quicker to access a variable directly than to find a class and then read the variable.

Finally, we build a wrapper, fill it with the menu's <ul> tree, and return the wrapper.

The <ul> tree itself is built using a second function, menu_build_fg(), which we'll add in a moment.

Before doing that, we need to add a new method to the Page object. We will be showing links to pages, and need to provide a function for creating the right address. Edit /ww.php_classes/Page.php and add these methods to the Page class:

```
function getRelativeURL(){
    if(isset($this->relativeURL))return $this->relativeURL;
    $this->relativeURL='';
    if($this->parent){
        $p=Page::getInstance($this->parent);
        if($p)$this->relativeURL.=$p->getRelativeURL();
    }
    $this->relativeURL.='/'.$this->getURLSafeName();
    return $this->relativeURL;
}
function getURLSafeName(){
    if(isset($this->getURLSafeName))
        return $this->getURLSafeName;
    $r=$this->urlname;
    $r=preg_replace('/[^a-zA-Z0-9,-]/','-',$r);
    $this->getURLSafeName=$r;
    return $r;
}
```

The getRelativeUrl() method ensures that a page's link includes its parents and so on. For example, if a page's name is page2 and it is contained under the parent page page1, then the returned string is /page1/page2, which can be used in <a> elements in the HTML.

The getURLSafeName() ensures that if the admin used any potentially harmful characters such as !£$%^&*? in the page name, then they are converted to - in the page name. When used in a MySQL query, the hyphen character - acts as a wildcard. So for example, if there is a page name "who are tom & jerry?", then the returned string is who-are-tom---jerry-. This method is commonly used in blog software where its desired that the page name is used in the URL.

Combined, these methods allow the admin to provide "SEO-friendly" page addresses without needing them to remember what characters are allowed or not. Of course, it means that there may be clashes if someone creates one page called "test?" and another called "test!", but those are rare and it is easy for the admin to spot the problem.

Back to the menu—let's add the menu_build_fg() function to /ww.incs/common. php. This will be a large function, so I'll explain it a bit at a time:

```
function menu_build_fg($parentid,$depth,$options){
  $PARENTDATA=Page::getInstance($parentid);
  // { menu order
  $order='ord,name';
  if(isset($PARENTDATA->vars->order_of_sub_pages)){
    switch($PARENTDATA->vars->order_of_sub_pages){
      case 1: // { alphabetical
        $order='name';
        if($PARENTDATA->vars->order_of_sub_pages_dir)
            $order.=' desc';
        break;
      // }
      case 2: // { associated_date
        $order='associated_date';
        if($PARENTDATA->vars->order_of_sub_pages_dir)
            $order.=' desc';
        $order.=',name';
        break;
      // }
      default: // { by admin order
        $order='ord';
        if($PARENTDATA->vars->order_of_sub_pages_dir)
            $order.=' desc';
        $order.=',name';
      // }
    }
  }
  // }
  $rs=dbAll("select id,name,type from pages where parent='"
      .$parentid."' and !(special&2) order by $order");
  if($rs===false || !count($rs))return '';
```

This first section gets the list of pages in this level of the menu from the database.

First, we get data about the parent page.

Next we figure out what sorting order the admin wanted that parent page's sub-pages to be displayed in, and we build up an SQL statement based on that.

Note the `and !(special&2)` part of the SQL statement. As explained in the previous chapter, we're using the `special` field as a bitfield. The `&` here is a Boolean AND function and returns true if the 2 bit is set (the 2 bit corresponds to "Does not appear in navigation"). So what this section means is "and not hidden".

If no pages are found, then an empty string is returned.

Now add this part of the function to the file:

```
$items=array();
foreach($rs as $r){
  $item='<li>';
  $page=Page::getInstance($r['id']);
  $item.='<a href="'.$page->getRelativeUrl().'">'
      .htmlspecialchars($page->name).'</a>';
  $item.=menu_build_fg($r['id'],$depth+1,$options);
  $item.='</li>';
  $items[]=$item;
}
$options['columns']=(int)$options['columns'];

// return top-level menu
if(!$depth)return '<ul>'.join('',$items).'</ul>';
```

What happens here is that we take the result set we got from the database in the previous section, and we build a list of links out of them using the `getRelativeURL()` method to generate safe URLs, and then display the admin-defined name using `htmlspecialchars()`.

Before each `<li>` is closed, we then recursively check `menu_build_fg()` with the current link as the new parent (the highlighted line). If there are no results, then the returned string will be blank. Otherwise it will be a sub-`<ul>` which will be inserted here.

If we are at the top level of the menu, then this generated list is immediately returned, wrapped in `<ul>...</ul>` tags.

The next section of code is triggered only if the call was to a sub-menu where `$depth` is 1 or more, for example from the call in the highlighted line in the last code section:

```
$s='';
if($options['background'])$s.='background:'
    .$options['background'].';';
if($options['opacity'])$s.='opacity:'
    .$options['opacity'].';';
if($s){
  $s=' style="'.$s.'"';
}
// return 1-column sub-menu
if($options['columns']<2)return '<ul'.$s.'>'
    .join('',$items).'</ul>';
```

This section checks to see if the `options` array had background or opacity rules for sub-menus, and applies them.

This is useful in the case that you are switching themes in the admin area, and the theme you switch to hasn't written CSS rules about sub-menus. It is very hard to think of every case that can occur, so designers sometimes don't cover all cases. As an example of this, imagine you have just created a new plugin for the CMS, and it looks good in a new theme designed specifically for it. The admin however, might prefer the general look of an older theme and selects it in the admin area (we'll get to that in this chapter). Unfortunately, that older theme does not have CSS rules to handle the new code.

In these cases, we need to provide workarounds so the code looks okay no matter the theme. In a later chapter, we'll look at how the menu options can be adjusted from the admin area, so that an admin can choose the sub-menu background color and opacity to fit any design they choose (in case the theme has not covered the case already).

The final line of the example returns the sub-menu wrapped in a `<ul>` element in the case that only one column is needed (the most common sub-menu type, and the default).

Now, let's add some code for multi-column sub-menus:

```
// return multi-column submenu
$items_count=count($items);
$items_per_column=ceil($items_count/$options['columns']);
$c='<table'.$s.'><tr><td><ul>';
for($i=1;$i<$items_count+1;++$i){
  $c.=$items[$i-1];
  if($i!=$items_count && !($i%$items_per_column))
      $c.='</ul></td><td><ul>';
}
$c.='</ul></td></tr></table>';
return $c;
}
```

In a number of places throughout the book, I've used HTML tables to display various layouts. While modern designers prefer to avoid the use of tables for layout, sometimes it is much easier to use a table for multi-columned layouts, then to try to find a working cross-browser CSS alternative. Sometimes the working alternative is too complex to be maintainable.

Another reason is that if we were to use a CSS alternative, we would be pushing CMS-specific CSS into the theme, which may conflict with the theme's own CSS. This should be avoided whenever possible.

In this case, we return the sub-menu broken into multiple columns. Most sites will not need this, but in sites that have a huge number of entries in a sub-menu and the sub-menu stretches longer than the height of the window, it's sometimes easier to use multiple columns to fit them all in the window than to get the administrator to break the sub-menu down into further sub-categories.

We can now see this code in action. Load up your home page in the browser, and it should look something like the next screenshot:

In my own database, I have two pages under /Home, but one of them is marked as hidden.

So, this shows how to create the navigation tree.

In the next chapter, we will improve on this menu using jQuery, and will then write a theme management system.

Summary

In this chapter, we advanced the CMS engine to the stage where you can now create a designed template, including page menus, and embed the page content within that.

In the next chapter, we will improve the menu, write a theme management system, and add the ability to embed Smarty templating code within page content.

6
Design Templates – Part Two

In the previous chapter we built the basics of templating, including how to use Smarty, and how to set up a theme so the CMS can display pages through the templates.

We also built a basic HTML navigation menu.

In this chapter, we will: Finish the templating engine. Improve the navigation menu using the Filament Group menu.

At the end of this chapter, the CMS will be complete enough to use in simple sites.

Adding jQuery to the menu

For a very long time, I was using a home-grown JavaScript navigational menu.

It was capable of displaying in many different ways—drop downs, slide downs (like jQuery-UI accordions), fade-ins.

It had built-in collision checks to make sure it was always visible and didn't try to render past the sides, bottom, or top of a screen.

It was complex, and I would only ever touch it when I was asked to add yet another feature to it by a client, or when a bug was discovered.

That's never the ideal situation. In an ideal situation, the components you use in your system are constantly being improved and added to, even when you are not working on it yourself.

That's where open source comes into its own. I really do love using a piece of software for a few months, then finding it has been updated by the developers and now has a load of new features that I wasn't aware that I wanted, but now "need".

In my CMS, I've replaced my home-grown solution with an existing project by the Filament Group, which can be seen in action here: `http://www.filamentgroup.com/lab/jquery_ipod_style_and_flyout_menus/`.

If you read through that document, you will see that the group is no longer working on the project, because they've given it to the jQuery-UI team to help create a jQuery-UI menu plugin.

At the time of writing, the jQuery-UI menu is still in development, and should be available by version 1.9. It's currently in a very basic state and unusable, but whenever the jQuery-UI team focuses on anything, the end result is always comprehensive and amazingly stable.

In the meantime, the existing **Filament Group Menu** (**fg-menu** from now on) is probably the best "general use" menu out there, and I'm certain that when the jQuery-UI version is released, porting from the fg-menu system to the new plugin will be easy.

By "general use", I mean that it is not designed specifically to be a drop down or fly-out menu. It's not designed to look exactly one way, or work exactly one way. It can work in a few different ways, so the site designers are not constrained too much by what we developers force on them.

So, let's install it.

Preparing the Filament Group Menu

Download the fg-menu code from the previously mentioned page (search for **Download the script, CSS, and sample HTML** on the page) and unzip it in /j. A /j/__MACOSX directory and a /j/fg-menu directory will both be created. Delete the /j/__MACOSX directory.

One problem with downloading plugins is that sometimes, the writers will associate colors and other styles to the elements that you will need to overwrite.

In most cases, I'd advocate adding a CSS sheet which overrides the fg-menu by using more specific selectors. This has a disadvantage of having the browser download two sheets when only one is needed.

However, since we know that the current version of the plugin is the last ever until jQuery-UI 1.9 is released, I feel it is okay to edit the downloaded files themselves.

This includes the JavaScript files. There are a number of things I didn't like about the fg-menu JavaScript, and the easiest way to address them was by editing the source itself.

I won't describe the CSS changes here (they're in the downloadable code bundle available on Packt's website) other than to say it was purely to remove colors.

The JavaScript gripes are minor as well, but they were enough that I felt the need to hack the source.

The default code forces the user to click the menu to activate its sub-menus.

This has the disadvantage that if you have say two pages, "Page1" and "Page1>Page2", where Page2 is a sub-page of Page1, then how do you tell the menu that you want to go to Page1? Clicking should do it, but instead, it opens the sub-menu!

The solution for this is easy: Just replace the responsible `.click()` events with `.mouseover()` events (lines 26 and 363) in the file `/j/fg-menu/fg.menu.js`.

Another problem has to do with widths and heights. I only noticed this on IE (no other browser) with jQuery 1.4.

fg-menu has two custom functions, `jQuery.fn.getTotalWidth()` and `jQuery.fn.getTotalHeight()` (lines 549 to 556), but those are no longer necessary, because you can use jQuery's `.outerWidth()` and `.outerHeight()` functions.

So, delete the source for those two custom functions, and edit lines 468 and 469 to refer to `outerWidth()` and `outerHeight()` instead.

 I'm walking through the process that I used to fix the code to try to explain how it was done. If you prefer to skip copying the process yourself, you can download the finished code as part of this chapter's downloadable code bundle from the Packt website.

Another thing is the `this.chooseItem()` function. In fg-menu, this is called when an item is clicked. In our case, we always want this to actually go to the page that's clicked. So add this line to the beginning of the function (after line 244):

```
location.href = $(item).attr('href');return;
```

I've placed both commands on the same line because I want to make as few changes to the original structure as possible, so that if I ever need to refer to a line number, it's as close to the original source as possible.

There are some other minor issues, but not important enough to mention here (they're all fixed in the chapter's code bundle).

The final change I made to the plugin is something that was actually requested of the Filament Group by an interested user, but they'd passed on responsibility by that time and it was never answered.

When a menu is opened and you take the mouse off it, it is expected that the menu will close. This doesn't happen in fg-menu (you need to actually click the document to close it).

To fix this, I added the following jQuery code to the end of the file:

```
$('.fg-menu,.fg-menu-top-level')
  .live('mouseover',function(){
    this.mouse_is_over=true;
    clearTimeout(window.fgmenu_mouseout_timer);
  })
  .live('mouseout',function(){
    this.mouse_is_over=false;
    window.fgmenu_mouseout_timer=setTimeout(function(){
      var o=0;
      $('.fg-menu,.fg-menu-top-level').each(function(){
        if (this.mouse_is_over) o++;
      });
      if(!o){
        $.each(allUIMenus, function(i){
          if (allUIMenus[i].menuOpen) {
            allUIMenus[i].kill();
          };
        });
      }
    },2000);
  });
```

In short, this code tells `fg-menu` to close all menus two seconds after the mouse has left it.

Let's examine this in more detail.

When you move your mouse between two elements that appear to be right next to each other, it is possible that the browser will interpret even the slightest gap (border, margin, and so on) as meaning the mouse is not in either of them.

For this reason, we need to create a "grace" period, which allows the mouse time to move from one to the other.

How we do that is when the mouse enters a menu item, you set a variable `mouse_is_over` on it. When the mouse leaves the item, we unset that variable, and start a countdown to the destruction code.

The countdown (a two second `setTimeout`) gives us enough time to move the mouse to another item and disable the timer.

If by chance the timer still goes off, for example the menu you left overlaps or is contained in another menu, and the `mouseenter` event never triggered on the "container", then the destruction code does a test to see if `mouse_is_over` is set.

If so, it does nothing. If not, then all menu entries are killed.

Integrating the menu

We've already embedded a `<ul>` tree version of the menu where `{{MENU}}` appears in the template. Enhancing this involves simply applying the fg-menu plugin to that `<ul>`.

Using the plugin involves adding the source of the plugin as an external JavaScript reference.

If we simply echo out a `<script>` tag every time we need to reference a file, we may end up with redundant loads.

For example, let's say you had two menus on the page. It is silly to have to load a static script twice (once for each menu), so let's create a global array which holds a list of external scripts and CSS files that need to be loaded, and whenever we want to output a script, we'll check against it.

Edit /`index.php` and add the following highlighted lines:

```
// { common variables and functions
include_once('ww.incs/common.php');
$page=isset($_REQUEST['page'])?$_REQUEST['page']:'';
$id=isset($_REQUEST['id'])?(int)$_REQUEST['id']:0;
$external_scripts=array();
$external_css=array();
// }
```

And we will add these functions to /`ww.incs/common.php`:

```
function import_script_once($script){
  global $external_scripts;
  if(isset($external_scripts[$script]))return '';
  $external_scripts[$script]=1;
  return '<script src="'.htmlspecialchars($script).'">
      </script>';
}
function import_css_once($css){
  global $external_css;
  if(isset($external_css[$css]))return '';
  $external_css[$css]=1;
  return '<link rel="stylesheet" href="'
      .htmlspecialchars($css).'"/ >';
}
```

It is easier to ensure that `$array[$filename]` is unique (as an array key), than to ensure that `$filename` is unique in `$array[]` as a value.

Now let's add the fg-menu script references. Edit `/ww.incs/common.php` and add these highlighted lines to the top of the `fg_menu_show()` function:

```
function menu_show_fg($opts){
  $c='';
  $c.=import_script_once('/j/fg-menu/fg.menu.js');
  $c.=import_css_once('/j/fg-menu/fg.menu.css');
  $options=array(
```

And now we add the code to activate the conversion from `<ul>` tree to `flyOut` menu. Add this to the end of the same function in the same file. I've highlighted the lines that the code goes between:

```
  $c.='<div class="menu-fg menu-fg-'.$options['direction']
    .'" id="menu-fg-'.$menuid.'">'
    .menu_build_fg($options['parent'],0,$options).'</div>';
  if($options['direction']=='vertical'){
    $posopts="positionOpts: { posX: 'left', posY: 'top',
      offsetX: 40, offsetY: 10, directionH: 'right',
      directionV: 'down', detectH: true, detectV: true,
      linkToFront: false },";
  }
  else{
    $posopts='';
  }
  $c.="<script>
jQuery.fn.outer = function() {
  return $( $('<div></div>').html(this.clone()) ).html();
}
$(function(){
  $('#menu-fg-$menuid>ul>li>a').each(function(){
    if(!$(this).next().length)return; // empty
    $(this).menu({
      content:$(this).next().outer(),
      choose:function(ev,ui){
        document.location=ui.item[0].childNodes(0).href;
      },
      $posopts
      flyOut:true
    });
  });
  $('.menu-fg>ul>li').addClass('fg-menu-top-level');
});
</script>";
  return $c;
}
```

First off, we set up the $posopts variable, which will tell fg-menu where sub-menus should be positioned relative to their parents. For example, where the top-level menu is vertical, the sub-menu should be offset to the right-hand side. In horizontal top-level menus, the sub-menu should appear directly below its parent (the default).

Next, we output the JavaScript which sets up the menu.

Notice that we've added a short jQuery plugin inline—because most browsers don't provide a method to get the outer HTML of an element, and fg-menu generates its sub-menus from an HTML string, we need to add this function so we can generate the HTML from the <ul> tree.

Now when you reload the browser, the screen will look like this, with the sub-menus hidden:

Because we are using an absolutely basic template, there is no margin or padding set up (in fact, the theme's CSS sheet is still blank at this point of the chapter). Remember that we set up the template initially to have the menu embedded with its direction set to "horizontal".

Embedding the {{MENU}} template function will automatically set up a basic menu. You need to then add your own CSS to make it look better. As an example, here is some simple CSS which I've added to the example template's CSS file, /ww.skins/ basic/c/style.css:

```
.fg-menu-container a{
  border:1px solid #000;
  text-decoration:none;
  font-style:italic;
  background:#fff;
}
.menu-fg a{
  border:1px solid #000;
  padding:5px;
```

```
    text-decoration:none
  }
  .menu-fg li{
    width:120px;
  }
  .menu-fg ul{
    list-style:none;
    padding:0;
  }
```

That's enough to make the menu more usable.

Here's a screenshot with the first item opened:

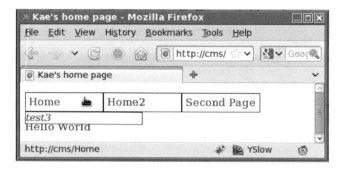

And if we edit the template and replace the "horizontal" with "vertical", we get this:

That's it for now with the menus. We'll come back to them later on when we're working on a menu plugin (so administrators can add menus to template without needing to actually edit the template source).

Until then, if you only plan on having one theme in your CMS, with only one template, there is enough of the engine built now for you to create simple sites.

However, if you want to provide multiple themes, we will need to build that into the administration area of the CMS. Let's do that now.

Choosing a theme in the administration area

Okay—let's write the theme switcher.

First, we will add the `Themes` page to the admin menu. The menu is getting a bit full, but we'll take care of that in the next chapter when we consider plugins.

Edit `/ww.admin/header.php` and add the highlighted line:

```
<li><a href="/ww.admin/users.php">Users</a></li>
<li><a href="/ww.admin/themes.php">Themes</a></li>
<li>
  <a href="/ww.incs/logout.php?redirect=/ww.admin/">
    Log Out
  </a>
</li>
```

Eventually, we will want to group the site-management (versus page-management) functions together, so we will add this to the `Users` admin page menu as well. Edit `/ww.admin/users.php` and add this highlighted line:

```
echo '<a href="/ww.admin/users.php">Users</a>';
echo '<a href="/ww.admin/themes.php">Themes</a>';
echo '</div>';
```

Similar to the Users page, we will have a "wrapper" file in `/ww.admin` that loads up sub-requirements. You can create this file by copying `/ww.admin/users.php`, making the small changes necessary (highlighted) to make it themes-based, and save it as `/ww.admin/themes.php`:

```
<?php
require 'header.php';
echo '<h1>Theme Management</h1>';

echo '<div class="left-menu">';
echo '<a href="/ww.admin/users.php">Users</a>';
echo '<a href="/ww.admin/themes.php">Themes</a>';
echo '</div>';

echo '<div class="has-left-menu">';
echo '<h2>Theme Management</h2>';
```

```
require 'themes/list.php';
echo '</div>';

echo '<script src="/ww.admin/themes/themes.js"></script>';
require 'footer.php';
```

Now create the directory /ww.admin/themes. We will place the dependent files in there.

Anything up to twenty or thirty themes can be easily displayed on one page to be chosen from by the administrator.

If there are more, then a more advanced selection script will need to be created than the one described in this section.

It is unanticipated, though, that in a single-site CMS, any more than two or three would be added to the repository at any time—after all, people don't switch their designs every two weeks!

In a larger system, though, where the CMS may be one of many instances which are accessing a common repository (in the case of a large hosting company that offers off-the-shelf websites, for example), there could be hundreds or even possibly thousands.

So, we've already created one simple theme, called "Basic", which really could not be any simpler.

However, when offering it up for selection (along with others), the name of the design is not really enough—it is better to show a screenshot so the admin has a visual idea of what they are choosing.

In larger systems, you may also have a description, describing the basic colors, whether the theme has columns, requires certain plugins, and so on. We will not need these.

So, first, load up your site, and take a screenshot of the design. Save that design as /ww.skins/basic/screenshot.png.

This is the convention that we will use—inside each theme directory, there will be a screenshot.png, sized 240x172 pixels. If there is no such file, then it will not be displayed in the admin area. As a side benefit, this will also allow you to "deprecate" any old designs, by hiding them from the admin, yet still allowing the design to work if it is already selected.

To demonstrate this sub-project, I've added eleven directories to my /ww.skins directory, with screenshots in each taken from freely-available WordPress designs (available here: http://wordpress.org/extend/themes/browse/popular/)— while WordPress themes will not work directly in the CMS, it is actually very simple to convert them so they do, either by hand or with a script.

Here is my /ww.skins directory:

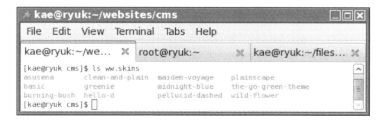

A shrewd reader will note that at the moment, the CMS does not currently save which theme it is using, and instead simply chooses the first it finds in that directory.

The order of files in a directory is not necessarily alphabetical.

When I load up my browser and check the front page again, I find it is no longer using the Basic theme, but the one named "Bakery":

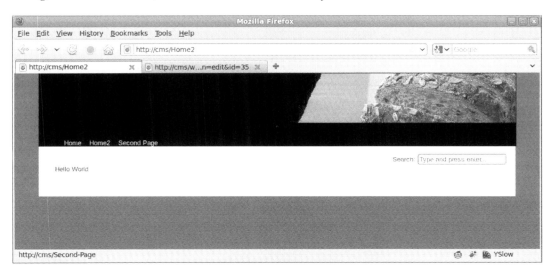

So how do we get the CMS to store one theme and not randomly choose others?

Earlier in the chapter we wrote some code which checked to see if the theme was defined in the /.private/config.php file's $DBVARS array, and if not, then choose from the /ww.skins directory. So we need to be able to change that array on-the-fly from the admin area.

The way to manage this is to make the file writable by the web server, as described back in the KFM section of *Chapter 3, Page Management – Part One*, then add this function to /ww.incs/basics.php:

```
function config_rewrite(){
    global $DBVARS;
    $tmparr=$DBVARS;
    $tmparr2=array();
    foreach($tmparr as $name=>$val)$tmparr2[]=
        '\''.addslashes($name).'\'=>\''.addslashes($val).'\'';
    $config="<?php\n\$DBVARS=array(\n "
        .join(",\n ",$tmparr2)
        ."\n);";
    file_put_contents(CONFIG_FILE,$config);
}
```

What this does is to take the current global $DBVARS array, and re-create it as an executable PHP string, and write it back into CONFIG_FILE (/.private/config.php by default).

Now in order to set the theme, all we need to do is to add a theme field to the global $DBVARS array and then call config_rewrite().

There is one more function needed. Add this to the same file:

```
function cache_clear($type){
    if(!is_dir(SCRIPTBASE.'/ww.cache/'.$type))return;
    $d=new DirectoryIterator(SCRIPTBASE.'/ww.cache/'.$type);
    foreach($d as $f){
        $f=$f->getFilename();
        if($f=='.' || $f=='..')continue;
        unlink(SCRIPTBASE.'/ww.cache/'.$type.'/'.$f);
    }
}
```

The reason for this is that Smarty caches the templates based on the filename in the template directory. But, because each template contains the same filenames, Smarty gets confused and reuses the old cache.

To solve this, we clear the cache whenever a new theme is chosen. We'll talk more about caches later on in the chapter.

Now let's create /ww.admin/themes/list.php:

```php
<?php
// { handle actions
if(isset($_REQUEST['action']) && $_REQUEST['action']=='set_theme'){
  if(is_dir(THEME_DIR.'/'.$_REQUEST['theme'])){
    $DBVARS['theme']=$_REQUEST['theme'];
    config_rewrite();
    cache_clear('pages');
  }
}
// }
// { display list of themes
  $dir=new DirectoryIterator(THEME_DIR);
  $themes_found=0;
  foreach($dir as $file){
    if($file->isDot())continue;
    if(!file_exists(THEME_DIR.'/'.$file.'/screenshot.png'))
        continue;
    $themes_found++;
    echo '<div style="width:250px;text-align:center;
        border:1px solid #000;margin:5px;height:250px;
        float:left;';
    if($file==$DBVARS['theme'])echo 'background:#ff0;';
    echo '"><form method="post" action="./themes.php">
        <input type="hidden" name="page" value="themes" />
        <input type="hidden" name="action"
            value="set_theme" />';
    echo '<input type="hidden" name="theme"
        value="'.htmlspecialchars($file).'" />';
    $size=getimagesize(
        '../ww.skins/'.$file.'/screenshot.png');
    $w=$size[0]; $h=$size[1];
    if($w>240){
      $w=$w*(240/$w);
      $h=$h*(240/$w);
    }
    if($h>172){
      $w=$w*(172/$h);
      $h=$h*(172/$h);
    }
    echo '<img src="/ww.skins/'.htmlspecialchars($file)
        .'/screenshot.png" width="'.(floor($w)).'"
        height="'.(floor($h)).'" /><br />';
```

```
        echo '<strong>',htmlspecialchars($file),'</strong><br />';
        echo '<input type="submit" value="set theme" />
            </form></div>';
    }
    if($themes_found==0){
        echo '<em>No themes found. Create a theme and place it
            into the /ww.skins/ directory.</em>';
    }
// }
```

At the head of the file, we check to see if any action was requested (to see if a theme was chosen).

If so, we set that in $DBVARS and rewrite the config file, then clear the Smarty cache so the new template is used instead of the old cached one.

Next, we display a form for each theme in /ww.skins that has a screenshot.png file in it.

We display the screenshot, making sure to resize it down if it's larger than a certain size (I chose 240x172), keeping the aspect ratio so it doesn't look weird.

With all this, you should now be able to click on **set theme** and have it update the configuration file. Make sure of this by checking /.private/config.php after clicking, to see if you got the file permissions right.

Here's an example before clicking:

```
<?php
$DBVARS=array(
    'username'=>'cmsuser',
    'password'=>'cmspass',
    'hostname'=>'localhost',
    'db_name'=>'cmsdb'
);
```

And after clicking, that file is updated to this, with the selected theme highlighted:

```
<?php
$DBVARS=array(
    'username'=>'cmsuser',
    'password'=>'cmspass',
    'hostname'=>'localhost',
    'db_name'=>'cmsdb',
    'theme'=>'basic'
);
```

Oh, and here is what the theme selection page looks like (with the **pellucid-dashed** theme selected—upper right-hand side corner):

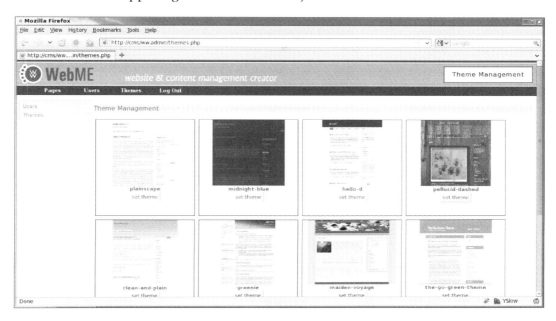

Next, we will update the Basic theme to have multiple templates, and add the ability to choose those templates.

Choosing a page template in the administration area

In the Basic theme, we created just one template, which we named `/ww.skins/basic/h/_default.html`. Edit that file, and make sure the menu is back to `horizontal`.

Now let's create a second template, called `/ww.skins/basic/h/menu-on-left.html`:

```
<!doctype html>
<html>
  <head>
    {{$METADATA}}
    <link rel="stylesheet"
        href="/ww.skins/basic/c/style.css" />
  </head>
  <body class="menu-on-left">
    <div id="menu-wrapper">{{MENU direction="vertical"}}</div>
```

```
        <div id="page-wrapper">{{$PAGECONTENT}}</div>
    </body>
</html>
```

Notice the class `menu-on-left`. That lets us add the following to the CSS sheet at
`/ww.skins/basic/c/style.css`:

```
.menu-on-left #menu-wrapper{
  float:left;
  width:130px;
}
.menu-on-left #page-wrapper{
  margin-left:140px;
}
```

This will only affect the menu wrapper and page wrapper in that specific template.

Now open `/ww.admin/pages/forms.php` and where it says `we'll add this in
the next chapter`, replace that block with this:

```
// { template
echo '<tr><th>template</th><td>';
$d=array();
if(!file_exists(THEME_DIR.'/'.THEME.'/h/')){
  echo 'SELECTED THEME DOES NOT EXIST<br />Please
      <a href="/ww.admin/siteoptions.php?page=themes">select
      a theme</a>';
}
else{
  $dir=new DirectoryIterator(THEME_DIR.'/'.THEME.'/h/');
  foreach($dir as $f){
    if($f->isDot())continue;
    $n=$f->getFilename();
    if(preg_match('/\.html$/',$n))
        $d[]=preg_replace('/\.html$/','',$n);
  }
  asort($d);
  if(count($d)>1){
    echo '<select name="template">';
    foreach($d as $name){
      echo '<option ';
      if($name==$page['template'])echo ' selected="selected"';
      echo '>',$name,'</option>';
    }
    echo '</select>';
  }
  else echo 'no options available';
}
```

```
echo '</td></tr>';
// }
```

Straightforward enough—this block first checks that the selected theme actually exists, and then displays template options if there are any, with the already-selected one selected (or the first on the list if none are already selected).

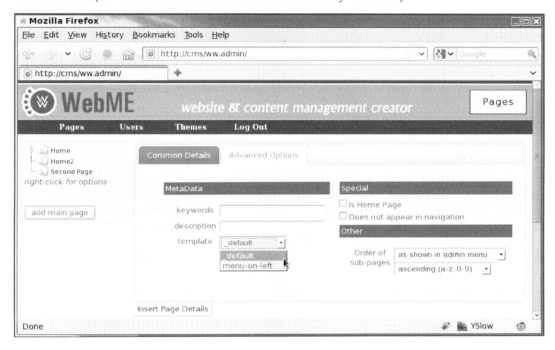

In the screenshot, you can see the list of templates. _default is at the top alphabetically.

Now, you need to edit /ww.admin/pages/action.edit.php, and change the create SQL block to this:

```
// { create SQL
$q='template="'.addslashes($_REQUEST['template']).'",
    edate=now(),type="'.addslashes($_REQUEST['type']).'",
    associated_date="'.addslashes($associated_date).'",
    keywords="'.addslashes($keywords).'",
    description="'.addslashes($description).'",
    name="'.addslashes($name).'",
    title="'.addslashes($title).'",
    body="'.addslashes($body).'",parent='.$pid.',
    special='.$special.',vars="'.addslashes($vars).'"';
// }
```

And with that done, you can now switch templates for each page on the front-end.

Running Smarty on page content

Let's say you want to embed some templated stuff into the actual content of the page.

For example, let's say that we've already done the next few chapters and have build the "image transitions" plugin. You want to have a load of images fading into each other in the page you are writing.

To do that, you would either have to write the source code of the transition effect into the page itself, or embed just the code for it. `{{IMAGE_TRANSITION directory="img"}}` is much easier to write than a whole code block, so it makes sense to use Smarty to handle not just the wrapping template, but also the page content itself.

To do that, you need to have the page content saved in a file, as Smarty works on actual files, and not on database stuff.

Edit `/ww.php_classes/Page.php` and add this method to the `Page` class:

```
function render(){
    $smarty=smarty_setup('pages');
    $smarty->compile_dir=SCRIPTBASE . '/ww.cache/pages';
    if(!file_exists(SCRIPTBASE.'/ww.cache/pages/template_'
        .$this->id)){
      file_put_contents(SCRIPTBASE.'/ww.cache/pages/template_'
          .$this->id,$this->body);
    }
    return $smarty->fetch(SCRIPTBASE
        .'/ww.cache/pages/template_'.$this->id);
}
```

When called, this method first sets up Smarty, as we saw earlier in the chapter.

Then it checks to see if a copy of the page body exists as a file in `SCRIPTBASE . '/ww.cache/pages/'`. If not, then the file is created.

Then, Smarty is run against that file and the result is returned.

Now we need to make sure it is used. Edit `/index.php`, and in the `set up pagecontent` section, change the first case to this:

```
case '0': // { normal page
  $pagecontent=$PAGEDATA->render();
  break;
// }
```

And finally, to make sure that the Smarty cache is cleared every time a page is changed, we add this (highlighted line) to the end of /ww.admin/pages/action.edit.php:

```
echo '<em>Page Saved</em>';
cache_clear('pages');
```

And also to the end of /ww.admin/pages/delete.php:

```
}
echo 1;
cache_clear('pages');
```

That will do it!

Now, as a test, change your home page to use the _default template (the one with the horizontal menu), and then edit the page body to this:

Before you save, there's something important to fix first. The CKeditor RTE (Rich-text Editor) converts the double-quote character " to the HTML entity code " in the background. This can cause problems, so we will edit /ww.admin/pages/action.edit.php, and where the $body variable is initialised, convert that line to this highlighted one:

```
$name          =pages_setup_name($id,$pid);
$body          =str_replace('&quot;','"',$_REQUEST['body']);
$special       =pages_setup_specials($id);
```

Then click on **Update** to save the page.

Now when you view the front-end, you should see this:

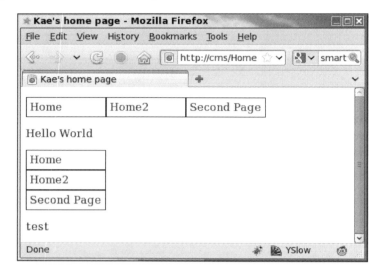

And that demonstrates that you can now call Smarty functions from within the page body itself!

Summary

In this chapter, we advanced the CMS engine to the stage that you can now create a designed template, including page menus, and embed the page content within that.

Not only that, but you can also now use Smarty functions within the page body as well, meaning that when we create plugins, we can use some of them "inline" in the page body.

In the next chapter, we will start on the plugin framework, allowing us to add or remove modules of code without affecting the core code at all.

7
Plugins

In this chapter, we will enhance the CMS engine so it can use plugins or external code modules, which can be "plugged" into the engine to add new abilities to it.

This chapter will include the following topics:

- What are plugins and triggers and why must a CMS handle them
- The creation of the plugin architecture
- Enabling plugins
- Handling of plugin database tables and upgrades
- Creating an example plugin, Page Comments

After completing this chapter, the CMS could be considered "complete", in that almost every other requested feature can be supplied by writing a plugin for it.

However, it should be noted that a CMS never is actually complete, because each new website may bring a new request that is not yet catered for.

Having said that, using plugins lets you at least complete a "core" engine and concentrate on providing hooks that allow further development to be done, outside that core.

What are plugins?

A **plugin** is a module of code that can be dropped into a directory and enabled, to give a CMS extra capabilities.

Plugins need to be able to change the output and do other tasks, so it is necessary to add various "hooks" throughout the code where the plugins can apply their code.

A very important reason for adding a plugin architecture to a CMS is that it lets you stabilize the core code. The **core** is basically the code that will be available in every instance of the CMS, as opposed to plugin code, which may or may not be present in any particular instance of the CMS.

With a core piece of code that is deemed "complete", it becomes easier to manage bugs. Because you are not always adding to the core code, you are not actively adding to the potential number of bugs.

In a CMS which does not have a stable core, any change to the central code can affect just about anything else.

You really need to get your CMS to a stage where you are no longer developing the central engine. Instead, you are working mostly on external plugins and maybe occasional bug fixes to the core, as they are found.

In my case, for example, I worked for years on building up a CMS before getting around to building in plugins. Every change that was requested was built into the core code. Usually, only the fully-tested code at that time would be the new code, so very often we would miss a problem that the new code would have caused somewhere else in the CMS. Often, this problem would not show up for weeks, so it would not be obvious what the problem was related to!

When all the development of a CMS is shifted to plugins, it becomes less likely that the core is at fault when a problem occurs. Because plugins, by their nature, tend to be isolated pieces of code, if a bug does appear, it is very likely the bug is within the plugin's code and not anywhere else.

Also, because plugins allow a person to develop without touching the core engine, it is possible for the external teams or individuals to create their own plugins that they can use with the engine, without needing to understand all the parts of the core engine.

One more advantage is that if the plugin architecture is solid, it is possible for development to continue on the core completely separately from the plugins, knowing that plugins from one version of the CMS will most likely work with a core from another version.

Events in the CMS

One example of a hook is event triggers.

In JavaScript (and therefore jQuery), there is the concept of **events**, where you can set a block of code to run when a certain trigger happens.

For example, when you move your mouse over an element, there are a number of potential trigger points—`onmouseover`, `onmouseenter`, `onmousemove` (and possibly others, depending on the context).

Obviously, PHP does not have those events, as it's a server-side language. But it is possible to conceive of triggers for your CMS that you could potentially hook onto.

For example, let's say you've just finished figuring out the page content. At this point, you may want to trigger a `page-content-created` event. This could (and will, in this chapter) be used by a **Page Comments** plugin to tack on the comments thread, and any required forms, to the end of that page content.

Another example: Let's say you want to create a custom log for your own purposes. You would then be interested in a **start trigger** that can be used to initialize certain values, such as a timer. After the output has been sent, a **finish trigger** that can be used to tally up a number of figures (compilation time, memory used, size of rendered output, and so on) and record them in a file or database before the script finishes.

Page types

In some cases, you will want the page content to be totally converted. Instead of showing a page body as normal, you may want to show an image gallery or a store checkout.

In this case, you would need to create a "page type" block of code, which the front-end will use instead of the usual page data `render()` call.

In the admin area, this might also require using a customized form instead of the usual rich text editor.

Admin sections

The admin area may need to have new sections added by a plugin. In the Events section, we described a logging plugin. A perfect complement to that is a graphing log viewer, which would be shown as a completely new admin section and have its own entry in the admin menu.

Page admin form additions

You may also want to add extra forms to all the Page forms in the admin, regardless of what page type it is. For example, if you create a security plugin and want to protect various pages depending on who is viewing it, you will need to be able to choose which users or groups have access and what to display if the current user does not have full access. This requires an additional form in the Page admin.

It is very difficult to describe all the possible plugin uses, and the number of triggers that may be required.

The easiest way to proceed is to just adjust the engine as required. If it turns out you forgot to add an event trigger at some point, it should be a small matter to just add it in at that point without affecting the core code beyond that addition.

Example plugin configuration

Create a directory called /ww.plugins.

Each plugin you create will be placed in a directory—one directory per plugin.

For our first example, we're going to build a Page Comments plugin, which will allow visitors to your site to leave comments on your pages.

On the admin side, we will need to provide methods to maintain the submitted comments per page and for the whole site.

Anyway, create a directory to hold the plugin called /ww.plugins/page-comments.

The CMS will expect the plugin configuration for each plugin to be in a file named plugin.php. So the configuration for the Page Comments plugin /ww.plugins/page-comments/plugin.php is as follows:

```php
<?php
$plugin=array(
   'name' => 'Page Comments',
   'description' => 'Allow your visitors to comment on pages.',
   'version' => '0',
   'admin' => array(
     'menu' => array(
       'Communication>Page Comments' => 'comments'
     ) ,
     'page_tab' => array(
       'name' => 'Comments',
       'function' => 'page_comments_admin_page_tab'
     )
   ),
   'triggers' => array(
     'page-content-created' => 'page_comments_show'
   )
);
```

The plugin.php files at least contain an array named $plugin, which describes the plugin.

We will expand on the possible configurations of this array throughout the book. For now, let's look at what the current example says. All of these options, except the first two, are optional.

First, we define a name, "Page Comments". This is only ever used in the admin area, when you are choosing your plugins. The same is true of the description field.

The version field is used by the CMS to tell whether a plugin is up-to-date or if some automatic maintenance is needed. This will be explained in more detail later in this chapter.

Next, we have the admin array, which holds details of the admin-only functions.

The menu array is used to edit the admin menu, in case you need to add an admin section for the plugin. In this case, we will add an admin section for Page Comments, which will let you set site-wide settings and view comments site-wide.

If a new tab is to be added to the page admin section, this tab is described in the `page_tab` array. `name` is what appears in the tab header, and `function` is the name of a PHP function that will be called to generate the tab content.

Finally, the triggers array holds details of the various triggers that the plugin should react to. Each trigger calls a function.

Obviously, this is not a complete list, and it is not possible to ever have a complete list, as each new circumstance you are requested to write for may bring up a need for a trigger or plugin config setting that you had not thought of.

You will see as we go through the book that we add on new settings as we go. However, you should also note that as we get closer to the end of the book, there are less and less additions, as the plugin architecture becomes more complete.

From the plugin configuration, you can see that there are some functions named, which we have not defined.

You should define those functions in the same file:

```
function page_comments_admin_page_tab($PAGEDATA){
  require_once SCRIPTBASE.'ww.plugins/page-comments/'
      .'admin/page-tab.php';
  return $html;
}
function page_comments_show($PAGEDATA){
  if(isset($PARENTDATA->vars->comments_disabled) &&
      $PARENTDATA->vars->comments_disabled=='yes')
    return;
  require_once SCRIPTBASE.'ww.plugins/page-comments/'
      .'frontend/show.php';
}
```

The functions are prefixed with an identifier to make sure that they don't clash with the functions from other plugins. In this case, because the plugin is named Page Comments, the prefix is `page_comments_`.

The functions here are essentially stubs. Plugins will be loaded every time any request is made to the server. Because of this, and the obvious fact that not all the functions would be needed in every request, it makes sense to keep as little code in it as possible in the `plugin.php` files.

In most cases, triggers will be called with just the `$PAGEDATA` object as a parameter. Obviously, in cases in the admin area where you're not editing any particular page this would not make sense, but for most plugins, to keep the function calls consistent, the only parameter is `$PAGEDATA`.

Enabling plugins

We have defined a plugin. We could make it such that when you place a plugin in the `/ww.plugins` directory, it is automatically enabled. However, if you are creating a CMS that you intend to reuse for a lot of other clients, it is a lot easier to simply copy the entire CMS source and reconfigure, than to copy the CMS source and then clear out the existing plugins and repopulate carefully with new ones that you would download from a repository that you keep somewhere else.

So, what we do is we give the admin a maintenance page where they choose the plugins they want to load. The CMS then only loads those and does not even look at the other directories.

Edit the `/ww.admin/header.php` file and add a new link (highlighted) to the plugin admin section:

```
<li><a href="/ww.admin/themes.php">Themes</a></li>
<li><a href="/ww.admin/plugins.php">Plugins</a></li>
<li><a href="/ww.incs/logout.php?redirect=/ww.admin/"
    >Log Out</a></li>
```

We will be changing the admin menu later in this chapter to make it customizable more easily, but for now, add in that link manually.

Now create the `/ww.admin/plugins.php` file:

```php
<?php
require 'header.php';
echo '<h1>Plugin Management</h1>';
echo '<div class="left-menu">';
echo '<a href="/ww.admin/users.php">Users</a>';
```

```
echo '<a href="/ww.admin/themes.php">Themes</a>';
echo '<a href="/ww.admin/plugins.php">Plugins</a>';
echo '</div>';

echo '<div class="has-left-menu">';
echo '<h2>Plugin Management</h2>';
require 'plugins/list.php';
echo '</div>';

require 'footer.php';
```

You'll have noticed that this is similar to the /ww.admin/themes.php and /ww.admin/users.php files. They're all related to site-wide settings, so I've placed links to them all in the left-menu. Edit those files and add in the new Plugins link to their menus.

Before we create the page for listing the enabled plugins, we must first set up the array of enabled plugins in /ww.incs/basics.php, by adding this to the end of the file:

```
// { plugins
$PLUGINS=array();
if (isset($DBVARS['plugins'])&&$DBVARS['plugins']) {
  $DBVARS['plugins']=explode(',',$DBVARS['plugins']);
  foreach($DBVARS['plugins'] as $pname){
    if (strpos('/',$pname)!==false) continue;
    require SCRIPTBASE . 'ww.plugins/'.$pname.'/plugin.php';
    $PLUGINS[$pname]=$plugin;
  }
}
else $DBVARS['plugins']=array();
// }
```

As you can see, we are again referencing the $DBVARS array in the /.private/config.php.

Because we already have a function for editing that (config_rewrite(), created in the previous chapter), all we need to do to change the list of enabled or disabled plugins, and create and maintain the $DBVARS['plugins'] array, making sure to resave the config file after each change.

What the code block does is that it reads in the plugin.php file for each enabled plugin, and saves the $plugin array from each file into a global $PLUGINS array.

The $DBVARS['plugins'] variable is an array, but we'll store it as a comma-delimited string in the config file. Edit config_rewrite() in the same file and add this highlighted line:

```
$tmparr=$DBVARS;
$tmparr['plugins']=join(',',$DBVARS['plugins']);
$tmparr2=array();
```

We'll enhance the plugin loader in a short while. In the meantime, let's finish the admin plugin maintenance page.

Create the directory /ww.admin/plugins, and in it, add /ww.admin/plugins/list.php:

```php
<?php
echo '<table id="plugins-table">';
echo '<thead><tr><th>Plugin Name</th><th>Description</th>
    <th> </th></tr></thead><tbody>';
// { list enabled plugins first
foreach($PLUGINS as $name=>$plugin){
  echo '<tr><th>',htmlspecialchars(@$plugin['name']),'</th>',
    '<td>',htmlspecialchars(@$plugin['description']),'</td>',
    '<td><a href="/ww.admin/plugins/disable.php?n=',
        htmlspecialchars($name),'">disable</a></td>',
    '</tr>';
}
// }
// { then list disabled plugins
$dir=new DirectoryIterator(SCRIPTBASE . 'ww.plugins');
foreach($dir as $plugin){
  if($plugin->isDot())continue;
  $name=$plugin->getFilename();
  if(isset($PLUGINS[$name]))continue;
  require_once(SCRIPTBASE.'ww.plugins/'.$name.'/plugin.php');
  echo '<tr id="ww-plugin-',htmlspecialchars($name),
        '" class="disabled">',
    '<th>',htmlspecialchars($plugin['name']),'</th>',
    '<td>',htmlspecialchars($plugin['description']),'</td>',
    '<td><a href="/ww.admin/plugins/enable.php?n=',
        htmlspecialchars($name),'">enable</a></td>',
    '</tr>';
}
// }
echo '</tbody></table>';
```

When viewed in a browser, it displays like this:

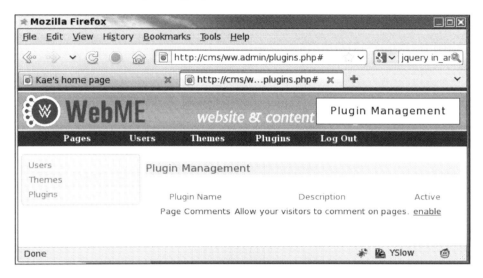

The script displays a list of already-enabled plugins (we have none so far), and then reads the `/ww.plugins` directory for any other plugins and adds them along with an "enable" link.

Now we need to write some code to do the actual selection/enabling of the plugins.

While it would be great to write some jQuery to do it in an Ajaxy way (so you click on the **enable** link and the plugin is enabled in the background, without reloading the page), there are too many things that might cause problems. For instance, if the plugin caused new items to appear in the menu, we'd have to handle that. If the plugin changed the theme, or did anything else that caused a layout change, we'd have to handle that as well.

So instead, we'll do it the old-fashioned PHP way—you click on **enable** or **disable**, which does the job on the server, and then reloads the plugin page so you can see the change.

Create the `/ww.admin/plugins/enable.php` file:

```php
<?php
require '../admin_libs.php';
if(!in_array($_REQUEST['n'],$DBVARS['plugins'])){
  $DBVARS['plugins'][]=$_REQUEST['n'];
  config_rewrite();
}
header('Location: /ww.admin/plugins.php');
```

It simply adds the requested plugin to the `$DBVARS['plugins']` array, then rewrites the config and redirects the browser back to the plugins page.

When clicked, the page apparently just reloads, and the plugin's link changes to **disable**.

The opposite script is just as simple. Write this code block in the file /ww.admin/plugins/disable.php:

```php
<?php
require '../admin_libs.php';
if(in_array($_REQUEST['n'],$DBVARS['plugins'])){
  unset($DBVARS['plugins'][
    array_search($_REQUEST['n'],$DBVARS['plugins'])
  ]);
  config_rewrite();
}
header('Location: /ww.admin/plugins.php');
```

In this case, all we needed to do was to remove the plugin name from `$DBVARS['plugins']` by unsetting its position in the array.

Plugins are now very simply set up. Here's a screenshot of that page with a number of plugins enabled and disabled. I copied some plugins from a more mature copy of the CMS that I have. We won't cover all of them in this book, but will be looking at a few of them, and building one or two others:

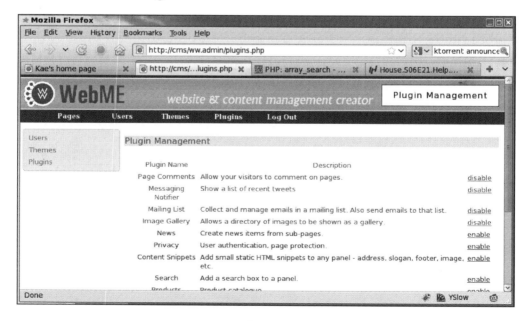

The enabled plugins are moved to the top of the list to make them more visible and the rest are shown below them.

Handling upgrades and database tables

Plugins frequently require database tables to be created or amended.

Because we are not doing a traditional installation when we install a plugin and simply clicking on **enable**, the CMS needs to know if anything needs to be done to the database (or other things, as we'll see).

For this, the CMS needs to keep a record of what version of the plugin is installed.

The way I handle upgrades in the CMS is that there are two copies of the plugin version numbers. One is kept in the $DBVARS array and another is kept hardcoded in the plugin's $plugin array.

If there is a discrepancy between the two, for example, if you've simply never used the plugin before or if you downloaded a later version of the plugin that has a different version number, you know an upgrade needs to be done.

I'll explain as we create the upgrade architecture. First, edit /ww.incs/basics.php and add the following highlighted lines to the plugins section:

```
require SCRIPTBASE . 'ww.plugins/'.$pname.'/plugin.php';
if(isset($plugin['version']) && $plugin['version'] && (
    !isset($DBVARS[$pname.'|version'])
    || $DBVARS[$pname.'|version']!=$plugin['version']
)){
  $version=isset($DBVARS[$pname.'|version'])
    ?(int)$DBVARS[$pname.'|version']
    :0;
  require SCRIPTBASE.'ww.plugins/'.$pname.'/upgrade.php';
  $DBVARS[$pname.'|version']=$version;
  config_rewrite();
  header('Location: '.$_SERVER['REQUEST_URI']);
  exit;
}
$PLUGINS[$pname]=$plugin;
```

How it works is that if the $plugin version is greater than 0 and either the $DBVARS-recorded version doesn't exist or is not equal to the $plugin version, we run an upgrade.php script in the plugin's directory and then reload the page.

Note the `$DBVARS[$pname.'|version']` variable name. In the Page Content plugin's case, that will be `$DBVARS['page-content|version']`.

Even if a plugin is eventually disabled, we don't clear that value. Because the upgrade may have made database changes, there's no point removing the value and potentially ruining the database, if you eventually re-enable the plugin.

Let's create the Page Comments `upgrade.php`, `/ww.plugins/page-comments/upgrade.php`:

```php
<?php
if($version==0){ // create tables
  dbQuery('create table `page_comments_comment` (
    `id` int(11) NOT NULL auto_increment,
    `comment` text,
    `author_name` text,
    `author_email` text,
    `author_website` text,
    `page_id` int,
    `status` int,
    `cdate` datetime,
    PRIMARY KEY  (`id`)
    ) ENGINE=MyISAM DEFAULT CHARSET=utf8');
  $version++;
}
```

And add a version number to the end of the array in `/ww.incs/page-comments/plugin.php`:

```php
  ) ,
  'version' => 1
);
```

Now, let's say you've just enabled the Page Comments plugin. What will happen is:

- 'page-comments' is added to `$DBVARS` and the plugins admin page is reloaded.
- As part of the reload, the `/ww.incs/basics.php` plugins section notices that the plugin has a version number, but the `$DBVARS['page-content|version']` value does not exist. `$version` is set to 0, and the plugin's `upgrade.php` script is run.
- The upgrade script creates the `page_comments_comment` table and increments `$version` to 1.
- The new `$version` is then recorded in `$DBVARS['page-content|version']` and the page is reloaded (again).

So in this case, clicking on **enable** triggered two reloads, one of which also ran an upgrade script.

Now, let's say that you later decided that you needed to also record a moderation e-mail address and whether or not moderation was turned on.

It doesn't make sense to create a whole new database table just to record single values.

Luckily, we already have some code in place that can record single values efficiently. Edit the `upgrade.php` script again and add the following code at the end:

```
if($version==1){ // add moderation details
   $DBVARS[$pname.'|moderation_email']='';
   $DBVARS[$pname.'|moderation_enabled']='no';
   $version++;
}
```

Change the version number in the `plugin.php` file to 2.

Remember that the first run of the script set `$DBVARS['page-content|version']` equal to 1. In this case, when a page is loaded, the upgrade script will skip the first `if` statement and will run the second.

If the plugin was being enabled for the first time, both `if` statements would be run.

The script we just wrote adds the moderation values directly to the `/.private/config.php` file. Notice that we prefixed the values with `page-comments|` so that they would not clash with other plugins.

In my case, that means `/.private/config.php` now looks like this:

```
<?php
$DBVARS=array(
    'username'=>'cmsuser',
    'password'=>'cmspass',
    'hostname'=>'localhost',
    'db_name'=>'cmsdb',
    'theme'=>'basic',
    'plugins'=>'page-comments',
    'page-comments|moderation_email'=>'',
    'page-comments|moderation_enabled'=>'no',
    'page-comments|version'=>'2'
);
```

Also, notice that the second change was not a database one. You can do file updates, send a notification ping to a remote server, send an e-mail, or anything else you want, in those updates.

Custom admin area menu

If you remember, we had the following code lines in `plugin.php`:

```
'menu' => array(
  'Communication>Page Comments' => 'comments'
),
```

Those indicate that we want to add a Page Comments link under a **Communication** top-level menu. When clicked, it should load up an admin maintenance script kept in `/ww.plugins/page-comments/admin/comments.php`.

To make this work, we will need to rewrite the admin menu.

Luckily, we've already installed the Filament Group menu, so we can use that. All we need to do is build a customized `<ul>` menu in the admin header instead of the hardcoded one we already have.

In `/ww.admin/header.php`, remove the entire `#menu-top` element and its contents. We will replace that code with the custom form. Here is the start of it:

```php
<?php
  $menus=array(
    'Pages'=>array(
      '_link'=>'/ww.admin/pages.php'
    ),
    'Site Options'=>array(
      'Users'  => array('_link'=>'/ww.admin/users.php'),
      'Themes' => array('_link'=>'/ww.admin/themes.php'),
      'Plugins'=> array('_link'=>'/ww.admin/plugins.php')
    )
  );
// }
```

First, we create the basic menu array. Any of the plugins that have menu items will add theirs to this.

```php
// { add custom items (from plugins)
foreach($PLUGINS as $pname=>$p){
  if(!isset($p['admin'])
      || !isset($p['admin']['menu']))continue;
  foreach($p['admin']['menu'] as $name=>$page){
    if(preg_match('/[^a-zA-Z0-9 >]/',$name))continue;
    $json='{"'.str_replace('>','":{"',$name)
        .'":{"_link":"plugin.php?_plugin='
        .$pname.'&amp;_page='.$page.'"}}'
```

```
            .str_repeat('}',substr_count($name,'>'));
        $menus=array_merge_recursive($menus,
            json_decode($json,true));
        }
    }
    // }
```

Our Page Comments plugin has a menu address **Communication** > **Page Comments**. This code block takes that string and creates a recursive JSON object from it (**Page Comments** contained in **Communication**), which it then converts to a PHP array, and merges it with $menus.

I know it looks difficult to understand—it was a pain to write it as well! I couldn't think of a simpler way to do it which was as concise. If you do, please e-mail me. I prefer my code to be readable by other people.

```
        $menus['Log Out']=array('_link'=>
            '/ww.incs/logout.php?redirect=/ww.admin/');
```

Finally, we add the **Log Out** button at the end of the $menus array.

And now, let's output the data in a nested <ul> list.

```
    // { display menu as UL list
    function admin_menu_show($items,$name=false,
                             $prefix,$depth=0){
      if(isset($items['_link']))
          echo '<a href="'.$items['_link'].'">'.$name.'</a>';
      else if($name!='top')
          echo '<a href="#'.$prefix.'-'.$name.'">'.$name.'</a>';
      if(count($items)==1 && isset($items['_link']))return;
      if($depth<2)echo '<div id="'.$prefix.'-'.$name.'">';
      echo '<ul>';
      foreach($items as $iname=>$subitems){
        if($iname=='_link')continue;
        echo '<li>';
        admin_menu_show($subitems,$iname,
            $prefix.'-'.$name,$depth+1);
        echo '</li>';
      }
      echo '</ul>';
      if($depth<2)echo '</div>';
    }
    admin_menu_show($menus,'top','menu');
    // }
  ?>
```

If an item does not explicitly have a _link associated with it, the name is shown and it is not clickable (or at least doesn't do anything when clicked).

With that in place, we have the following menu:

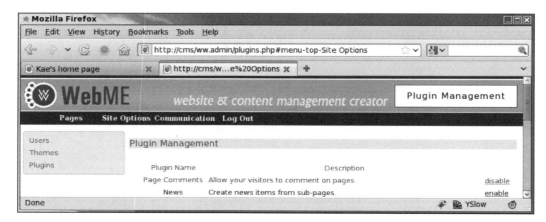

The sub-menus do not yet appear because we haven't enabled the fg-menu.

Edit /ww.admin/j/admin.js and add the following highlighted lines to the final section:

```
$('input.date-human').each(convert_date_to_human_readable);
$('#menu-top>ul>li>a').each(function(){
  if(!(/#/.test(this.href.toString())))return;
  $(this).menu({
    content: $(this).next().html(),
    flyOut:true,
    showSpeed: 400,
    callerOnState: '',
    loadingState: '',
    linkHover: '',
    linkHoverSecondary: '',
    flyOutOnState: ''
  });
});
});
```

That piece of code runs fg-menu on all the items in the menu that do not link to #.

After this, we can see that the **Site Options** menu now makes sense:

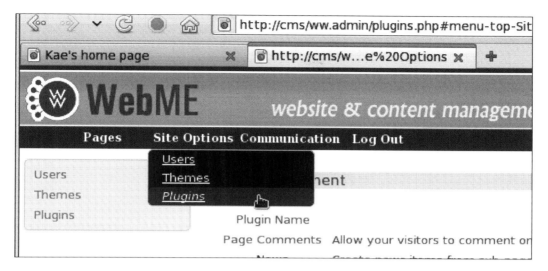

And we have our **Page Comments** menu item:

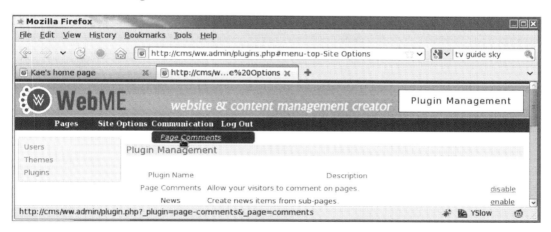

Notice the URL in the status bar.

```
http://cms/ww.admin/plugin.php
    ?_plugin=page-comments&_page=comments
```

All the menu items created from plugins are directed to /ww.admin/plugin.php
(not /ww.admin/plugins.php; that has a different purpose), telling the script what
plugin is being used (page-comments) and what admin form (comments) should be
used from the plugin's /admin directory.

Create the file /ww.admin/plugin.php:

```php
<?php
require 'header.php';
$pname=$_REQUEST['_plugin'];
$pagename=$_REQUEST['_page'];
if(preg_match('/[^\-a-zA-Z0-9]/',$pagename) || $pagename=='')
    die('illegal character in page name');
if(!isset($PLUGINS[$pname]))die('no plugin of that name ('
    .htmlspecialchars($pname).') exists');
$plugin=$PLUGINS[$pname];
$_url='/ww.admin/plugin.php?_plugin='.urlencode($pname)
    .'&amp;_page='.$pagename;
echo '<h1>'.htmlspecialchars($pname).'</h1>';
if(!file_exists(SCRIPTBASE.'/ww.plugins/'.$pname.'/admin/'
    .$pagename.'.php')){
  echo '<em>The <strong>'.htmlspecialchars($pname).'</strong>
      plugin does not have an admin page named <strong>'
      .$pagename.'</strong>.</em>';
}
else{
  if(file_exists(SCRIPTBASE.'/ww.plugins/'.$pname
      .'/admin/menu.php')){
    include SCRIPTBASE.'/ww.plugins/'
        .$pname.'/admin/menu.php';
    echo '<div class="has-left-menu">';
    include SCRIPTBASE.'/ww.plugins/'.$pname.'/admin/'
        .$pagename.'.php';
    echo '</div>';
  }
  else include SCRIPTBASE.'/ww.plugins/'.$pname.'/admin/'
      .$pagename.'.php';
}
require 'footer.php';
```

When called, this displays the standard admin area header, including the menu, and then checks the requested plugin data.

If the plugin doesn't exist, the requested page doesn't exist in the plugin's /admin directory, or if the other tests fail, an explanation is shown to the admin and the script is exited.

If all is well, we display the plugin's admin page.

If a `menu.php` file exists in the plugin's `/admin` directory, the menu is shown in a column on the left-hand side and the rest of the page is on the right-hand side.

Otherwise, the page takes over the entire space available.

We haven't created the admin page for comments yet, so here's what the error message looks like:

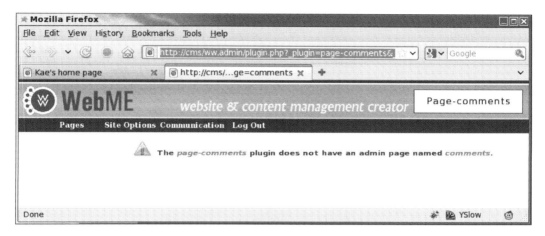

Ideally, the admin should never see that page at all, but if they go playing around with the contents of the URL bar, we need to take care of any eventualities.

Now, we'll write a simple script for that. Create the `/ww.plugins/page-comments/ admin/` directory, and create a file in it called `comments.php`, with the following code:

```php
<?php
$htmlurl=htmlspecialchars('/ww.admin/plugin.php?_plugin='
  .'page-comments&_page=comments');
// { moderation settings
echo '<form action="',$htmlurl,'" method="post">'
  ,'<h2>Moderation</h2><table><tr><th>Enabled</th>'
  ,'<th>Moderator\'s email</th></tr>';
// { moderation enabled
echo '<tr><td><select name="moderation_enabled">'
  ,'<option value="no">No</option><option value="yes"';
if($DBVARS['page-comments|moderation_enabled']=='yes')
  echo ' selected="selected"';
echo '>yes</option></select></td>';
// }
// { moderation email
echo '<td><input name="moderation_email" value="'
```

```
    ,htmlspecialchars(
      $DBVARS['page-comments|moderation_email'])
    ,'" /></td>';
// }
echo '<td><input type="submit" name="action" value="save" '
    ,'/></td></tr></table></form>';
```

This code, when viewed in the browser, shows the following:

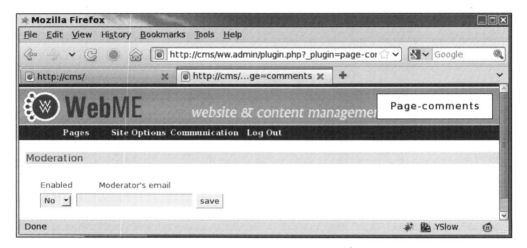

The first thing we do is to set $htmlurl. This is the HTML-encoded URL of the current plugin admin page. You will need to use this in all the actions so that the CMS knows what plugin you're working with.

We use it, for example, in the <form> that we set to use the POST method (otherwise, when the form is submitted, it may override the ?_plugin=page-comments&_page=comments part of the URL).

Let's add the code for saving that now. Add it after the opening the <?php line in the file.

```
if(isset($_REQUEST['action']) && $_REQUEST['action']=='save'){
    $mod=($_REQUEST['moderation_enabled']=='yes')?'yes':'no';
    $email=$_REQUEST['moderation_email'];
    if(($mod=='yes' && $email=='') ||
        ($mod=='yes' && !
        filter_var($email,FILTER_VALIDATE_EMAIL))){
      echo '<em>error: email is not valid. please retry</em>';
    }
    else{
      $DBVARS['page-comments|moderation_email']=$email;
```

```
    $DBVARS['page-comments|moderation_enabled']=$mod;
    config_rewrite();
    echo '<em>Moderation options saved</em>';
  }
}
```

This just does a bit of validation on the submitted form, then saves it using the
config_rewrite() function to write it directly to the config file.

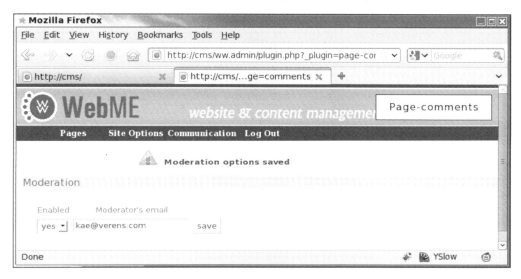

Okay, that's enough from the admin area for now. Let's work on the front-end.

Adding an event to the CMS

We want it so that after the content of a page is figured out, we can trigger a plugin
to run some code on it. The obvious place for this trigger to run is immediately at the
end of the "set up pagecontent" block in /ww.index.php (highlighted):

```
    // other cases will be handled here later
  }
  plugin_trigger('page-content-created',$PAGEDATA);
  // }
  // { set up metadata
```

We will create that function in /ww.incs/basics.php:

```
function plugin_trigger($trigger_name){
  global $PLUGIN_TRIGGERS,$PAGEDATA;
```

```
    if(!isset($PLUGIN_TRIGGERS[$trigger_name]))return;
    foreach($PLUGIN_TRIGGERS[$trigger_name] as $fn)
      $fn($PAGEDATA);
}
```

This checks to see if a plugin trigger of that name (page-content-created) exists in the global $PLUGIN_TRIGGERS array, which we'll create in a moment, and if so, it runs all functions associated with the name, sending $PAGEDATA as a parameter.

In the same file as we are creating the $PLUGINS array, we should also be creating the $PLUGINS_TRIGGERS array.

Change the start of the plugins block to this:

```
// { plugins
$PLUGINS=array();
$PLUGINS_TRIGGERS=array();
if(isset($DBVARS['plugins'])&&$DBVARS['plugins']){
```

And near the end of the block:

```
    $PLUGINS[$pname]=$plugin;
    if(isset($plugin['triggers'])){
      foreach($plugin['triggers'] as $name=>$fn){
        if(!isset($PLUGIN_TRIGGERS[$name]))
            $PLUGIN_TRIGGERS[$name]=array();
        $PLUGIN_TRIGGERS[$name][]=$fn;
      }
    }
  }
}
else $DBVARS['plugins']=array();
```

And it's as simple as that. We can now create triggers anywhere in the CMS core, and they will execute any that are in the plugins.

If you remember, the Page Comments plugin triggers the function page_comments_show() when page-content-created is triggered.

We've already written a stub function for this, which then loads up the file /ww.plugins/page-comments/frontend/show.php.

Create that file now (create the directory `ww.plugins/page-comments/frontend` first):

```php
<?php
global $pagecontent,$DBVARS;

$c='';
$message='';
// { add submitted comments to database
// }
// { show existing comments
// }
// { show comment entry form
$c.='<a name="page-comments-submit"></a>'
    .'<h3>Add a comment</h3>';
if($message)$c.=$message;
$c.='<form action="'.$PAGEDATA->getRelativeURL()
    .'#page-comments-submit" method="post"><table>';
$c.='<tr><th>Name</th><td><input name="page-comments-name" />'
    .'</td></tr>';
$c.='<tr><th>Email</th><td><input type="email" '
    .'name="page-comments-email" /></td></tr>';
$c.='<tr><th>Website</th><td><input '
    .'name="page-comments-website" /></td></tr>';
$c.='<tr><th>Your Comment</th><td><textarea '
    .'name="page-comments-comment"></textarea></td></tr>';
$c.='<tr><th colspan="2"><input name="action" '
    .'value="Submit Comment" /></th></tr>';
$c.='</table></form>';
// }
$pagecontent.='<div id="page-comments-wrapper">'.$
    c.'</div>';
```

Simple enough; this adds a comment box onto the global `$pagecontent` variable.

Note that the `#page-comments-submit` anchor appended to the page URL. If someone submits a comment, they will be brought back to the comment form.

I've adjusted the basic theme we've been using, to make it a little neater and added some Lorem Ipsum text to the body of the home page, so we can see what it looks like with some text in it.

Here's what the home page looks like with the Page Comments plugin enabled:

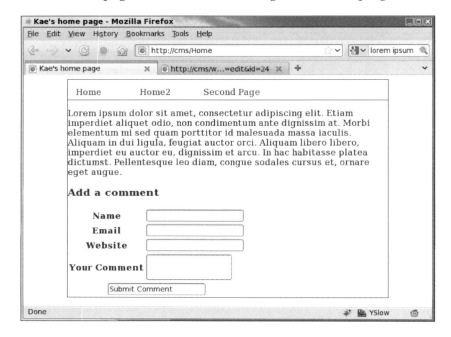

Now we need to take care of what happens when the comment is submitted.

Edit the `/ww.plugins/page-comments/frontend/show.php` file, changing the "add submitted comments to database" section to this:

```
// { add submitted comments to database
if(isset($_REQUEST['action']) &&
    $_REQUEST['action']=='Submit Comment'){
  if(!isset($_REQUEST['page-comments-name']) ||
      $_REQUEST['page-comments-name']==''')
      $message.='<li>Please enter your name.</li>';
  if(!isset($_REQUEST['page-comments-email']) ||
      !filter_var($_REQUEST['page-comments-email'],
      FILTER_VALIDATE_EMAIL))
      $message.='<li>Please enter your email address.</li>';
  if(!isset($_REQUEST['page-comments-comment']) ||
      !$_REQUEST['page-comments-comment'])
      $message.='<li>Please enter a comment.</li>';
  if($message)$message='<ul
      class="error page-comments-error">'.$message.'</ul>';
  else{
    $website=isset($_REQUEST['page-comments-website'])
```

```
        ?$_REQUEST['page-comments-website']:'';
    if($DBVARS['page-comments|moderation_enabled']=='yes'){
      $status=0;
      mail($DBVARS['page-comments|moderation_email'],
        '['.$_SERVER['HTTP_HOST'].'] comment submitted',
        'A new comment has been submitted to the page "'
        .$PAGEDATA->getRelativeUrl().'". Please log into '
        'the admin area of the site and moderate it using '
        'that page\'s admin.',
        'From: noreply@'.$_SERVER['HTTP_HOST']
        ."\nReply-to: noreply@".$_SERVER['HTTP_HOST']);
      $message='<p>Comments are moderated. It may be a '
          .'few minutes before your comment appears.</p>';
    }
    else $status=1;
    dbQuery('insert into page_comments_comment set comment="'
      .addslashes($_REQUEST['page-comments-comment'])
      .'",author_name="'
      .addslashes($_REQUEST['page-comments-name'])
      .'",author_email="'
      .$_REQUEST['page-comments-email']
      .'",author_website="'.addslashes($website)
      .'",cdate=now(),page_id='.$PAGEDATA->id.',status='
      .$status);
  }
}
// }
```

This will record the comment in the database. Notice the status field. This says whether a comment is visible or not.

This can be enhanced in many ways. You can change the e-mail that's sent to the moderator to add links back to the right places, you can add an is_spam field to the database and check the comment using the Akisment service (http://akismet.com/), or you can have client-side jQuery form validation.

I haven't added these, as I am currently simply explaining how plugins work.

Finally in this section, we need to display any comments that have been successfully entered and moderated. To simulate this, I temporarily turned off moderation in my own copy before doing the following (so comments go through with status set to 1).

Before we write the code for showing comments, we will add a new function to /ww.incs/basics.php:

```
function date_m2h($d, $type = 'date') {
  $date = preg_replace('/[- :]/', ' ', $d);
  $date = explode(' ', $date);
  if ($type == 'date') {
    return date('l jS F, Y', mktime(0, 0, 0,
        $date[1], $date[2], $date[0]));
  }
  return date(DATE_RFC822, mktime($date[5],
      $date[4], $date[3], $date[1], $date[2], $date[0]));
}
```

This function m2h (stands for "mysql to human") takes a MySQL date and converts it to a format that can be read by humans.

It's easy to write two or three lines and get the same result (or one complex line), but why bother, when it just takes a single function call?

Now, edit /ww.plugins/page-comments/frontend/show.php again and this time change the "show existing comments" section to this:

```
// { show existing comments
$c.='<h3>Comments</h3>';
$comments=dbAll('select * from page_comments_comment where
    status=1 and page_id='.$PAGEDATA->id.' order by cdate');
if(!count($comments)){
  $c.='<p>No comments yet.</p>';
}
else foreach($comments as $comment){
  $c.=htmlspecialchars($comment['author_name']);
  if($comment['author_website'])$c.=' (<a href="'
      .htmlspecialchars($comment['author_website']).'">'
      .htmlspecialchars($comment['author_website']).'</a>)';
  $c.=' said, at '.date_m2h($comment['cdate'])
    .':<br /><blockquote>'
    .nl2br(htmlspecialchars($comment['comment']))
    .'</blockquote>';
}
// }
```

This code takes comments from the page_comments_comment table and shows them in the page, as long as they have already been accepted/moderated (their status is 1), and they belong to that page.

Here's a screenshot of our home page now, with a submitted comment:

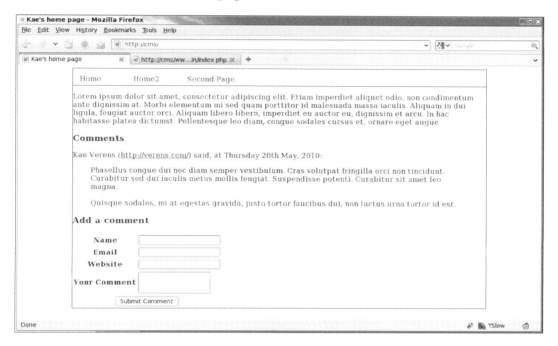

And now we get to the final major plugin method for the CMS in this chapter (there is still more to come): adding a tab to the page admin.

Adding tabs to the page admin

When a comment is submitted (by the way, turn moderation back on), an e-mail is sent to the moderator, who is asked to log into the admin area to check messages that may have been sent.

We had this in the `plugin.php` file:

```
'page_tab' => array(
  'name' => 'Comments',
  'function' => 'page_comments_admin_page_tab'
)
```

We will use this information to add a new tab to the page admin named Comments, which will be populated by calling a function `page_comments_admin_page_tab()`, which we've already built as a stub. It loads and runs the file `/ww.plugins/page-comments/admin/page-tab.php`, which generates a string named `$html` (it contains HTML) and returns that to the page admin to be displayed.

Note that it is also very useful to have a central area where comments from all pages can be moderated. This chapter does not discuss that, but if you wish to see how that would be implemented, please see the comments plugin here: `http://code.google.com/p/webworks-webme/source/browse/#svn/ww.plugins/comments`.

So first, let's adapt the page admin so it will run the plugin's function. Edit / `ww.admin/pages/forms.php` and before the line which opens the `<form>`, add the highlighted code given as follows:

```
// }
// { generate list of custom tabs
$custom_tabs=array();
foreach($PLUGINS as $n=>$p){
  if(isset($p['admin']['page_panel'])){
    $custom_tabs[$p['admin']['page_panel']['name']]
        =$p['admin']['page_panel']['function'];
  }
}
// }
echo '<form id="pages_form" method="post">';
```

This code builds up a `$custom_tabs` array from the global `$PLUGINS` array.

Next, we display the tab names . Replace the "// add plugin tabs here" line with this highlighted line:

```
        ,'<li><a href="#tabs-advanced-options">Advanced
            Options</a></li>';
foreach($custom_tabs as $name=>$function)echo '<li><a
    href="#tabs-custom-'
    ,preg_replace('/[^a-z0-9A-Z]/','',$name)
    ,'">',htmlspecialchars($name),'</a></li>';
echo '</ul>';
```

Finally, we add in the actual tab content (highlighted code) after the "Advanced Options" section:

```
// }
// { tabs added by plugins
foreach($custom_tabs as $n=>$p){
  echo '<div id="tabs-custom-'
      ,preg_replace('/[^a-z0-9A-Z]/','',$n),'">'
      ,$p($page,$page_vars),'</div>';
}
```

```
    // }
    echo '</div><input type="submit" name="action" value="',
        ($edit?'Update Page Details':'Insert Page Details')
        ,'" /></form>';
```

This creates the tab bodies by calling the plugin functions with two parameters; the main $page table data, and the custom variables of the page, $page_vars.

The result is then echoed to the screen.

So, let's create the /ww.plugins/page-comments/admin/page-tab.php file:

```php
<?php
$html='';
$comments=dbAll('select * from page_comments_comment where
    page_id='.$PAGEDATA['id'].' order by cdate desc');
if(!count($comments)){
  $html='<em>No comments yet.</em>';
  return;
}
$html.='<table id="page-comments-table"><tr><th>Name</th>'
    ,'<th>Date</th><th>Contact</th>'
    ,'<th>Comment</th><th> </th></tr>';
foreach($comments as $comment){
  $html.='<tr class="';
  if($comment['status'])$html.='active';
  else $html.='inactive';
  $html.='" id="page-comments-tr-'.$comment['id'].'">';
  $html.='<th>'.htmlspecialchars($comment['author_name'])
    .'</th>';
  $html.='<td>'.date_m2h($comment['cdate'],'datetime')
    .'</td>';
  $html.='<td>';
  $html.='<a href="mailto:'
    .htmlspecialchars($comment['author_email']).'">'
    .htmlspecialchars($comment['author_email']).'</a><br />';
  if($comment['author_website'])$html.='<a href="'
    .htmlspecialchars($comment['author_website']).'">'
    .htmlspecialchars($comment['author_website']).'</a>';
  $html.='</td>';
  $html.='<td>'.htmlspecialchars($comment['comment']).'</td>';
  $html.='<td></td></tr>';
}
$html.='</table><script src="/ww.plugins/page-comments'
  .'/admin/page-tab.js"></script>';
```

In this code block, we build up a string variable named `$html` that holds details on all the comments for a specified page.

We've left a blank `<td>` at the end of each row, which will be filled by jQuery with some actionable links.

Enhancements that you could build in here might be to limit the number of characters available in each table cell or also to add pagination for pages with vast numbers of comments.

We can already see that the tab is working:

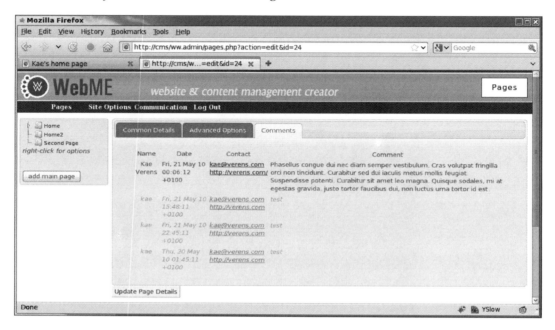

Now we need to add in the actions.

Create the file `/ww.plugins/page-comments/admin/page-tab.js`:

```
function page_comments_build_links(){
  var stat=this.className;
  if(!stat)return;
  var id=this.id.replace('page-comments-tr-','');
  var html='<a href="javascript:page_comments_'+(
    (stat=='active')
      ?'deactivate('+id+');">deactivate'
      :'activate('+id+');">activate'
    )+'</a> | <a href="javascript:'
```

```
          +'page_comments_delete('+id+');">delete</a>';
    $(this).find('td:last-child').html(html);
}
$(function(){
  $('#page-comments-table tr')
    .each(page_comments_build_links);
});
```

This script takes all the `<tr>` rows in the table, checks their classes, and builds up links based on whether the link is currently active or inactive.

The reason we do this through JavaScript and not straight in the PHP is that we're going to moderate the links through AJAX, so it would be a waste of resources to do it in both PHP and jQuery.

The page now looks like this:

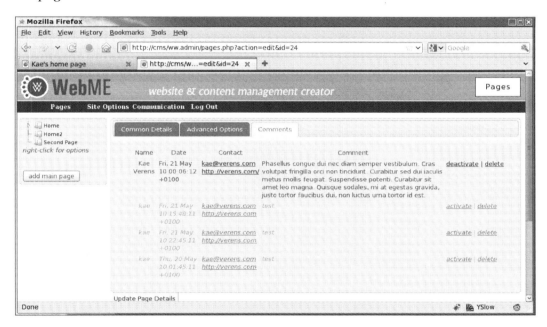

Okay, now we just need to make those links work. Add these functions to the same file:

```
function page_comments_activate(id){
  $.get('/ww.plugins/page-comments/admin/activate.php'
      +'?id='+id,function(){
    var el=document.getElementById('page-comments-tr-'+id);
    el.className='active';
```

```
    $(el).each(page_comments_build_links);
  });
}
function page_comments_deactivate(id){
  $.get('/ww.plugins/page-comments/admin/deactivate.php'
    +'?id='+id,function(){
    var el=document.getElementById('page-comments-tr-'+id);
    el.className='inactive';
    $(el).each(page_comments_build_links);
  });
}
function page_comments_delete(id){
  $.get('/ww.plugins/page-comments/admin/delete.php'
    +'?id='+id,function(){
    $('#page-comments-tr-'+id).fadeOut(500,function(){
      $(this).remove();
    });
  });
}
```

These handle the deletion, activation, and deactivation of comments from the client-side. I haven't included tests to see if they were successful (this is a demo).

The deletion event is handled by fading out the table row and then removing it. The others simply change classes on the row and links in the right cell.

First, let's build the activation PHP script /ww.plugins/page-comments/admin/activate.php:

```
<?php
require $_SERVER['DOCUMENT_ROOT'].'/ww.admin/admin_libs.php';
$id=(int)$_REQUEST['id'];
dbQuery('update page_comments_comment set status=1
    where id='.$id);
echo '1';
```

The next one is to deactivate the comment, /ww.plugins/page-comments/admin/deactivate.php:

```
<?php
require $_SERVER['DOCUMENT_ROOT'].'/ww.admin/admin_libs.php';
$id=(int)$_REQUEST['id'];
dbQuery('update page_comments_comment set status=0
    where id='.$id);
echo '0';
```

Yes, they're the same except for two numbers. I have them as two files because it might be interesting in the future to add in separate actions that happen after one or the other, such as sending an e-mail when a comment is activated and other such actions.

The final script is the deletion one, `/ww.plugins/page-comments/admin/delete.php`:

```php
<?php
require $_SERVER['DOCUMENT_ROOT'].'/ww.admin/admin_libs.php';

$id=(int)$_REQUEST['id'];
dbQuery('delete from page_comments_comment where id='.$id);
echo '1';
```

Very simple and it completes our Page Comments example!

As pointed out, there are a load of ways in which this could be improved. For example, we didn't take into account people that are already logged in (they shouldn't have to fill in their details and should be recorded in the database), there is no spam control, we did not use client-side validation, you could add "gravatar" images for submitters, and so on.

All of these things can be added on at any point. We're onto the next plugin now!

Summary

In this chapter, we built the framework for enabling plugins and looked at a number of ways that the plugin can integrate with the CMS.

We also changed the admin menu so it could incorporate custom items from the plugins.

We built an example plugin, Page Comments, which used a few different plugin hook types, page admin tabs, a standalone admin page, and a `page-content-created` trigger.

In the next chapter, we will create a plugin that allows the admin to create a form page for submission as an e-mail or for saving in the database.

8
Forms Plugin

In this chapter, we will create a plugin for providing a form generator which can be used for sending the submitted data as an e-mail, or saving in the database.

By building this plugin, we will extend the core engine so that it can display custom content forms in the page admin and custom page types. We will also adjust the output on the front-end so it can display from the plugin instead of straight from the page's body field.

How it will work

There are a number of ways to create a form. Probably the simplest way is to allow the administrator to "draw" the form using a rich text editor, and treat the submitted `$_POST` values as being correct.

There are a number of reasons why POST should be used for forms instead of GET:

A form may contain file-upload inputs, requiring multi-part encoded POST data.

A form may contain textareas, which could have arbitrarily long tracts of text pasted in them (GET has a rather short limit on the number of characters allowed).

When a form is submitted through POST, and the user reloads the page, the browser pops up a warning asking if the user is sure that he/she wants to post the form data again. This is better than accidentally sending forms over and over again.

This method has the disadvantage that the server doesn't know what type of data was supposed to be inputted, so it can't validate it.

A more robust method is to define each field that will be in the form, then create a template which will be shown to the user.

This allows us to autogenerate server-side and client-side validation. For example, if the input is to be an e-mail address, then we can ensure that only e-mails are entered into it. Similar tests can be done for numbers, select-box values, and so on.

We could make this comprehensive and cover all forms of validation. In this chapter, though, we will build a simple forms plugin that will cover most cases that you will meet when creating websites.

We will also need to define what is to be done with the form after it's submitted—e-mail it or store in a database.

Because we're providing a method of saving to database, we will also need a way of exporting the saved values so they can be read in an office application. CSV is probably the simplest format to use, so we'll write a CSV exporter.

And finally, because we don't want robots submitting rubbish to your form or trying to misuse it, we will have the option of using a captcha.

The plugin config

Plugins are usually started by creating the definition file. So, create the directory /ww.plugins/forms and add this file to it:

```php
<?php
$plugin=array(
    'name' => 'Form',
    'admin' => array(
        'page_type' => array(
            'form' => 'form_admin_page_form'
        )
    ),
    'description' =>
        'Generate forms for sending as email or saving in the database',
    'frontend' => array(
        'page_type' => array(
            'form' => 'form_frontend'
        )
    ),
    'version' => 3
);
function form_admin_page_form($page,$page_vars){
    $id=$page['id'];
    $c='';
    require dirname(__FILE__).'/admin/form.php';
```

```php
  return $c;
}
function form_frontend($PAGEDATA){
  require dirname(__FILE__).'/frontend/show.php';
  return $PAGEDATA->render().form_controller($PAGEDATA);
}
```

In the `admin` section of the `$plugin` array, we have a new value, `page_type`. We are going to handle forms as if they were full pages. For example, you may have a contact page where the page is predominantly taken over by the form itself.

The `page_type` value tells the server what function to call in order to generate custom forms for the page admin.

It's an array, in case one plugin handles a number of different page types.

Because we've provided an admin-end `page_type`, it also makes sense to provide the front-end equivalent, so we also add a `page_type` to the `frontend` array.

I've set the version to 3 here, because while developing it, I made three adjustments to the database.

Here's the `upgrade.php` file, which should go in the same directory:

```php
<?php
if($version==0){ // forms_fields
  dbQuery('CREATE TABLE IF NOT EXISTS `forms_fields` (
    `id` int(11) NOT NULL auto_increment,
    `name` text,
    `type` text,
    `isrequired` smallint(6) default 0,
    `formsId` int(11) default NULL,
    `extra` text,
    PRIMARY KEY  (`id`)
    ) ENGINE=MyISAM DEFAULT CHARSET=utf8');
  $version=1;
}
if($version==1){ // forms_saved
  dbQuery('CREATE TABLE IF NOT EXISTS `forms_saved` (
    `forms_id` int(11) default 0,
    `date_created` datetime default NULL,
    `id` int(11) NOT NULL auto_increment,
    PRIMARY KEY  (`id`)
    ) ENGINE=MyISAM DEFAULT CHARSET=utf8');
  $version=2;
}
```

```
if($version==2){ // forms_saved_values
   dbQuery('CREATE TABLE IF NOT EXISTS `forms_saved_values` (
      `forms_saved_id` int(11) default 0,
      `name` text,
      `value` text,
      `id` int(11) NOT NULL auto_increment,
      PRIMARY KEY  (`id`)
      ) ENGINE=MyISAM DEFAULT CHARSET=utf8');
   $version=3;
}
```

When the plugin is enabled (enable it in the plugins section of the admin area), that script will be run, and the tables added to the database.

- The `forms_fields` table holds information about the fields that will be shown in the form.

- The `formsId` value links to the page ID, and the extra value is used to hold values in cases where the input type needs extra data—such as select-boxes, where you need to tell the form what the select-box options are.

- The `forms_saved` table holds data on forms that have been saved in the database, including the date and time that the form was saved.

- The `forms_saved_values` holds the saved data and is related via `forms_saved_id` to the `forms_saved` table.

Okay—we have the config and the database tables installed. Now let's get down to the administration.

Page types in the admin

When you click on **add main page** in the page admin section, the pop up appears as seen here:

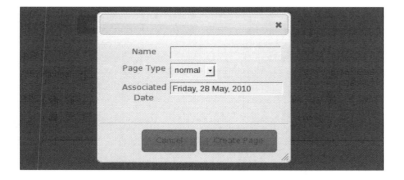

The **Page Type** in the form only holds one value at the moment, **normal**. We need to change this so that it can add types created by plugins.

We first assume that most pages will be "normal", so we can leave that as the single value in the select-box; we then use the RemoteSelectOptions plugin described earlier in the book to add any others if the select-box is used.

Edit /ww.admin/pages/menu.js and add the following highlighted line to the pages_new() function:

```
$('#newpage_date').each(convert_date_to_human_readable);
$('#newpage_dialog select[name=type]')
  .remoteselectoptions({
    url:'/ww.admin/pages/get_types.php'
  });
return false;
```

And here's the /ww.admin/pages/get_types.php file:

```
<?php
require '../admin_libs.php';
echo '<option value="0">normal</option>';
foreach($PLUGINS as $n=>$plugin){
  if(!isset($plugin['admin']['page_type']))continue;
  foreach($plugin['admin']['page_type'] as $n=>$p){
    echo '<option value="'.htmlspecialchars($n).'">'
        .htmlspecialchars($n).'</option>';
  }
}
```

All it does is to echo out the normal type as an option, then goes through all installed plugins and displays their page_type values as well.

The **add main page** pop up now has the new `form` page type added, as seen in the next screenshot:

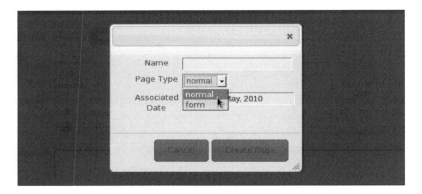

When you submit this form, a new page is created. The new page's form says its type is `normal`, but that's because we haven't added the code yet to the main form.

You can see that it's been done correctly by checking the database, as seen in the next screenshot:

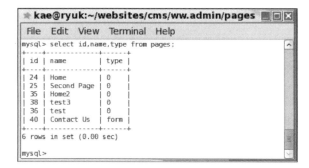

We add the page types to the main page form in the same way as we did with the **add main page** form.

Edit the `/ww.admin/pages/pages.js` file and add these highlighted lines to the `$(function...)` section:

```
    other_GET_params:currentpageid
  });
  $('#pages_form select[name=type]').remoteselectoptions({
    url:'/ww.admin/pages/get_types.php'
  });
});
```

This does exactly the same as the previous one. However, on doing it you'll see that the page form still says `normal`:

The reason for this is that the HTML of the page is generated without knowing about the other page types. We need to add code to the form itself.

Because the name of the type is stored in the page table (except if it's `normal`, in which case it's stored as `0`), all we need to do is to output that name on its own.

Edit `/ww.admin/pages/forms.php`, in the **Common Details** section, change the `type` section to this:

```
// { type
echo '<th>type</th><td><select name="type"><option';
if(!$page['type'])echo ' value='0'>normal';
else echo '>'.htmlspecialchars($page['type']);
echo '</option></select></td>';
// }
```

Now, let's get back to the plugin and adding its admin forms to the page.

Adding custom content forms to the page admin

The page admin form appears as seen in the next screenshot:

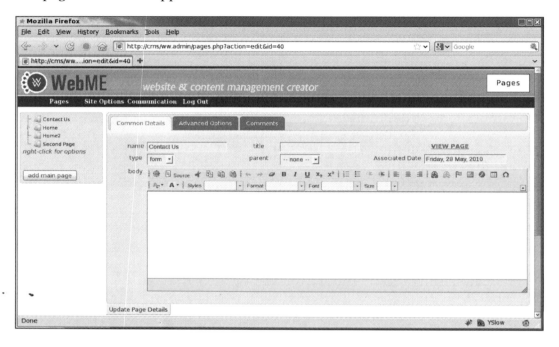

We saw in the previous chapter how to add another tab along the top.

When creating the custom form for the plugin, we could use the same method and add another tab.

However, it makes more sense to convert the body section so that it can be tabbed.

In the end, it all gets added to the database in the same way, but visually, tabs along the top of the page appear to be "meta" data (data about the page), whereas tabs in the body section appear to be "content" data.

The difference is subtle, but in my experience, admins tend to find it easier to use forms that are arranged in this way.

So, we will add the forms to the body section.

Open /ww.admin/pages/forms.php again, and change the generate list of custom tabs section to this (changed lines are highlighted):

```
// { gather plugin data
$custom_tabs=array();
$custom_type_func='';
foreach($PLUGINS as $n=>$p){
  if(isset($p['admin']['page_tab'])){
    $custom_tabs[$p['admin']['page_tab']['name']]
        =$p['admin']['page_tab']['function'];
  }
  if(isset($p['admin']['page_type'])){
    foreach($p['admin']['page_type'] as $n=>$f){
      if($n==$page['type'])$custom_type_func=$f;
    }
  }
}
// }
```

We rename it to `gather plugin data` because it's no longer specifically about tabs.

This loops through all installed plugins, getting any tabs that are defined, and setting `$custom_type_func` to the plugin's `page_type` function if it exists.

And later in the same file, change the `page-type-specific data` section to this:

```
// { page-type-specific data
if($custom_type_func && function_exists($custom_type_func)){
  echo '<tr><td colspan="6">'
    .$custom_type_func($page,$page_vars).'</td></tr>';
}
else{
  echo '<tr><th>body</th><td colspan="5">';
  echo ckeditor('body',$page['body']);
  echo '</td></tr>';
}
// }
```

This outputs the result of the `page_type` function if it was set and the function exists.

The function requires a file that we haven't yet created, so loading the admin page will display only half the form before crashing.

Create the directory `/ww.plugins/forms/admin` and create the file `form.php` in it:

```
<?php
$c.='<div class="tabs">';
// { table of contents
$c.='<ul><li><a href="#forms-header">Header</a></li>'
```

```
      .'<li><a href="#forms-main-details">Main Details</a></li>'
      .'<li><a href="#forms-fields">Fields</a></li>'
      .'<li><a href="#forms-success-message">Success Message</a></li>'
      .'<li><a href="#forms-template">Template</a></li></ul>';
// }
// { header
$c.='<div id="forms-header"><p>Text to be shown
    above the form</p>';
$c.=ckeditor('body',$page['body']);
$c.='</div>';
// }
// { main details
// }
// { fields
// }
// { success message
// }
// { template
// }
$c.='</div>';
```

I've left the main details, fields (and other) sections empty on purpose. We'll fill them in a moment.

This code creates a tab structure. You can see the table of contents matches the commented sections.

Creating a "skeleton" of a config form can be useful because it lets you view your progress in the browser, and you can leave reminders to yourself in the form of commented sections that have not yet been filled in.

Doing this also helps you to develop the habit of commenting your code, so that others can understand what is happening at various points of the file.

The previous code snippet can now be viewed in the browser, and renders as seen in the following screenshot:

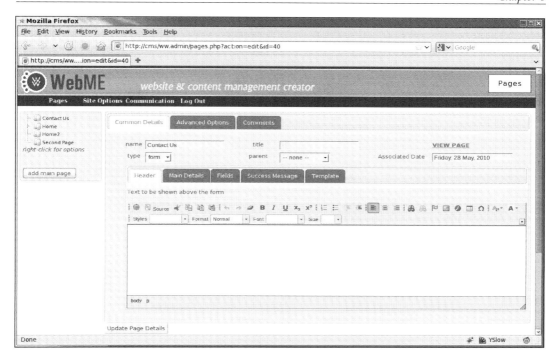

So we have two rows of tabs. You can now see what I meant—the bottom collection of tabs is obviously about the page content, while the others are more about the page itself.

Before we work on the `fields` tab, let's do the other three.

First, replace the `template` section with this:

```
// { template
$c.= '<div id="forms-template">';
$c.= '<p>Leave blank to have an auto-generated
    template displayed.</p>';
$c.= ckeditor('page_vars[forms_template]',
    $page_vars['forms_template']);
$c.= '</div>';
// }
```

The template defines how you want the form to appear on the front-end. We start off with the assumption that the admin does not know (or want to know) how to fill this in, so we leave a message saying that if the template is left blank, it will be auto-generated on the front-end.

When we get to displaying the form on the front-end, we'll discuss this one more.

Notice that we use `page_vars[forms_template]` as the name for the template's input box. With this, we will not need to write server-side code to save the data, as it will be handled by the page admin's own saving mechanism.

Next, replace the `success message` section with this:

```
// { success message
$c.= '<div id="forms-success-message">';
$c.= '<p>What should be displayed on-screen after the
    message is sent.</p>';
if(!$page_vars['forms_successmsg'])
  $page_vars['forms_successmsg']=
    '<h2>Thank You</h2>
    <p>We will be in contact as soon as we can.</p>';
$c.= ckeditor('page_vars[forms_successmsg]',
    $page_vars['forms_successmsg']);
$c.= '</div>';
// }
```

This defines the message which is shown to the form submitter after they've submitted the form. We initialize this with a simple non-specific message (**We will be in contact as soon as we can**), as we cannot be certain what the form will be used for.

The final straightforward tab is the `main details` section. Replace it with the following code. It may be a little long, but it's just a few fields. A screenshot after the code will explain what it does:

```
// { main details
$c.= '<div id="forms-main-details"><table>';
// { send as email
if(!isset($page_vars['forms_send_as_email']))
  $page_vars['forms_send_as_email']=1;
$c.= '<tr><th>Send as Email</th><td><select
    name="page_vars[forms_send_as_email]"><option
    value="1">Yes</option><option value="0"';
if(!$page_vars['forms_send_as_email'])
  $c.=' selected="selected"';
$c.= '>No</option></select></td>';
// }
// { recipient
if(!isset($page_vars['forms_recipient']))
  $page_vars['forms_recipient']=
      $_SESSION['userdata']['email'];
```

```
$c.= '<th>Recipient</th><td><input
    name="page_vars[forms_recipient]"
    value="'.htmlspecialchars($page_vars['forms_recipient'])
    .'" /></td></tr>';
// }

// { captcha required
if(!isset($page_vars['forms_captcha_required']))
  $page_vars['forms_captcha_required']=1;
$c.= '<tr><th>Captcha Required</th><td><select
    name="page_vars[forms_captcha_required]"><option
    value="1">Yes</option><option value="0"';
if(!$page_vars['forms_captcha_required'])
  $c.=' selected="selected"';
$c.='>No</option></select></td>';
// }

// { reply-to
if(!isset($page_vars['forms_replyto'])
    || !$page_vars['forms_replyto'])
  $page_vars['forms_replyto']='FIELD{email}';
$c.= '<th>Reply-To</th><td><input
    name="page_vars[forms_replyto]"
    value="'.htmlspecialchars($page_vars['forms_replyto']).'"
    /></td></tr>';
// }

// { record in database
if(!isset($page_vars['forms_record_in_db']))
  $page_vars['forms_record_in_db']=0;
$c.= '<tr><th>Record In DB</th><td><select
    name="page_vars[forms_record_in_db]"><option
    value="0">No</option><option value="1"';
if($page_vars['forms_record_in_db'])
  $c.=' selected="selected"';
$c.='>Yes</option></select></td>';
// }

// { export
if($id){
  $c.= '<th>Export<br /><i style="font-size:small">(requires
      Record In DB)</i></th><td>from: <input id="export_from"
      class="date" value="'
    .date('Y-m-d',mktime(0,0,0,date("m")-1,date("d"),
        date("Y")))
    .'" />. <a href="javascript:form_export('.$id
    .')">export</a></td></tr>';
```

```
    }
    else{    $c.='<td colspan="2"> </td></tr>';
    }
    // }
    $c.= '</table></div>';
    // }
```

This code builds up the **Main Details** tab, which looks like this in the browser:

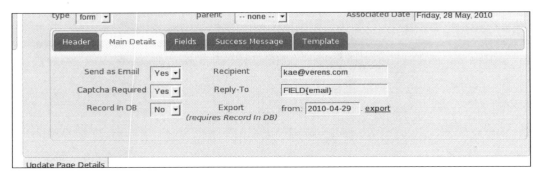

The **Send as Email** and **Captcha Required** are defaulted to **Yes**, while the **Record in DB** is defaulted to **No**.

Recipient is the person that the form is e-mailed to, which is set initially to the e-mail address of the administrator that created the form.

If the form is e-mailed to the recipient, and the recipient replies to the e-mail, then we need to know who we're replying to. We default this to FIELD{email}, which is a code indicating that the reply-to should be equal to whatever was filled in in the form in its email field (assuming it has one). We'll talk more on this later on. You could just as well enter an actual e-mail address such as no-reply@no-such.domain.

The **Export** field lets you export saved form details to a CSV file. We'll work on this later in the chapter as well.

For now, let's define the form fields.

Defining the form fields

Before we look at the code, we should define what it is that we are trying to achieve with the fields tab.

We want to be able to define each field that will be entered in the form by the user.

While some validation will be available, we should always be aware that the forms plugin will be used by an administrator who may be daunted by complex controls, so we will try to keep the user interface as simple as possible.

Validation will be kept to a minimum of whether the field must be entered in the form, and whether the entered value matches the field type. For example, if the field is defined as an e-mail, then the entered value must be an e-mail address. If the field is a select-box, then the entered value must match one of the entries we've defined as belonging to that select-box, and so on.

We will not use complex validation, such as if one entry is entered, then another must not. That kind of validation is rarely required by a simple website, and it would make the user interface much more cluttered and difficult to use.

Now, the `fields` tab is made of two parts—first, any fields that are already associated with the form will be printed out by the PHP, and we will then add some JavaScript to allow more fields to be added "on-the-fly".

Here is the PHP of it (replace the `fields` section in the file with this):

```
// { fields
$c.= '<div id="forms-fields">';
$c.= '<table id="formfieldsTable" width="100%"><tr><th
    width="30%">Name</th><th width="30%">Type</th><th
    width="10%">Required</th><th id="extrasColumn"><a
    href="javascript:formfieldsAddRow()">add
    field</a></th></tr></table><ul id="form_fields"
    style="list-style:none">';
$q2=dbAll('select * from forms_fields where formsId="'.$id.'"
    order by id');
$i=0;
$arr=array('input box','email','textarea','date',
    'checkbox','selectbox','hidden');
foreach($q2 as $r2){
  $c.= '<li><table width="100%"><tr>';
  // { name
  $c.='<td width="30%"><input name="formfieldElementsName['
    .$i.']" value="'.htmlspecialchars($r2['name']).'" />'
    .'</td>';
  // }
  // { type
  $c.='<td width="30%"><select name="formfieldElementsType['
    .$i.']">';
  foreach($arr as $v){
```

```
        $c.='<option value="'.$v.'"';
        if($v==$r2['type'])$c.=' selected="selected"';
        $c.='>'.$v.'</option>';
    }
    $c.='</select></td>';
    // }

    // { is required
    $c.='<td><input type="checkbox"
        name="formfieldElementsIsRequired['.($i).']"';
    if($r2['isrequired'])$c.=' checked="checked"';
    $c.=' /></td>';
    // }

    // { extras
    $c.='<td>';
    switch($r2['type']){
        case 'selectbox':case 'hidden':{
            $c.='<textarea class="small"
                name="formfieldElementsExtra['.($i++)
                .']">'.htmlspecialchars($r2['extra']).'</textarea>';
            break;
        }
        default:{
            $c.='<input type="hidden"
                name="formfieldElementsExtra['.($i++).']"
                value="'.htmlspecialchars($r2['extra']).'" />';
        }
    }
    $c.= '</td>';
    // }
    $c.='</tr></table></li>';
}
$c.= '</ul></div>';
// }
```

If you've read through that, you'll see that it simply outputs a number of rows of field data. We'll have a look at a screenshot shortly. First, let's add the JavaScript.

At the end of the file, add these lines:

```
$c.='<script>var formfieldElements='.$i.';</script>';
$c.='<script src="/ww.plugins/forms/admin/forms.js">
    </script>';
```

The variable $i here was set in the previous code-block, and represents the number of field rows that are already printed on the screen.

Now create the file `/ww.plugins/forms/admin/forms.js`:

```
window.form_input_types=['input box','email','textarea',
    'date','checkbox','selectbox','hidden'];
function formfieldsAddRow(){
  formfieldElements++;
  $('<li><table width="100%"><tr><td width="30%"><input '
    +'name="formfieldElementsName['+formfieldElements+']" '
    +'/></td><td width="30%"><select class="form-type" name="'
    +'formfieldElementsType['+formfieldElements+']"><option>'
    +form_input_types.join('</option><option>')
    +'</option></select></td><td width="10%"><input '
    +'type="checkbox" name="'
    +'formfieldElementsIsRequired['+formfieldElements+']" '
    +'/></td><td><textarea name="'
    +'formfieldElementsExtra['+formfieldElements+']" '
    +'style="display:none" class="small"></textarea></td>'
    +'</tr></table></li>'
    ).appendTo($('#form_fields'));
  $('#form_fields').sortable();
  $('#form_fields input,#form_fields select,#form_fields
      textarea').bind('click.sortable mousedown.sortable',
    function(ev){
      ev.target.focus();
    });
}
$('select.form-type').live('change',function(){
  var val=$(this).val();
  var display=(val=='selectbox' || val=='hidden')
    ?'inline':'none';
  $(this).closest('tr').find('textarea')
    .css('display',display);
});

if(!formfieldElements)var formfieldElements=0;
$(function(){
  formfieldsAddRow();
});
```

First, we define the list of available field types.

The `formfieldsAddRow()` function adds a new field row to the `fields` tab. The row is a simple line of HTML, replicating what we did in the PHP earlier.

Notice that we add a hidden textarea. This is to hold data on select-box values or hidden values if we choose to set the field type to either of those.

Next, we make the rows sortable using the jQuery UI's `.sortable()` plugin. This is so that the admin can reorder the field values if they want to.

Note that the `.sortable()` plugin makes it tricky to click on the input, select, and textarea boxes in the field row, as it hijacks the click and mousedown events, so the next line overrides the `.sortable()` event grab if you click on one of those elements. If you want to sort the rows, you should drag from a point outside those elements.

Next, we add a `live` event, which says that whenever a select-box with the class `form-type` is changed, we should change the visibility of the `extras` textarea in that row based on what you changed it to.

And finally, we initialize everything by calling `formfieldsAddRow()` so that the form has at least one row in it.

Note that we could have replaced the last three lines with this:

```
$( formfieldsAddRow);
```

However, when we get around to exporting saved data, we will want to add some more to the initialization routine, so we do it the long way.

In the screenshot, you can see the result of all this. I took this snapshot as I was dragging the **Request** field above the **Comment** one. Notice that the **Request** field has its extras textarea visible and filled in, one option per line.

Next we need to save the inputs.

Edit the file /ww.plugins/forms/plugin.php, and change the function form_ admin_page_form() to the following (changes are highlighted):

```
function form_admin_page_form($page,$page_vars){
  $id=$page['id'];
  $c='';
  if(isset($_REQUEST['action'])
      && $_REQUEST['action']=='Update Page Details')
    require dirname(__FILE__).'/admin/save.php';
  require dirname(__FILE__).'/admin/form.php';
  return $c;
}
```

And then all that's required is to do the actual save. Create the file /ww.plugins/ forms/admin/save.php:

```
<?php
dbQuery('delete from forms_fields where formsId="'.$id.'"');
if(isset($_POST['formfieldElementsName'])
      &&is_array($_POST['formfieldElementsName'])){
  foreach($_POST['formfieldElementsName'] as $key=>$name){
    $name=addslashes(trim($name));
    if($name!=''){
      $type=addslashes($_POST['formfieldElementsType'][$key]);
      $isrequired=
        (isset($_POST['formfieldElementsIsRequired'][$key]))
        ?1:0;
      $extra=
        addslashes($_POST['formfieldElementsExtra'][$key]);
      $query='insert into forms_fields set name="'.$name.'"
        ,type="'.$type.'", isrequired="'.$isrequired.'"
        ,formsId="'.$id.'",extra="'.$extra.'"';
      dbQuery($query);
    }
  }
}
```

First, the old existing fields are deleted if they exist, and then a fresh set are added to the database.

This happens each time you edit the form, because updating existing entries is much more complex than simply starting from scratch each time. This is especially true if you are moving them around, adding new ones, and so on.

Note that we check to see if the field's name was entered. If not, that row is not added to the database. So, to delete a field in your form, simply delete the name and update the page.

Now, let's show the form on the front-end.

Showing the form on the front-end

Showing the form is a matter of taking the information from the database and rendering it in the page HTML.

First, we need to tell the controller (/index.php) how to handle pages which are of a type other than normal.

Edit the /index.php file, and in the switch in set up pagecontent, replace the other cases will be handled here later line with the following default case:

```
default: // { plugins
  $not_found=true;
  foreach($PLUGINS as $p){
    if(isset($p['frontend']['page_type'][$PAGEDATA->type])){
      $pagecontent=$p['frontend']['page_type']
        [$PAGEDATA->type]($PAGEDATA);
      $not_found=false;
    }
  }
  if($not_found)$pagecontent='<em>No plugin found to handle
    page type <strong>'.htmlspecialchars($PAGEDATA->type)
    .'</strong>. Is the plugin installed and
    enabled?</em>';
// }
```

If the page type is not normal (type 0 in the switch that we've edited), then we check to see if it's a plugin.

This code runs through the array of plugins that are loaded, and checks to see if any of them have a frontend page_type that matches the current page. If so, then the associated function is run, with the $PAGEDATA object as a parameter.

We've already created the function as part of the plugin.php file. Now let's work on rendering the form.

Create the file /ww.plugins/forms/frontend/show.php (create the directory first):

```
<?php
require_once SCRIPTBASE.'ww.incs/recaptcha.php';
function form_controller($page){
  $fields=dbAll('select * from forms_fields where
    formsId="'.$page->id.'" order by id');
  if(isset($_POST['_form_action']))
    return form_submit($page,$fields);
  return form_display($page,$fields);
}
```

The first thing we do is to load up the field data from the database, as this is used when submitting and when rendering.

When the page is first loaded, there is no `_form_action` value in the `$_POST` array, so the function `form_display()` is then run and returned.

Add that function to the file now:

```
function form_display($page,$fields){
  if(isset($page->vars->forms_template)){
    $template=$page->vars->forms_template;
    if($template==' ')$template=false;
  }
  else $template=false;
  if(!$template)
    $template=form_template_generate($page,$fields);
  return form_template_render($template,$fields);
}
```

We first check the form's template to see that it is created and is not blank.

Next, if the template was blank, we build one using the field data as a guide.

And finally, we render the template and return it to the page controller.

Okay—the first thing we're missing is the `form_template_generate()` function. Add that to the file as follows:

```
function form_template_generate($page,$fields){
  $t='<table>';
  foreach($fields as $f){
    if($f['type']=='hidden')continue;
    $name=preg_replace('/[^a-zA-Z0-9_]/','',$f['name']);
    $t.='<tr><th>'.htmlspecialchars($f['name'])
      .'</th><td>{{$'.$name.'}}</td></tr>';
  }
  if($page->vars->forms_captcha_required){
    $t.='<tr><td> </td><td>{{CAPTCHA}}</td></tr>';
  }
  return $t.'</table>';
}
```

Simple enough—we iterate through each row, and generate some Smarty-like code. Here's an example output of the function (formatted for easier reading):

```
<table class="forms-table">
  <tr><th>Name</th><td>{{$Name}}</td></tr>
```

```
<tr><th>Email</th><td>{{$Email}}</td></tr>
<tr><th>Address</th><td>{{$Address}}</td></tr>
<tr><th>Request</th><td>{{$Request}}</td></tr>
<tr><th>Comment</th><td>{{$Comment}}</td></tr>
<tr><td> </td><td>{{CAPTCHA}}</td></tr>
</table>
```

We're not going to actually use Smarty on this one, as it would be too much—we just want to do a little bit of code replacement, so adding the full power of Smarty would be a waste of resources.

We use the Smarty-like code so that the admin doesn't have to remember different types of code. We could have also used BBCode, or simply placed % on either end of the field names, and so on.

Note that we don't output a line for hidden fields. Those fields are only ever seen by the administrator when the form is submitted.

Finally, we get to the rendering.

This function is kind of long, so we'll do it in bits.

```
function form_template_render($template,$fields){
  if(strpos($template,'{{CAPTCHA}}')!==false){
    $template=str_replace('{{CAPTCHA}}',
      recaptcha_get_html(RECAPTCHA_PUBLIC),$template);
  }
  foreach($fields as $f){
    $name=preg_replace('/[^a-zA-Z0-9_]/','',$f['name']);
    if($f['isrequired'])$class=' required';
    else $class='';
    if(isset($_POST[$name])){
      $val=$_POST[$name];
    }
    else $val='';
```

We first initialize the function and render the captcha if it's turned on. We're using the same captcha code that we used for the admin authentication.

Next, we start looping through each field value.

If the form has already been submitted, and we're showing it again, then we set $val to the value that was submitted. This is so we can show it in the form again.

Next, we figure out what should go into the template for the field:

```
switch($f['type']){
  case 'checkbox': // {
    $d='<input type="checkbox" id="forms-plugin-'.$name
      .'" name="'.$name.'"';
    if($val)$d.=' checked="'.$_REQUEST[$name].'"';
    $d.=' class="'.$class.'" />';
    break;
  // }
  case 'date': // {
    if(!$val)$val=date('Y-m-d');
    $d='<input id="forms-plugin-'.$name.'" name="'.$name
      .'" value="'.htmlspecialchars($val).'" class="date'
      .$class.'" />';
    break;
  // }
  case 'email': // {
    $d='<input type="email" id="forms-plugin-'.$name.'"
      name="'.$name.'" value="'.htmlspecialchars($val).'"
      class="email'.$class.'" />';
    break;
  // }
  case 'selectbox': // {
    $d='<select id="forms-plugin-'.$name.'" name="'.$name
      .'" class="'.$class.'">';
    $arr=explode("\n",htmlspecialchars($f['extra']));
    foreach($arr as $li){
      if($li=='')continue;
      $li=trim($li);
      if($val==$li)$d.='<option selected="selected">'.$li
        .'</option>';
      else $d.='<option>'.$li.'</option>';
    }
    $d.='</select>';
    break;
  // }
  case 'textarea': // {
    $d='<textarea id="forms-plugin-'.$name.'" name="'
      .$name.'" class="'.$class.'">'
      .htmlspecialchars($val).'</textarea>';
    break;
  // }
  default: // {
    $d='<input id="forms-plugin-'.$name.'" name="'.$name
      .'" value="'.htmlspecialchars($val).'" class="text'
      .$class.'" />';
  // }
}
```

This switch block checks what type of field it is, and generates an appropriate HTML string to represent it.

Note that we've added classes to the inputs. These classes can be used for client-side validation, or for CSS.

Finally:

```
    $template=str_replace('{{$'.$name.'}}',$d,$template);
  }
  return '<form method="post" id="forms-plugin">'.$template
    .'<input type="submit" name="_form_action"
    value="submit" /></form>
    <script src="/ww.plugins/forms/frontend/forms.js">
    </script>';
}
```

We replace the Smarty-like code with the HTML string for each field, and finally return the generated form with the submit button attached.

We also load up a JavaScript file, to handle validation on the client-side. We'll get to that shortly.

Having finished all of this, here's a screenshot of an example filled-in form:

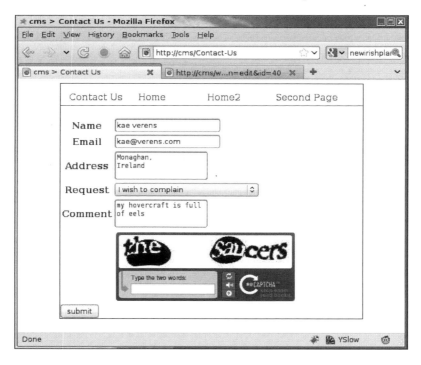

The form can be easily marked up in CSS to make it look better. But we're not here to talk style—let's get on with the submission of the form.

Handling the submission of the form

When submit is clicked, the form data is sent to the same page (we didn't put an `action` parameter in the `<form>` element, so it goes back to the same page by default).

The submit button itself has the name `_form_action` which, when the form controller is loaded, triggers `form_submit()` to be called.

Add that function to the same file:

```
function form_submit($page,$fields){
  $errors=form_validate($page,$fields);
  if(count($errors)){
    return '<ul id="forms-plugin-errors"><li>'
      .join('</li><li>',$errors)
      .'</ul>'
      .form_display($page,$fields);
  }
  if($page->vars->forms_send_as_email)
    form_send_as_email($page,$fields);
  if($page->vars->forms_record_in_db)
    form_record_in_db($page,$fields);
  return $page->vars->forms_successmsg;
}
```

The first thing we do is validate any submitted values.

Always write your validation for the server-side first.

If you do your validation on the client-side first, then you may forget to do it on the server-side. You'd also have to disable your client-side validation in order to test the server-side work.

After validation, we send the form off in an e-mail and save the form in the database if that's how it was set up in the admin area.

Finally, we return the success message to the page controller.

There are three functions to add.

The first is the validation function:

```
function form_validate($page,$fields){
  $errors=array();
  if($page->vars->forms_captcha_required){
    $resp=recaptcha_check_answer(
      RECAPTCHA_PRIVATE,
      $_SERVER["REMOTE_ADDR"],
      $_POST["recaptcha_challenge_field"],
      $_POST["recaptcha_response_field"]
    );
    if(!$resp->is_valid)$errors[]='Please fill in
        the captcha.';
  }
  foreach($fields as $f){
    $name=preg_replace('/[^a-zA-Z0-9_]/','',$f['name']);
    if(isset($_POST[$name])){
      $val=$_POST[$name];
    }
    else $val='';
    if($f['isrequired'] && !$val){
      $errors[]='The "'.htmlspecialchars($f['name']).'" field
          is required.';
      continue;
    }
    if(!$val)continue;
    switch($f['type']){
      case 'date': // {
        if(preg_replace('/[0-9]{4}-[0-9]{2}-[0-9]{2}/','',
          $val)=='')continue;
        $errors[]='"'.htmlspecialchars($f['name']).'" must be
            in yyyy-mm-dd format.';
        break;
      // }
      case 'email': // {
        if(filter_var($val,FILTER_VALIDATE_EMAIL))continue;
        $errors[]='"'.htmlspecialchars($f['name']).'" must be
            an email address.';
        break;
      // }
      case 'selectbox': // {
        $arr=explode("\n",htmlspecialchars($f['extra']));
        $found=0;
        foreach($arr as $li){
```

```
        if($li=='')continue;
        if($val==trim($li))$found=1;
      }
      if($found)continue;
      $errors[]='You must choose one of the options in
         "'.htmlspecialchars($f['name']).'".';
      break;
    // }
   }
  }
  return $errors;
}
```

If you create dummy functions for `form_send_as_email()` then you can test the given code, and its output should appear as seen in the next screenshot:

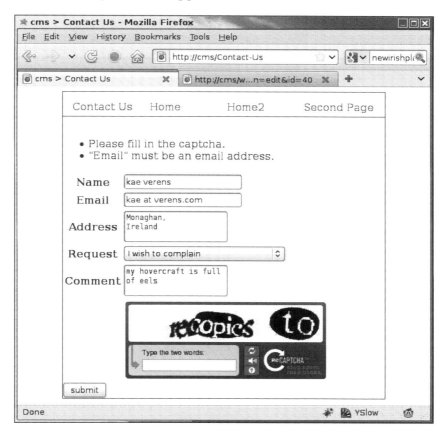

Okay, so validation works.

Sending by e-mail

Next, we will add the e-mail sender function.

The e-mail that we create does not need to be fancy—we're submitting a simple list of questions and responses, and it's not to a client, so it doesn't need a template to be created.

With that in mind, it's reasonable to create the following simple function:

```
function form_send_as_email($page,$fields){
  $m="-----------------------------\n";
  foreach($fields as $f){
    $name=preg_replace('/[^a-zA-Z0-9_]/','',$f['name']);
    if(!isset($_POST[$name]))continue;
    $m.=$f['name']."\n\n";
    $m.=$_POST[$name];
    $m.="-----------------------------\n";
  }
  $from=preg_replace('/^FIELD{|}$/','',
    $page->vars->forms_replyto);
  $to=preg_replace('/^FIELD{|}$/','',
    $page->vars->forms_recipient);
  if($page->vars->forms_replyto!=$from)
    $from=$_POST[preg_replace('/[^a-zA-Z0-9_]/','',$from)];
  if($page->vars->forms_recipient!=$to)
    $to=$_POST[preg_replace('/[^a-zA-Z0-9_]/','',$to)];
  mail($to,'['.$_SERVER['HTTP_HOST'].'] '
    .addslashes($page->name),$m,
    "From: $from\nReply-to: $from");
}
```

With this in place, the system will send the form contents as an e-mail:

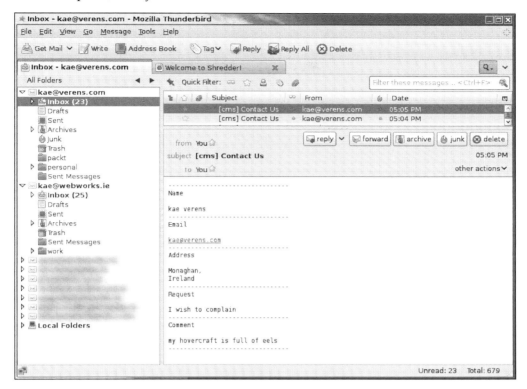

Perfectly readable and simple.

Saving in the database

Next, we tackle saving the form into the database:

```
function form_record_in_db($page,$fields){
  $formId=$page->id;
  dbQuery("insert into forms_saved (forms_id,date_created)
values($formId,now())");
  $id=dbOne('select last_insert_id() as id','id');
  foreach($fields as $r){
    $name=preg_replace('/[^a-zA-Z0-9_]/','',$r['name']);
    if(isset($_POST[$name]))$val=addslashes($_POST[$name]);
    else $val='';
    $key=addslashes($r['name']);
    dbQuery("insert into forms_saved_values (forms_saved_
id,name,value) values($id,'$key','$val')");
  }
}
```

This records the values of the form in the database:

```
mysql> select * from forms_saved;
+----------+---------------------+----+
| forms_id | date_created        | id |
+----------+---------------------+----+
|       40 | 2010-06-01 05:58:16 |  1 |
+----------+---------------------+----+
1 row in set (0.00 sec)
mysql> select * from forms_saved_values \G
*************************** 1. row ***************************
forms_saved_id: 1
         name: Name
        value: Kae Verens
           id: 6
*************************** 2. row ***************************
forms_saved_id: 1
         name: Email
        value: kae@verens.com
           id: 7
*************************** 3. row ***************************
forms_saved_id: 1
         name: Address
        value: Monaghan,
Ireland
           id: 8
*************************** 4. row ***************************
forms_saved_id: 1
         name: Request
        value: I wish to complain
           id: 9
*************************** 5. row ***************************
forms_saved_id: 1
         name: Comment
        value: my hovercraft is full of eels
           id: 10
5 rows in set (0.00 sec)
```

We cannot expect the admin to use the MySQL, so we need to write the export function now.

Exporting saved data

Back in the admin area, we had the following part of the **Forms** config:

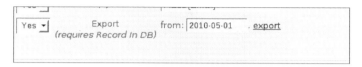

First, let's make that date area more interesting.

Edit the file `/ww.plugins/forms/admin/forms.js` and add the following
highlighted line to the `$(function)` part:

```
$(function(){
  formfieldsAddRow();
  $('#export_from').datepicker({dateFormat:'yy-m-d'});
});
```

This simple line then adds calendar functionality to that input, as seen in the
next screenshot:

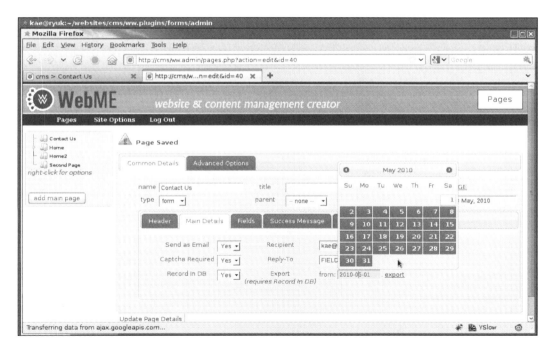

When the input is clicked, the calendar pops up, so the admin doesn't have to write
the date and get the format right.

Now let's add the function for handling the export (to that same file):

```
function form_export(id){
   if(!id)return alert('cannot export from an empty
      form database');
   if(!(+$('select[name="page_vars\\[forms_record_in_db\\]"]')
      .val()))
      return alert('this form doesn\'t record to database');
   var d=$('#export_from').val();
   document.location='/ww.plugins/forms/admin/export.php?date='
      +d+'&id='+id;
}
```

This function checks first to see if the form is marked to save in the database. If so, then it does a redirect to /ww.plugins/forms/admin/export.php. Create that file now:

```
<?php
require $_SERVER['DOCUMENT_ROOT'].'/ww.admin/admin_libs.php';
if(isset($_REQUEST['id']))$id=(int)$_REQUEST['id'];
else exit;
if(!$id)exit;
$date=$_REQUEST['date'];
if(!preg_match('/^20[0-9][0-9]-[0-9][0-9]-[0-9][0-9]$/',
   $date))die('invalid date format');
header('Content-type: application/octet-stream');
header('Content-Disposition: attachment; filename="form'
   .$id.'-export.csv"');
// { ids
$ids=array();
$rs=dbAll("select id,date_created from forms_saved where
   forms_id=$id and date_created>'$date'");
foreach($rs as $r){
   $ids[$r['id']]=$r['date_created'];
}
// }
// { columns
$cols=array();
$rs=dbAll('select name from forms_fields where formsId="'
   .$id.'" order by id');
foreach($rs as $r){
   $cols[]=$r['name'];
}
// }
// { do the export
```

```
echo '"Date Submitted","';
echo join('","',$cols).'"'."\n";
foreach($ids as $id=>$date){
  echo '"'.$date.'",';
  for($i=0;$i<count($cols);++$i){
    $r=dbRow('select value from forms_saved_values where
      forms_saved_id='.$id.' and name="'.addslashes($cols[$i])
      .'"');
    echo '"'.str_replace('\\"','""',addslashes($r['value']))
      .'"';
    if($i<count($cols)-1)echo ',';
    else echo "\n";
  }
}
// }
```

This exports the data as a CSV file.

Because the Content-type is application/octet-stream and browsers would not normally know how to handle that, the file is forced to download, instead of displaying in the browser. You can then open that exported file up in a spreadsheet:

	A	B	C	D	E	F
1	Date Submitted	Name	Email	Address	Request	Comment
2	2010-06-01 05:58:16	Kae Verens	kae@verens.com	Monaghan, Ireland	I wish to complain	my hovercraft is full of eels
3						

With the export finished, we've completed a functional forms plugin.

Summary

In this chapter, we added the ability for a plugin to create a full page type, instead of just a trigger.

We also added content tabs to the page admin.

With the Forms plugin created, the admin can now create contact pages, questionnaires, and other types of page that request data in the form of user input.

In the next chapter, we will create an Image Gallery plugin.

9
Image Gallery Plugin

When the time comes to display images in a website, whether it is a family album, a portfolio, or a series of product shots, there are a few ways to do this:

- You can insert each image manually using a rich-text editor to build up a large table
- You can select the images one-by-one from a list of images that exists on your server
- You can upload your images into a directory and have them automatically converted into a gallery

Option one can be done by using the rich-text editor—CKeditor, which we've already integrated into pages—but it's horribly tedious work building a gallery that way.

Option two would take some work to achieve, as we would need to create a list of all the images first and then create a method to select the images, store them in a database, and then, finally, create the gallery. Even then, selecting images one-by-one is probably more work than an admin should need to do.

Option three is perfect—the admin simply uploads images into a folder and a gallery is automatically created. It's even easier than that, as we will see, because we don't even need the admin to realize a directory is in use.

In this chapter, we will create an Image Gallery plugin, allowing an admin to upload a lot of images and have them automatically converted to either a slide-show gallery or a tabular gallery (we'll offer the choice).

We will not need to extend the plugin architecture any further for this one, so there will be minimal core engine editing.

Plugin configuration

Create the directory /ww.plugins/image-gallery, and in it, create the plugin.php file:

```php
<?php
$kfm_do_not_save_session=true;
require_once SCRIPTBASE.'j/kfm/api/api.php';
require_once SCRIPTBASE.'j/kfm/initialise.php';

$plugin=array(
  'name' => 'Image Gallery',
    'page_type' => array(
      'image-gallery' => 'image_gallery_admin_page_form'
    )
  ),
  'description' => 'Allows a directory of images to be
      shown as a gallery.',
  'frontend' => array(
    'page_type' => array(
      'image-gallery' => 'image_gallery_frontend'
    )
  )
);
function image_gallery_admin_page_form($page,$vars){
  require dirname(__FILE__).'/admin/index.php';
  return $c;
}
function image_gallery_frontend($PAGEDATA){
  require dirname(__FILE__).'/frontend/show.php';
  return image_gallery_show($PAGEDATA);
}
```

Earlier in the book, we introduced KFM, which is an online file manager. Instead of writing a whole new file management system every time we need to manage uploads or other file stuff, it makes sense to use what we already have.

The first three lines of the plugin.php load up KFM in a way that can be used by the server without needing to have a pop-up window for the client.

The first line tells KFM not to bother recording or checking its database for session data. This vastly speeds up interaction with it. As we are not interested in reusing the session, it is fine to ignore it.

The second loads up some useful functions that are not used within KFM, but would be useful for external systems. For example, we will use the `kfm_api_getDirectoryId()` function, which translates a human-readable directory (such as `images/page-2`) to an internal KFM ID.

We then initialize KFM, loading the various classes and building up its base information.

The rest of the `plugin.php` is standard fare by now—we create a page type, "Image Gallery", and its associated helper functions.

Now, log in to your admin area and enable the plugin, then go to the Pages section.

Page Admin tabs

As we did with the Forms plugin, let's create a skeleton tabs list first before we fill them in.

Create the directory `/ww.plugins/image-gallery/admin` and add the file `index.php` to it:

```php
<?php
$c='<div class="tabs">';
// { table of contents
$c.='<ul><li><a href="#image-gallery-images">Images</a></li>'
  .'<li><a href="#image-gallery-header">Header</a></li>'
  .'<li><a href="#image-gallery-settings">Settings</a></li></ul>';
// }
// { images
$c.='<div id="image-gallery-images">';
$c.='</div>';
// }
// { header
$c.='<div id="image-gallery-header">';
$c.=ckeditor('body',$page['body']);
$c.='</div>';
// }
// { settings
$c.='<div id="image-gallery-settings">';
$c.='</div>';
// }
$c.='</div>';
$c.='<link rel="stylesheet"
    href="/ww.plugins/image-gallery/admin/admin.css" />';
```

As before, the only tab that we've fully completed is the **Header** one, which is simply a CKeditor object. This tab will appear in just about every page admin, so it makes sense to simply copy or paste it each time.

The other two tabs will be fleshed out shortly, and I won't explain the admin.css file (it's just style—download it from Packt's archived files for this chapter).

When viewed, this looks totally bare:

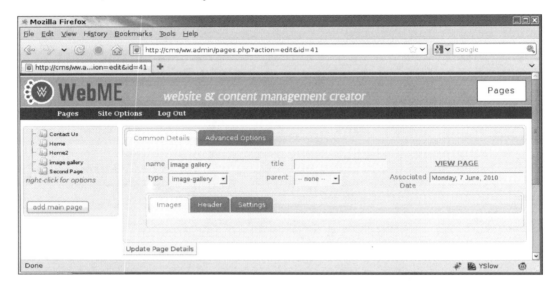

Notice that in the Forms plugin, we placed the **Header** tab first. In this one, it is the second tab.

The reason for this is that once a form is created, it is unlikely to be changed much, so if an admin is going to that page it is probably to adjust the header text, so we make that immediately available.

In an image gallery, however, the most likely reason an admin visits the page is to upload new images or delete old ones, so we make that one the first tab.

Initial settings

Before we get to work on the upload tab, we need to add some settings so the gallery knows how to behave.

Edit the index.php file again and add the following code after the opening <?php; the existing lines (beginning and end) have been highlighted:

```php
<?php
// { initialise variables
$gvars=array(
    'image_gallery_directory'    =>'',
    'image_gallery_x'            =>3,
    'image_gallery_y'            =>2,
    'image_gallery_autostart'    =>0,
    'image_gallery_slidedelay'   =>5000,
    'image_gallery_thumbsize'    =>150,
    'image_gallery_captionlength'=>100,
    'image_gallery_type'         =>'ad-gallery'
);
foreach($gvars as $n=>$v)if(isset($vars[$n]))$gvars[$n]=$vars[$n];
// }
$c='<div class="tabs">';
```

This reads the page variables and if any of the $gvars variables are not defined, the page variable of that name is created and set to the defaults set here.

Default	Function
image_gallery_directory	The directory that contains the images.
image_gallery_x	If the gallery type is a tabular one, then x is the width in cells of that table.
image_gallery_y	This is the height in rows of the images table.
image_gallery_autostart	If the gallery type is a slide-show, then this indicates where it should start sliding when the page loads.
image_gallery_slidedelay	How many milliseconds between each page slide.
image_gallery_thumbsize	This is the size of the image thumbnails.
image_gallery_captionlength	How many characters to show of the image's caption before cutting it off.
image_gallery_type	What type of gallery to use.

As we can save these variables directly into the page variables object, we don't need to provide an external database table for them or even to save them into the site's $DBVARS array (that should really only be used for data that is site-wide and not page-specific).

Uploading the Images

As we discussed earlier, the easiest way to manage images is to have them all uploaded to a single directory.

It is not necessary for the admin to know what directory that is. Whenever I do anything that involves uploading user-sourced files, it is always into the KFM-controlled files area, so that the files can be manipulated in more than one way.

We will upload the files into a directory /f/image-gallery/page-*n*, where the 'n' is a number corresponding to the page ID.

Let's build the **Images** tab. The code is medium long, so I'll describe it in a few blocks. In total, it should replace the current images comment block in the source:

```
// { images
$c.='<div id="image-gallery-images">';
if(!$gvars['image_gallery_directory'] || !is_dir(
    SCRIPTBASE.'f/'.$gvars['image_gallery_directory'])){
  mkdir(SCRIPTBASE.'f/image-galleries');
  $gvars['image_gallery_directory']=
      '/image-galleries/page-'.$page['id'];
  mkdir(SCRIPTBASE.'f/'.$gvars['image_gallery_directory']);
}
```

Here's how it goes:

The first thing that we do is check if the image_gallery_directory option is set and whether the directory actually exists.

If not, the option is set to /image-galleries/page- plus the page ID and this directory is then created.

```
$dir_id=kfm_api_getDirectoryId(preg_replace('/^\//','',
    $gvars['image_gallery_directory']));
$images=kfm_loadFiles($dir_id);
$images=$images['files'];
$n=count($images);
```

Next, we get the internal KFM ID of that directory (the ID is created if it doesn't already exist), and then load up all files in that directory.

$n is set to the number of files found.

```
$c.='<iframe src="/ww.plugins/image-gallery/admin/'
  .'uploader.php?image_gallery_directory='
  .urlencode($gvars['image_gallery_directory'])
  .'" style="width:400px;height:50px;'
```

```
.'border:0;overflow:hidden"></iframe>'
  .'<script>window.kfm={alert:function(){}};'
  .'window.kfm_vars={};function x_kfm_loadFiles(){}'
  .'function kfm_dir_openNode(){'
  .'document.location=document.location;}</script>';
```

Because all the tabs are contained in the page form, we can't have a sub-form to handle image uploads. So, we create an `<iframe>` to handle the upload.

This `<iframe>` will submit its files to KFM's `upload.php` file, which will handle their upload.

Upon a successful upload, KFM calls two functions, `x_kfm_loadFiles()` and `kfm_dir_openNode()`. We create dummy versions of these so there are no errors, and use the `kfm_dir_openNode()` call to reload the page to show the new images.

We'll create the `<iframe>`'s file after we finish this tab.

```
if($n){
  $c.='<div id="image-gallery-wrapper">';
  for($i=0;$i<$n;$i++){
    $c.='<div><img src="/kfmget/'.$images[$i]['id']
    .',width=64,height=64" title="'
    .str_replace('\\\\n','<br />',$images[$i]['caption'])
    .'" /><br /><input type="checkbox" id="image-gallery-'
    .'dchk-'.$images[$i]['id'].'" /><a href="javascript:;"'
    .' id="image-gallery-dbtn-'.$images[$i]['id']
    .'">delete</a></div>';
  }
  $c.='</div>';
}
```

If images were found in the directory, then we display the images, shrunk down to a maximum width of 64x64. The `/kfmget/...` bit will be explained shortly.

After the image is displayed, we add a check-box and **delete** link to delete the image. We'll add behaviors to those shortly.

```
else{
  $c.='<em>no images yet. please upload some.</em>';
}
$c.='</div>';
// }
```

Finally, we handle the case where there are no images, by simply asking for them to be uploaded.

Handling the uploads

In the same directory, /ww.plugins/image-gallery/admin, create the file
uploader.php:

```php
<?php
$dir=$_REQUEST['image_gallery_directory'];

echo '<form action="/j/kfm/upload.php" method="POST"
        enctype="multipart/form-data">
  <input type="file" name="kfm_file[]" multiple="multiple" />
  <input type="hidden" name="MAX_FILE_SIZE" value="9999999999"
    />
  <input type="hidden" name="directory_name"
      value="'.htmlspecialchars($dir).'" />
  <input type="submit" name="upload" value="Upload" />
  </form>';
```

This is a very simple upload form.

Note the use of multiple="multiple" in the file input box. Modern browsers will
allow you to upload multiple files, while older browsers will still work, but one
image at a time.

With that in place, we can now view the tab:

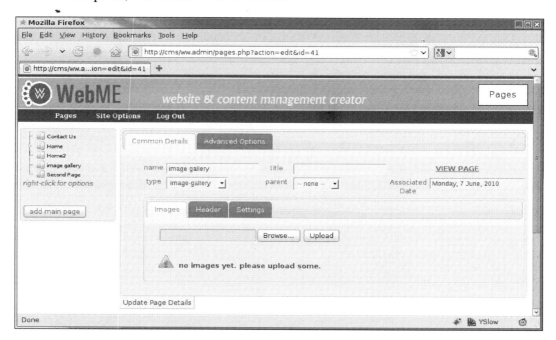

Uploading images will work, as you can verify by looking in your /f/image-galleries/page-*n* directory, but will appear broken:

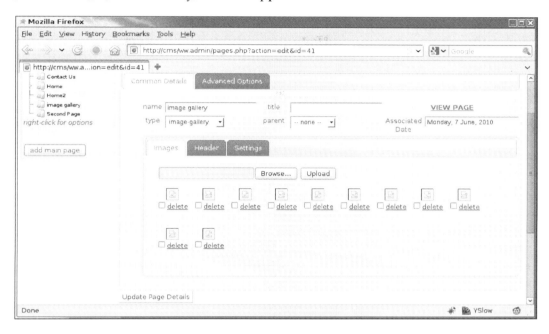

The reason for this is that the images are displayed using a mod_rewrite URL that we have not yet defined.

Adding a kfmget mod_rewrite rule

Here is what we provided in the source (for example):

```
<img src="/kfmget/13,width=64,height=64" ... />
```

The long version of this is:

```
/j/kfm/get.php?id=13,width=64,height=64
```

KFM understands that you want the file with ID 13 to be displayed and its size is constrained to 64x64.

Edit /.htaccess and add the following highlighted line:

```
RewriteEngine on
RewriteRule ^kfmget/(.*)$ /j/kfm/get.php?id=$1 [L]
RewriteRule ^([^./]{3}[^.]*)$ /index.php?page=$1 [QSA,L]
```

We place the rule before the main page rule because that one matches everything and `mod_rewrite` would not get to the `kfmget` rule.

The reason we use the shortcut in the first place is that by eliminating the `?` symbol, we allow the file to be cached. If you work a lot with images, it can be a drain on your network (and your wits) to constantly reload images that you were only viewing a moment ago.

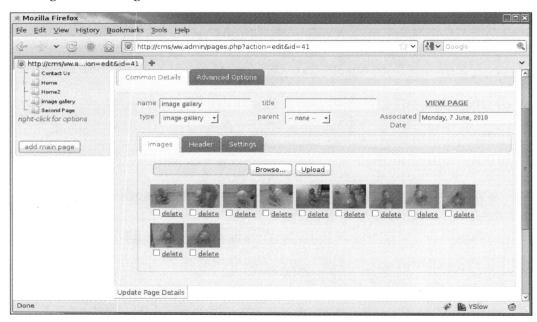

Much better.

Now, let's work on the **delete** links.

Deleting images

In the previous screenshot, you saw that each image had a check-box and link. The check-box must be ticked before the **delete** link is clicked to verify that the admin meant to delete the image.

Add the following highlighted line to the end of the `index.php` file:

```
$c.='</div>';
$c.='<link rel="stylesheet"
    href="/ww.plugins/image-gallery/admin/admin.css" />';
$c.='<script
    src="/ww.plugins/image-gallery/admin/js.js"></script>';
```

Then create the /ww.plugins/image-gallery/admin/js.js file:

```javascript
$('#image-gallery-wrapper a').bind('click',function(){
  var $this=$(this);
  var id=$this[0].id.replace('image-gallery-dbtn-','');
  if(!$('#image-gallery-dchk-'+id+':checked').length){
    alert('you must tick the box before deleting');
    return;
  }
  $.get('/j/kfm/rpc.php?action=delete_file&id='
      +id,function(ret){
    $this.closest('div').remove();
  });
});
```

First, we bind the click event to each of the delete links.

When clicked, we verify that the check-box was checked or return an alert explaining that it needs to be checked.

Finally, we call KFM through an **RPC (Remote Procedure Call)** to delete the file.

The RPC file is not yet a part of the official KFM distribution but was always on the plans for version 2, so here's the first implementation of /j/kfm/rpc.php:

```php
<?php
require 'initialise.php';
switch($_REQUEST['action']){
  case 'delete_file': // {
    $id=(int)$_REQUEST['id'];
    $file=kfmFile::getInstance($id);
    if($file){
      $file->delete();
      echo 'ok';
      exit;
    }
    else die('file does not exist');
  // }
}
```

Over time, that file will grow to include all sorts of RPC commands.

With this in place, we have completed the **Images** tab.

Before we get to the **Settings** tab, we will create the front-end part of the plugin.

Upload some images so we've something to look at and then let's get to work.

Front-end gallery display

There are many ways to show lists of images on the front-end.

If you look in the "Media" section of `http://plugins.jquery.com/`, you will find many galleries and other ways of representing multiple images.

When given the choice, most people in my experience want a gallery where a list of thumbnails is shown and clicking or hovering on one of them shows a larger version of the image.

The plugin we will use here is ad-gallery (`http://coffeescripter.com/code/ad-gallery/`) but we are writing the CMS plugin such that we can easily switch to another jQuery plugin by changing the "type" select-box in the admin area.

Create the directory `/ww.plugins/image-gallery/j/ad-gallery` (create the `j` first, obviously) and then download the JS and CSS files (in the **Downloads** section of `http://coffeescripter.com/code/ad-gallery/`) to there.

Create the `/ww.plugins/image-gallery/frontend` directory, and in there, create the file `show.php`:

```php
<?php
function image_gallery_show($PAGEDATA){
  $gvars=$PAGEDATA->vars;
  // {
  global $plugins_to_load;
  $c=$PAGEDATA->render();
  $start=isset($_REQUEST['start'])?(int)$_REQUEST['start']:0;
  if(!$start)$start=0;
  $vars=array(
    'image_gallery_directory'    =>'',
    'image_gallery_x'            =>3,
    'image_gallery_y'            =>2,
    'image_gallery_autostart'    =>0,
    'image_gallery_slidedelay'   =>5000,
    'image_gallery_thumbsize'    =>150,
    'image_gallery_captionlength'=>100,
    'image_gallery_type'         =>'ad-gallery'
  );
  foreach($gvars as $n=>$v)
    if($gvars->$n!='')$vars[$n]=$gvars->$n;
  $imagesPerPage=
    $vars['image_gallery_x']*$vars['image_gallery_y'];
  if($vars['image_gallery_directory']=='')
    $vars['image_gallery_directory']
```

```php
           ='/image-galleries/page-'.$PAGEDATA->id;
    //  }
    $dir_id=kfm_api_getDirectoryId(preg_replace('/^\//','',
        $vars['image_gallery_directory']));
    $images=kfm_loadFiles($dir_id);
    $images=$images['files'];
    $n=count($images);
    if($n){
      switch($vars['image_gallery_type']){
        case 'ad-gallery':
          require dirname(__FILE__).'/gallery-type-ad.php';
          break;
        default:
          return $c.'<em>unknown gallery type "'
            .htmlspecialchars($vars['image_gallery_type'])
            .'"</em>';
      }
      return $c;
    }else{
      return $c.'<em>gallery "'.$vars['image_gallery_directory']
        .'" not found.</em>';
    }
  }
```

This script acts as a controller for the gallery, making sure default variables are set before including the requested gallery type's script.

Notice the `switch` statement. If you want to add more jQuery gallery plugins, you can add them here.

Let's create the file `/ww.plugins/image-gallery/frontend/gallery-type-ad.php`. We'll build it up a bit at a time:

```php
<?php
$c.='<style type="text/css">img.ad-loader{
  width:16px !important;height:16px !important;}</style>
  <div style="visibility:hidden" class="ad-gallery">
    <div class="ad-image-wrapper"> </div>
    <div class="ad-controls"> </div>
    <div class="ad-nav"> <div class="ad-thumbs">
      <ul class="ad-thumb-list">';
for($i=0;$i<$n;$i++){
  $c.='<li> <a href="/kfmget/'.$images[$i]['id'].'">
    <img src="/kfmget/'.$images[$i]['id'].',width='
      .$vars['image_gallery_thumbsize'].',height='
```

```
        .$vars['image_gallery_thumbsize'].'" title="'
        .str_replace('\\\\n','<br />',$images[$i]['caption'])
        .'"> </a> </li>';
  }
  $c.='</ul> </div> </div> </div>';
```

First, we display the list of thumbnails, similar to how it was done in the admin area.

The styles and element structure are the `ad-gallery` plugin.

```
  $c.='<script src="/ww.plugins/image-gallery/j/ad-gallery/'
    .'jquery.ad-gallery.js"></script>'
    .'<style type="text/css">@import "/ww.plugins/image-'
    .'gallery/j/ad-gallery/jquery.ad-gallery.css";'
    .'.ad-gallery .ad-image-wrapper{ height: 400px;}'
    .'</style>';
```

Next, we import the `ad-gallery` plugin and its CSS file.

```
  $c.='<script>
  $(function(){
    $(".ad-gallery").adGallery({
      animate_first_image:true,
      callbacks:{
        "init":function(){
          $("div.ad-gallery").css("visibility","visible");
        }
      },
      loader_image:"/i/throbber.gif",
      slideshow:{';
  $slideshowvars=array();
  if($vars['image_gallery_autostart']){
    $slideshowvars[]='enable:true';
    $slideshowvars[]='autostart:true';
  }
  $sp=(int)$vars['image_gallery_slidedelay'];
  if($sp)$slideshowvars[]='speed:'.$sp;
  $c.=join(',',$slideshowvars);
  $c.='}
    });
  });</script>';
```

Finally, we build up the start-up function that will be called when the page loads.

And you can then view the page in your browser:

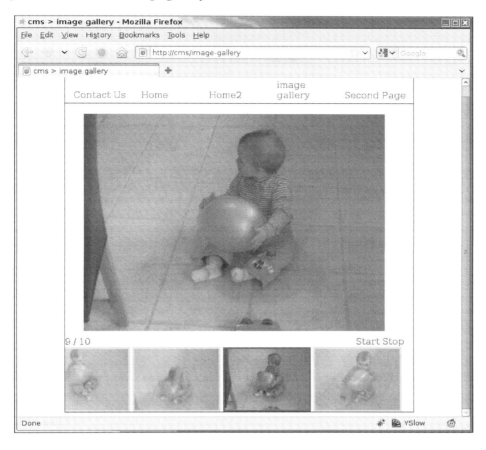

This gallery should cover the most basic needs, but if you wanted to use a different gallery type, it should be simple enough to add it to this.

We'll demonstrate this by building up a simple gallery in a grid fashion.

Settings tab

First, we need to write the **Settings** tab code so we can configure it. Edit the file / ww.plugins/image-gallery/admin/index.php and let's replace the settings comment block, starting with this:

```
// { settings
$c.='<div id="image-gallery-settings">';
$c.='<table><tr><th>Image Directory</th><td><select '
```

```
      .'id="image_gallery_directory" '
      .'name="page_vars[image_gallery_directory]">'
      .'<option value="/">/</option>';
  foreach(image_gallery_get_subdirs(SCRIPTBASE.'f','') as $d){
    $c.='<option value="'.htmlspecialchars($d).'"';
    if($d==$gvars['image_gallery_directory'])
      $c.=' selected="selected"';
    $c.='>'.htmlspecialchars($d).'</option>';
  }
  $c.='</select></td>';
  $c.='<td colspan="2"><a style="background:#ff0;'
    .'font-weight:bold;color:red;display:block;'
    .'text-align:center;" '
    .'href="#page_vars[image_gallery_directory]" '
    .'onclick="javascript:window.open(\'/j/kfm/?startup_folder='
    .'\'+$(\'#image_gallery_directory\').attr(\'value\')'
    .',\'kfm\',\'modal,width=800,height=600\');">Manage '
    .'Images</a></td></tr>';
```

This first section allows finer control over where the files are uploaded to.

After that, follow the next steps:

First, we create a select-box containing all the directories in the user uploads section (/f), using the `image_gallery_get_subdirs()`, which we'll define in a moment.

Next, we add a link that lets you open KFM straight to that directory, so you can edit the images with more control than what was in the first tab.

```
  // { columns
  $c.='<tr><th>Columns</th><td><input '
    .'name="page_vars[image_gallery_x]" value="'
    .(int)$gvars['image_gallery_x'].'" /></td>';
  // }
  // { gallery type
  $c.='<th>Gallery Type</th><td><select '
    .'name="page_vars[image_gallery_type]">';
  $types=array('ad-gallery','simple gallery');
  foreach($types as $t){
    $c.='<option value="'.$t.'"';
    if(isset($gvars['image_gallery_type']) &&
        $gvars['image_gallery_type']==$t)
      $c.=' selected="selected"';
    $c.='>'.$t.'</option>';
  }
```

```
$c.='</select></td></tr>';
// }
```

Next, we add an input box for columns (in case the type you choose is a grid-style gallery) and a drop-down select-box to choose the gallery type.

In the `$types` array, you name the types just as the `switch` in `show.php` on the front-end expects to find them. I've named our new one "simple gallery".

```
// { rows
$c.='<tr><th>Rows</th><td><input '
  .'name="page_vars[image_gallery_y]" value="'
  .(int)$gvars['image_gallery_y'].'" /></td>';
// }
// { autostart the slideshow
$c.='<th>Autostart slide-show</th><td><select '
  .'name="page_vars[image_gallery_autostart]"><option '
  .'value="0">No</option><option value="1"';
if($gvars['image_gallery_autostart'])
  $c.=' selected="selected"';
$c.='>Yes</option></select></td></tr>';
// }
```

Next, we add an input for the rows for grid-style galleries, followed by a select-box to choose whether slide-shows should be auto-started or not.

```
// { caption length
$cl=(int)@$gvars['image_gallery_captionlength'];
$cl=$cl?$cl:100;
$c.='<tr><th>Caption Length</th><td><input '
  .'name="page_vars[image_gallery_captionlength]" value="'
  .$cl.'" /></td>';
// }
// { slide delay
$sd=(int)@$gvars['image_gallery_slidedelay'];
$c.='<th>Slide Delay</th><td><input name="'
  .'page_vars[image_gallery_slidedelay]" class="small" '
  .'value="'.$sd.'" />ms</td></tr>';
// }
```

Next, we ask for the caption length. We set its default to 100 and if we are using a slide-show, we ask for the slide-show delay (default value is set to 5000 ms).

You can set an image's caption by either editing its embedded data before uploading it, or by using KFM to edit the caption after it's uploaded (right-click on the image | **edit** | **change caption**).

```
// { thumb size
$ts=(int)@$gvars['image_gallery_thumbsize'];
$ts=$ts?$ts:150;
$c.='<tr><th>Thumb Size</th><td><input name="'
  .'page_vars[image_gallery_thumbsize]" value="'.$ts
  .'" /></td></tr>';
// }
$c.='</table>';
$c.='</div>';
// }
```

Finally, we ask for the thumb-size, and then close up the tab.

Okay, before we can view the tab, we need to create that missing function. Add this at the top of the file (after the `<?php`):

```
function image_gallery_get_subdirs($base,$dir){
  $arr=array();
  $D=new DirectoryIterator($base.$dir);
  $ds=array();
  foreach($D as $dname){
    $d=$dname.'';
    if($d{0}=='.')continue;
    if(!is_dir($base.$dir.'/'.$d))continue;
    $ds[]=$d;
  }
  asort($ds);
  foreach($ds as $d){
    $arr[]=$dir.'/'.$d;
    $arr=array_merge($arr,image_gallery_get_subdirs(
      $base,$dir.'/'.$d));
  }
  return $arr;
}
```

This function recursively builds up a list of the directories contained in the user uploads section and returns it.

Finally, we can view the tab:

That's the admin area completed.

Now, we can get back to the front and finish our grid-based gallery.

Grid-based gallery

We've already added the ad-gallery. Now let's create our grid-based gallery that will be called `simple gallery`.

Edit `/ww.plugins/image-gallery/frontend/show.php` and add the following highlighted lines to the switch:

```
        break;
    case 'simple gallery':
      require dirname(__FILE__).'/gallery-type-simple.php';
      break;
    default:
```

After that, create `/ww.plugins/image-gallery/frontend/gallery-type-simple.php`, again explained in parts, as follows:

```php
<?php
$c.='<table id="image_gallery" class="image_gallery">';
if($n>$imagesPerPage){
  $prespage=$PAGEDATA->getRelativeURL();
  // { prev
    $c.='<th class="prev" style="text-align:left" '
      .'id="image_gallery_prev_wrapper">';
    if($start>0){
      $l=$start-$imagesPerPage;
      if($l<0)$l=0;
      $c.='<a href="'.$prespage.'?start='.$l.'">&lt;-- '
        .'prev</a>';
    }
    $c.='</th>';
  // }
  for($l=1;$l<$vars['image_gallery_x']-1;++$l)$c.='<th></th>';
  // { next
    $c.='<th class="next" style="text-align:right" '
      .'id="image_gallery_next_wrapper">';
    if($start+$imagesPerPage<$n){
      $l=$start+$imagesPerPage;
      $c.='<a href="'.$prespage.'?start='.$l.'">next '
        .'--&gt;</a>';
    }
    $c.='</th>';
  // }
}
```

This first section sets up pagination. If we have columns and rows set to 3 and 2, then there are six images per page.

If there are more than six images in the set, we need to provide navigation to those images.

This block figures out what page we're on and whether there is more to come.

```php
$all=array();
$s=$start+$vars['image_gallery_x']*$vars['image_gallery_y'];
if($s>$n)$s=$n;
for($i=$start;$i<$s;++$i){
  $cap=$images[$i]['caption'];
  if(strlen($cap)>$vars['image_gallery_captionlength'])
```

```
        $cap=substr($cap,0,$vars['image_gallery_captionlength']-3)
          .'...';
    $all[]=array(
      'url'=>'/kfmget/'.$images[$i]['id'],
      'thumb'=>'/kfmget/'.$images[$i]['id'].',width='
        .$vars['image_gallery_thumbsize'].',height='
        .$vars['image_gallery_thumbsize'],
      'title'=>$images[$i]['caption'],
      'caption'=>str_replace('\\\n',"<br />",
        htmlspecialchars($cap))
    );
  }
```

Next, we build up an array of the visible images, including details such as caption, link to original image, address of thumbnail, and so on.

```
for($row=0;$row<$vars['image_gallery_y'];++$row){
  $c.='<tr>';
  for($col=0;$col<$vars['image_gallery_x'];++$col){
    $i=$row*$vars['image_gallery_x']+$col;
    $c.='<td id="igCell_'.$row.'_'.$col.'">';
    if(isset($all[$i]))$c.='<div style="text-align:center" '
      .'class="gallery_image"><a href="'.$all[$i]['url']
      .'"><img src="'.$all[$i]['thumb'].'" />'
      .'<br style="clear:both" /><span class="caption">'
      .$all[$i]['caption'].'</span></a></div>';
    $c.='</td>';
  }
  $c.='</tr>';
}
$c.='</table>';
```

Finally, we generate the table of images.

This can be enhanced by generating jQuery to manage the pagination but as this is just a demonstration of having two gallery methods for the one CMS plugin, it's not necessary to go through that trouble.

In the admin area, go to the **Settings** tab and change the gallery type to **simple gallery** and click **Update** to save it.

Now, when viewed in a browser, the page looks like this:

And when the **next -->** link is clicked, it changes to this:

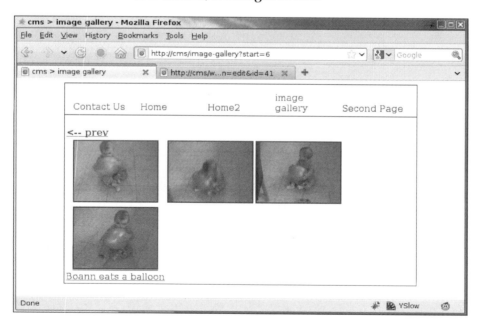

Notice that the URL has been changed to add a `start` parameter and the pagination has changed. There is no **next -->** and a **<-- prev** link is added.

Also, the bottom photo on the left-hand side has a caption on it.

That's it—a completed Image Gallery plugin.

Summary

In this chapter, we created an Image Gallery plugin for the CMS, which lets you upload multiple images to a directory and choose from a list of gallery types how you want to show the images on the front-end.

In the next chapter, we will build the basics of the Panels plugin. A **Panel** is basically a "wrapper", within which widgets can be placed by the admin. It greatly extends the customizability of a site design.

10
Panels and Widgets – Part One

A **panel** is an area in your design which can contain a number of widgets. These widgets can be installed by simply "dropping" them into place using the admin area.

A **widget** is a small visual object such as a poll, login box, search box, news scroller, and so on, which you may want to place on your site.

Items placed in a panel can be seen on every page of the site.

In this chapter, we will learn how to:

- Create the panel plugin
- Create the content snippet widget
- Add widgets to panels
- Display panels and widgets on the front-end

This is another two-part chapter.

This first chapter will develop panels and widgets enough that they can be created and seen on the front-end.

The next chapter will enhance this foundation and let you customize the widgets, and choose which pages the panels and widgets should be visible on.

Creating the panel plugin

Usually when creating a website, a header, footer, and sidebar will be written into the theme which are specific to the company the website is for.

The header would include the company name, logo, and maybe a collage of pertinent images.

The footer would include the company name, trademarks, maybe a contact number.

The sidebar would include contact details of the company.

If you replace those three areas with panels (named "header", "footer", "sidebar"), each of which can contain a widget which provides the required HTML for the company-specific details, then this allows you to create a generic web design which can be customized for a specific company, and yet be reused by another customer if you wish.

The Content Snippet widget is just that—it's a snippet of HTML content which you want to have shared among all your pages.

Create the directory /ww.plugins/panels and add this plugin.php to it:

```php
<?php
$plugin=array(
  'name'=>'Panels',
  'description'=>
    'Allows content sections to be displayed throughout the site.',
  'admin'=>array(
    'menu'=>array(
      'Misc>Panels'=>'index'
    )
  ),
  'frontend'=>array(
    'template_functions'=>array(
      'PANEL'=>array(
        'function' => 'panels_show'
      )
    )
  ),
  'version'=>4
);
function panels_show($vars){
}
```

We'll leave the front-end function blank for now.

Notice that we've added a template function to the configuration array. Because we are talking about adding panels to specific parts of the site design, we need to add code to the theme's template files to say where the panels go. We do this by adding the PANEL function to Smarty, which will call panels_show() when it is used in the design. The template_functions array will be explained later.

An example of its use:

```
<html>
  <body>
    {{$PANEL name="header"}}
    <p>page content goes here</p>
    {{$PANEL name="footer"}}
  </body>
</html>
```

At the moment, our CMS doesn't actually add that function to Smarty, but we'll get to that.

Notice as well that the configuration set the version number to 4. This is because there were four database table revisions I made while developing the plugin.

I've combined all four into one step here. Add the `/ww.plugins/panels/upgrade.php` file:

```
<?php
if($version<4){ // panels table
  dbQuery('CREATE TABLE IF NOT EXISTS `panels` (
    `id` int(11) NOT NULL auto_increment,
    `name` text,
    `body` text,
    `visibility` text,
    `disabled` smallint default 0,
    PRIMARY KEY  (`id`)
    ) ENGINE=MyISAM DEFAULT CHARSET=utf8');
  $version=4;
}
```

The panels table includes these fields:

`id`	Internal ID of the panel.
`name`	The name of the panel. This is used in the design template. For example: `{{PANEL name="footer"}}`
`body`	A JSON array containing details of any contained widgets.
`visibility`	A list of pages which this panel is visible on. If left blank, it's visible on all of them.
`disabled`	This allows you to "turn off" a panel so it's not visible at all on the front-end, yet keeps its settings.

The reason we detail the contained widgets in a JSON array instead of a related database table is that database access is usually slower than simply reading a text file, especially if there are quite a few records.

In any one panel, there would usually be only two or three widgets. Running a database search for that number of items is silly when you can include their details in the container panel's result instead.

Registering a panel

A panel is tied explicitly to a name, which is referred to in a template. When you create the template, you write into it where you want the panel to appear by using that name.

There are two ways to know the names of the panels that are contained in any template:

1. Decide beforehand what names are allowed.
2. Parse the templates to extract the names.

The first option is simply unreasonable. If we do decide on a certain list of allowed names, we may end up with a list of ten or more panel names, where any design may pick and choose from the list. However, we then still have the problem of showing only the active panel names to the administrator.

It is more reasonable to not restrict the list of names, but instead extract the names that the designer chose from the template itself.

The extraction itself also poses a problem. Do we parse the actual template file itself? If so, we would be writing the equivalent of a Smarty compiler.

Why not let Smarty do the work itself? The solution I've come to use is that the panel names in any template are figured out by viewing the template in the front-end and using Smarty to then register any unknown panels in a database table.

This means that by viewing the front-end of the site before you go to the administration page, we populate the table of panels with a list of actual panels that are in use by the site.

While this is not ideal, in actual usage, it's sufficient. Most website designs involve creating the pages before worrying about panels. This means that the list of panels is complete before the administrator goes to populate them.

So, first we need to edit the template and add in the panel. Open up the `/ww.skins/basic/h/_default.html` file and add in the following highlighted lines:

```
<div id="wrapper">
  <div id="menu-wrapper">{{MENU
    direction="horizontal"}}</div>
  {{PANEL name="right"}}
  <div id="page-wrapper">{{$PAGECONTENT}}</div>
  {{PANEL name="footer"}}
</div>
```

I've also edited the CSS file so the **right** panel, when generated, will be floated to the right-hand side and the #page-wrapper element leaves enough margin space for it. It's not essential for me to print that here.

Note that in the plugin.php file, we had this section:

```
'frontend'=>array(
  'template_functions'=>array(
    'PANEL'=>array(
      'function' => 'panels_show'
    )
  )
),
```

We will use the template_functions array to add custom functions to Smarty, which will be executed at the appropriate place in the template.

Edit /ww.incs/common.php, and add the highlighted code to the smarty_setup function:

```
$smarty->register_function('MENU', 'menu_show_fg');
foreach($GLOBALS['PLUGINS'] as $pname=>$plugin){
  if(isset($plugin['frontend']['template_functions'])){
    foreach($plugin['frontend']['template_functions']
        as $fname=>$vals){
      $smarty->register_function($fname,$vals['function']);
    }
  }
}
return $smarty;
}
```

Now any template_functions array items will be added to Smarty and can be called from the template itself.

Edit the /ww.plugins/panels/plugin.php file, and replace the panels_show() function:

```
function panels_show($vars){
  $name=isset($vars['name'])?$vars['name']:'';
  // { load panel data
  $p=dbRow('select visibility,disabled,body from panels where
      name="'.addslashes($name).'" limit 1');
  if(!$p){
    dbQuery("insert into panels (name,body)
        values('".addslashes($name)."','{\"widgets\":[]}')");
    return '';
  }
  // }
  // { is the panel visible?
  // }
  // { get the panel content
  $widgets=json_decode($p['body']);
  if(!count($widgets->widgets))return '';
  // }
}
```

This is a skeleton function. A lot of it has been left out. At the moment, all that it does is to verify that the panel is in the database and if not, the panel is added to the database.

When you view the page in the browser, there is no visible difference. The HTML source has not been changed. It's as if the {{PANEL}} lines weren't in the template at all.

This is because if a panel is empty, it is pointless having an empty space in the page.

It is possible to have CSS change the layout of the page depending on whether the panel exists or not. That is outside the scope of the book, but if you need to know how to do it, read the following article which I wrote a few months ago:

http://blog.webworks.ie/2010/04/27/creating-optional-columns-in-website-layouts/

Even though there is no visible difference in the HTML, the database table has been populated:

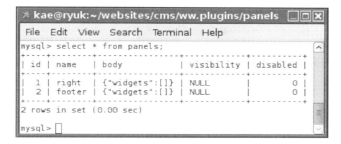

By decoding the JSON in the body field, the function knew there were no contained widgets and returned an empty string.

The panel admin area

Now we need to populate the panels.

The panel admin section will be easy to explain the look of, but is kind of complex underneath it.

The page will be a two-column layout, with a wide column on the left-hand side holding a list of all available widgets, and a narrow column on the right-hand side listing the available panels.

We will start by building that visual.

Create the `/ww.plugins/panels/admin` directory, and in there, place an `index.php` file:

```php
<?php
echo '<table style="width:95%"><tr>';
echo '<td><h3>Widgets</h3><p>Drag a widget into a panel on '
  .'the right.</p><div id="widgets"></div>'
  .'<br style="clear:both" /></td>';
echo '<td style="width:220px"><h3>Panels</h3><p>Click a '
  .'header to open it.</p><div id="panels"></div>'
  .'<br style="clear:both" /></td></tr>';
echo '</table>';
```

When viewed, we get a general idea of how this will work.

Next, we will show the panels that we inserted into the database in the previous section of the chapter.

Showing panels

Add the following code to the admin/index.php file that we just edited:

```
echo '<link rel="stylesheet" type="text/css"
    href="/ww.plugins/panels/admin/css.css" />';
// { panel and widget data
echo '<script>';
// { panels
echo 'ww.panels=[';
$ps=array();
$rs=dbAll('select * from panels order by name');
foreach($rs as $r)$ps[]='{id:'.$r['id'].',disabled:'
  .$r['disabled'].',name:"'.$r['name'].'",widgets:'
  .$r['body'].'}';
echo join(',',$ps);
echo '];';
// }
// { widgets
echo 'ww.widgets=[];';
// }
```

```
// { widget forms
echo 'ww.widgetForms={};';
// }
// }
?>
</script>
<script src="/ww.plugins/panels/admin/js.js"></script>
```

When viewed in a browser, the plugin now generates the following HTML:

```
<h1>panels</h1>
<table style="width:95%">
  <tr>
    <td><h3>Widgets</h3><p>Drag a widget into a panel on the
      right.</p><div id="widgets"></div>
      <br style="clear:both" /></td>
    <td style="width:220px"><h3>Panels</h3><p>Click a header
      to open it.</p><div id="panels"></div>
      <br style="clear:both" /></td>
  </tr>
</table>
<link rel="stylesheet" type="text/css"
    href="/ww.plugins/panels/admin/css.css" />
<script>
ww.panels=[
  {id:2,disabled:0,name:"footer",widgets:{"widgets":[]}},
  {id:1,disabled:0,name:"right",widgets:{"widgets":[]}}
];
ww.widgets=[];
ww.widgetForms={};
</script>
<script src="/ww.plugins/panels/admin/js.js"></script>
```

And now we can add some JavaScript to generate the panel wrappers. Create the file `/ww.plugins/panels/admin/js.js`:

```
function panels_init(panel_column){
  for(var i=0;i<ww_panels.length;++i){
    var p=ww_panels[i];
    $('<div class="panel-wrapper '
        +(p.disabled?'disabled':'enabled')+'" id="panel'
        +p.id+'">'
        +'<h4><span class="name">'+p.name+'</span></h4>'
        +'<span class="controls" style="display:none">'
          +'<a title="remove panel" href="'
```

```
          +'javascript:panel_remove('
          +i+');" class="remove">remove</a>, '
      +'<a href="javascript:panel_visibility('
          +p.id+');" class="visibility">visibility</a>, '
      +'<a href="javascript:panel_toggle_disabled('
          +i+');" class="disabled">'
          +(p.disabled?'disabled':'enabled')+'</a>'
        +'</span></div>'
      )
      .data('widgets',p.widgets.widgets)
      .appendTo(panel_column);
  }
}
$(function(){
  var panel_column=$('#panels');
  panels_init(panel_column);
  $('<span class="panel-opener">&darr;</span>')
    .appendTo('.panel-wrapper h4')
    .click(function(){
      var $this=$(this);
      var panel=$this.closest('div');
      if($('.panel-body',panel).length){
        $('.controls',panel).css('display','none');
        return $('.panel-body',panel).remove();
      }
      $('.controls',panel).css('display','block');
    });
});
```

So first, we get the `#panels` wrapper and run `panels_init` on it. This function builds up a simple element with a few links inside it:

remove	This link is for deleting the panel if your template doesn't use it or you just want to empty it quickly.
visibility	This will be used to decide what pages the panel is visible on. If you want this panel to only show on the front page, for example, you would use this.
enabled	This link lets you turn off the whole panel and its contained widgets so you can work on it in the admin area but it's not visible in the front-end.

Notice the usage of `.data('widgets',p.widgets.widgets)` — this saves the contained widget data to the panel element itself. We'll make use of that soon.

The panels start with their bodies hidden and only their names visible (in <h4> elements).

After `panels_init()` is finished, we then add a down-arrow link to each of those `<h4>` elements, which when clicked will toggle the panel body's visibility.

Here's what the page looks like now, with one of the panels opened up:

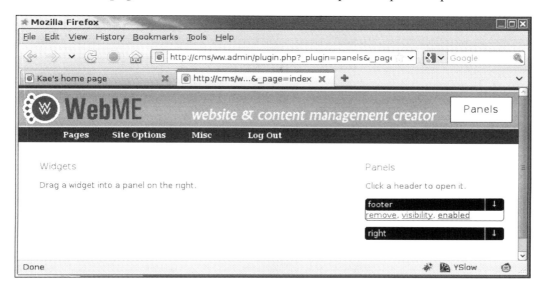

Before we write the code for those links, we will start building the widget code—otherwise, there'd be no visible proof that the links are working.

Creating the content snippet plugin

In order to demonstrate widgets, we will build a simple plugin called content snippet. This plugin will manage small snippets of code which can be displayed anywhere that a panel is.

In my own work, I use content snippets to add editable footers, headers, and side panel content sections (for addresses, contact details, and so on) to design templates. This allows the customer to update details without needing access to the template files themselves.

Create the directory `/ww.plugins/content-snippet`, and add the following `plugin.php` file in it:

```php
<?php
$plugin=array(
    'name' => 'Content Snippets',
    'admin' => array(
```

```
          'widget' => array(
            'form_url' => '/ww.plugins/content-snippet/admin/'
              .'widget-form.php'
          )
        ),
        'description' => 'Add small static HTML snippets to any '
          .'panel - address, slogan, footer, image, etc.',
        'frontend' => array(
          'widget' => 'contentsnippet_show'
        ),
        'version' => '1'
      );
      function contentsnippet_show($vars=null){
        require_once SCRIPTBASE.'ww.plugins/content-snippet/'
          .'frontend/index.php';
        return content_snippet_show($vars);
      }
```

Inside the admin array, we have a widget section. The form_url parameter points to the address of a PHP script which will be used to configure the panel.

And inside the front-end array, we have a corresponding widget section which points at a function which will display the widget.

We will need a database table for this plugin, so create the upgrade.php file:

```
<?php
if($version=='0'){ // add table
  dbQuery('create table if not exists content_snippets( id'
    .' int auto_increment not null primary key, html text)'
    .'default charset=utf8;');
  $version=1;
}
```

All we need for this panel is to record some HTML, which is then displayed as-is on the front-end.

After you finish writing the files, go to the **Plugins** area of the CMS and enable this new plugin, then go back to the **Panels** area.

Adding widgets to panels

We now have a very simple plugin skeleton ready to go. All we need to do is add it to a panel, configure it (by adding HTML), and then show it on the front-end.

Showing widgets

First, we need to show the list of available widgets.

Edit the file `/ww.plugins/panels/admin/index.php` and change the widgets section to this:

```
// { widgets
echo 'ww_widgets=[';
$ws=array();
foreach($PLUGINS as $n=>$p){
  if(isset($p['frontend']['widget']))$ws[]='{type:"'.$n
    .'",description:"'.addslashes($p['description']).'"}';
}
echo join(',',$ws);
echo '];';
// }
```

That will output the following to our browser:

```
ww_widgets=[{type:"content-snippet",description:"Add small static HTML
snippets to any panel - address, slogan, footer, image, etc."}];
```

Now we edit the `admin/js.js` file to show these widgets in the left-hand side column. This will involve a few small changes, so we'll step through them one at a time.

First, add the highlighted lines to the `$(function){` section:

```
panels_init(panel_column);
var widget_column=$('#widgets');
ww_widgetsByName={};
widgets_init(widget_column);
$('<span class="panel-opener">&darr;</span>')
```

Then add the `widgets_init()` function:

```
function widgets_init(widget_column){
  for(var i=0;i<ww_widgets.length;++i){
    var p=ww_widgets[i];
    $('<div class="widget-wrapper"><h4>'+p.type
        +'</h4><p>'+p.description+'</p></div>')
      .appendTo(widget_column)
      .data('widget',p);
    ww_widgetsByName[p.type]=p;
  }
}
```

This takes the global ww_widgets array and builds little box elements out of the data, attaching the widget data to the boxes, and then adding the boxes to the left column of the main table.

The page looks much better now, as you can see in the next screenshot:

The next step is to take widgets from the left-hand side of the page and associate them with panels on the right-hand side of the page.

Dragging widgets into panels

Drag-and-drop is handled by using jQuery UI's Sortable plugin, which allows you to drag items from one list (the widgets list on the left-hand side) and drop into another list (the list of contained widgets in each panel on the right).

Edit the $(function()){ section of js.js again and add these highlighted lines:

```
$('.controls',panel).css('display','block');
var widgets_container=$('<div class="panel-body">'
  +'</div>');
widgets_container.appendTo(panel);
$('<br style="clear:both" />')
  .appendTo(panel);
$('.panel-body').sortable({
});
});
```

```
$('#widgets').sortable({
  'connectWith':'.panel-body',
  'stop':function(ev,ui){
    var item=ui.item;
    var panel=item.closest('.panel-wrapper');
    if(!panel.length)return $(this).sortable('cancel');
  }
})
$('<br style="clear:both" />').appendTo(widget_column);
});
```

First we add a `panel-body` element to the right-hand side panels, which will hold the widgets.

Next, we make the contents of the right-hand side `pane-body` elements `sortable`, so we can link to them with the left-hand side column widgets.

Finally, we make the left-hand side column `sortable`, linking to the `panel-body` elements on the right-hand side.

With this done, we can now drag widgets into the panels:

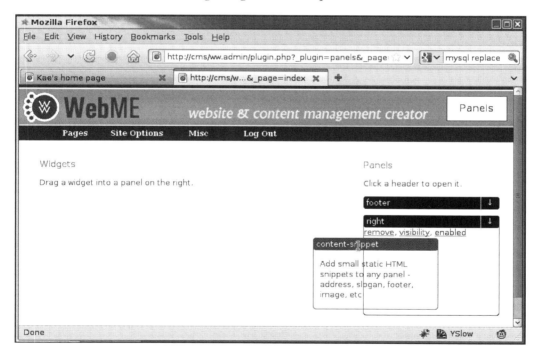

Unfortunately, this is not very useful, as the widget has been removed from the left-hand side column, and therefore can't be reused. For example, if you wanted to use a content snippet in each panel, you can't do that now.

So, what we need to do is "clone" the dragged item (or at least its data properties) and place the clone in the panel, then cancel the drag so the original dragged widget goes back to the **right** panel.

Edit the same file again, and add these highlighted lines:

```
'stop':function(ev,ui){
  var item=ui.item;
  var panel=item.closest('.panel-wrapper');
  if(!panel.length)return $(this).sortable('cancel');
  var p=ww_widgetsByName[$('h4',ui.item).text()];
  var clone=buildRightWidget({'type':p.type});
  panel.find('.panel-body').append(clone);
  $(this).sortable('cancel');
}
```

The above code calls a function buildRightWidget() with the widget name (the name of the plugin used to create the widget), and the resulting element is added to the panel instead of the actual dragged widget.

The dragged widget is then returned to its original place (by cancelling the sortable's drag) where it can be used again.

Here's the function buildRightWidget(), to be added to the file:

```
function buildRightWidget(p){
  var widget=$('<div class="widget-wrapper '
      +(p.disabled?'disabled':'enabled')+'"></div>')
    .data('widget',p);
  var h4=$('<h4></h4>')
    .appendTo(widget);
  var name=p.name||p.type;
  $('<input type="checkbox" class="widget_header_visibility"'
      +' title="tick this to show the widget title on the'
      +' front-end" />')
    .click(widget_header_visibility)
    .appendTo(h4);
  $('<span class="name">'+name+'</span>')
    .click(widget_rename)
    .appendTo(h4);
  $('<span class="panel-opener">&darr;</span>')
    .appendTo(h4)
```

```
        .click(showWidgetForm);
    return widget;
}
```

This code creates another wrapper similar to the panels wrappers, with the title of the widget visible.

There are a number of functions called with callbacks, for doing things such as renaming the widget, showing the widget name in the front-end, or showing the widget form.

We'll get to those. In the meantime, add some "stub" functions as placeholders:

```
function showWidgetForm(){}
function widget_header_visibility(){}
function widget_rename(){}
```

Now, after dragging, we have a visual similar to the following screenshot:

We'll do one more thing in the admin area, then we can show the widget in the front-end.

Saving panel contents

Whenever a new widget is added to a panel, we need to rebuild the panel's body JSON string (in the panels table in the database) and save it to the server.

Edit the `js.js` file again, and add the following highlighted lines:

```
widgets_container.appendTo(panel);
$('<br style="clear:both" />').appendTo(panel);
$('.panel-body').sortable({
  'stop':function(){
    updateWidgets($(this).closest('.panel-wrapper'));
  }
});
});
```

This code runs `updateWidgets()` whenever a widget in the **right** panel is moved around (rearranged, for instance).

Add the following highlighted code as well:

```
var clone=buildRightWidget({'type':p.type});
panel.find('.panel-body').append(clone);
$(this).sortable('cancel');
updateWidgets(panel);
}
})
```

This adds a behavior such that when the widget is dropped into a panel body, the function `updateWidgets()` is run.

Here is the `updateWidgets()` function:

```
function updateWidgets(panel){
  var id=panel[0].id.replace(/panel/,'');
  var w_els=$('.widget-wrapper',panel);
  var widgets=[];
  for(var i=0;i<w_els.length;++i){
    widgets.push($(w_els[i]).data('widget'));
  }
  panel.data('widgets',widgets);
  var json=json_encode({'widgets':widgets});
  $.post('/ww.plugins/panels/admin/save.php',{
    'id':id,
    'data':json
  });
}
```

This function takes a panel as its parameter. It then searches the panel for any contained widgets, adds all of their contained "widget" data to its own "widgets" array, and sends that to the server to be saved.

There is no built-in JSON encoder in jQuery, so you'll need to add one.

Edit /ww.admin/j/admin.js and add this:

```
function typeOf(value) {
  // from http://javascript.crockford.com/remedial.html
  var s = typeof value;
  if (s === 'object') {
    if (value) {
      if (value instanceof Array) {
        s = 'array';
      }
    } else {
      s = 'null';
    }
  }
  return s;
}
function json_encode(obj){
  switch(typeOf(obj)){
    case 'string':
      return '"'+obj.replace(/(["\\])/g,'\\$1')+'"';
    case 'array':
      return '['+obj.map(json_encode).join(',')+']';
    case 'object':
      var string=[];
      for(var property in obj)string.push(
          json_encode(property)+':'
          +json_encode(obj[property]));
      return '{'+string.join(',')+'}';
    case 'number':
      if(isFinite(obj))break;
    case false:
      return 'null';
  }
  return String(obj);
}
```

The first function, typeOf(), is there because JavaScript's built-in typeof keyword doesn't differentiate between objects and arrays, and those are very different in JSON!

Here is the server-side file that saves it— `/ww.plugins/panels/admin/save.php`.

```php
<?php
require $_SERVER['DOCUMENT_ROOT'].'/ww.admin/admin_libs.php';
$id=(int)$_REQUEST['id'];
$widgets=addslashes($_REQUEST['data']);
dbQuery("update panels set body='$widgets' where id=$id");
```

Now after dragging a content snippet widget into a panel, here is the database table:

```
 kae@ryuk:~/websites/cms/ww.plugins/panels/admin          [][][x]

File  Edit  View  Search  Terminal  Help
mysql> select * from panels;
+----+--------+------------------------------------------+------------+----------+
| id | name   | body                                     | visibility | disabled |
+----+--------+------------------------------------------+------------+----------+
|  3 | right  | {"widgets":[{"type":"content-snippet"}]} | NULL       |        0 |
|  4 | footer | {"widgets":[]}                           | NULL       |        0 |
+----+--------+------------------------------------------+------------+----------+
2 rows in set (0.00 sec)

mysql> █
```

We can now record what widgets are in what panels.

While interesting details of the widgets, such as customizing widget contents, are yet to be recorded, this is enough to display some stubs on the front-end, which we'll do next.

Showing panels on the front-end

We have the panel widgets in the database now, so let's write some code to extract and render them.

Edit `/ww.plugins/panels/plugin.php` and add the following highlighted code to the end of the `panels_show()` function:

```php
// { show the panel content
$h='';
global $PLUGINS;
foreach($widgets->widgets as $widget){
  if(isset($PLUGINS[$widget->type])){
    if(
      isset($PLUGINS[$widget->type]['frontend']['widget'])
    ){
      $h.=$PLUGINS[$widget->type]['frontend']['widget']
        ($widget);
    }
    else $h.='<em>plugin "'
```

```
        .htmlspecialchars($widget->type)
        .'" does not have a widget interface.</em>';
    }
    else $h.='<em>missing plugin "'
      .htmlspecialchars($widget->type)
        .'".</em>';
  }
// }
$name=preg_replace('/[^a-z0-9\-]/','-',$name);
return '<div class="panel panel-'.$name.'">'.$h.'</div>';
// }
}
```

The highlighted line does the trick. In the `plugin.php` for the content snippet plugin, we had this section:

```
'frontend' => array(
  'widget' => 'contentsnippet_show'
),
```

What the highlighted line does is to call the function `contentsnippet_show()` with a parameter `$widget` which is set to the contents of the panel's `$widgets` array at that point.

So, anything that's saved in the admin area for that widget is passed to the function on the front-end as an array. We'll see more on this later.

The function `contentsnippet_show()` loads up `frontend/index.php` and then returns the result of a call to its contained `content_snippet_show()`.

The functions have similar names—the only difference being the '_'. The one without the '_' is a stub, in case the other is not actually required. There is no point loading up a lot of code if only a little of it is actually used.

Create the directory `/ww.plugins/content-snippet/frontend`, and add the file `index.php` to it:

```php
<?php
function content_snippet_show($vars){
  if(is_object($vars) && isset($vars->id) && $vars->id){
    $html=dbOne('select html from content_snippets
        where id='.$vars->id,'html');
    if($html)return $html;
  }
  return '<p>this Content Snippet is not yet defined.</p>';
}
```

You can see that the function expects the parameter `$vars` to be an object with a variable `$id` in it.

We have not set that variable yet, which would correspond to a table entry in the database, so the alternative failure string is returned instead.

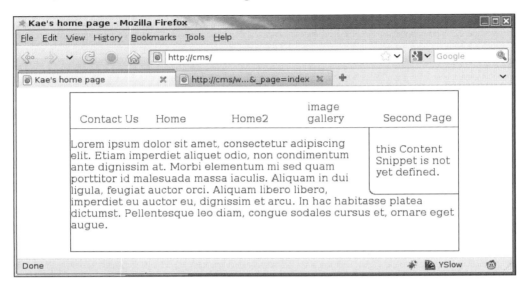

If you remember, we added two panels to the template—a **right** panel, visible in this screenshot, and a **footer** panel. The **footer** panel is not visible, because we haven't added anything to it yet.

Summary

In this chapter, we built the basics of a panels and widgets system.

Widgets are a way to add huge flexibility to any web design that has panels built into it.

In the next chapter, we will finish the system, letting the admin customize the widgets, and choose what pages the widgets and panels are visible on.

11

Panels and Widgets – Part Two

In the previous chapter, we built the basics of the panels and widgets system. You can now create panels, can drag widgets into them, and can see the results on the front-end of the site.

In this chapter, we will enhance the system letting you customize the widgets and letting you choose what pages the panels and widgets are visible on.

Widget forms

In the last chapter, we had widgets showing on the front-end, but with a default **This Content Snippet is not yet defined** message.

In order to change the message to something more useful, we will need to do more work in the admin area.

Firstly, when you reload the Panels area of the admin, you'll see that our right panel widget appears to have vanished. We've recorded it in the database, but have not set the page to show it on loading.

Edit `/ww.plugins/panels/admin/js.js` and where the `.panel-opener` is added to the `h4` of `.panel-wrapper`, add these highlighted lines:

```
widgets_container.appendTo(panel);
var widgets=panel.data('widgets');
for(var i=0;i<widgets.length;++i){
  var p=widgets[i];
  var w=buildRightWidget(p);
  w.appendTo(widgets_container);
  if(p.header_visibility)
```

```
$('input.widget_header_visibility',w)[0]
    .checked=true;
}
$('<br style="clear:both" />').appendTo(panel);
```

When we created the panels in the JavaScript, we set the wrapper's `data('widgets')` with data from the database. This code takes that data and adds the widgets on-the-fly, when the panel is opened.

Because each widget is different, we need to provide a way to load up external configuration forms.

To do this, replace the `showWidgetForm()` stub function with this:

```
function showWidgetForm(w){
  if(!w.length)w=$(this).closest('.widget-wrapper');
  var f=$('form',w);
  if(f.length){
    f.remove();
    return;
  }
  var form=$('<form></form>').appendTo(w);
  var p=w.data('widget');
  if(ww_widgetForms[p.type]){
    $('<button style="float:right">Save</button>')
      .click(function(){
        w.find('input,select').each(function(i,el){
          p[el.name]=$(el).val();
        });
        w.data('widget',p);
        updateWidgets(form.closest('.panel-wrapper'));
        return false;
      })
      .appendTo(form);
    var fholder=$('<div style="clear:both;border-bottom:1px solid
#416BA7">loading...</div>').prependTo(form);
    p.panel=$('h4>span.name',form.closest('.panel-wrapper')).eq(0).
text();
    fholder.load(ww_widgetForms[p.type],p);
  }
  else $('<p>automatically configured</p>').appendTo(form);

  $('<a href="javascript:;" title="remove widget">remove</a>')
    .click(function(){
      if(!confirm('Are you sure you want to remove this widget from
this panel?'))return;
```

```
            var panel=w.closest('.panel-wrapper');
            w.remove();
            updateWidgets(panel);
        })
        .appendTo(form);
    $('<span>, </span>').appendTo(form);
    $('<a href="javascript:;">visibility</a>')
        .click(widget_visibility)
        .appendTo(form);
    $('<span>, </span>').appendTo(form);
    $('<a class="disabled" href="javascript:;">'+(p.disabled?'disabled':
'enabled')+'</a>')
        .click(widget_toggle_disabled)
        .appendTo(form);
}
function widget_toggle_disabled(){}
function widget_visibility(){}
```

The first few lines toggle the form closed, if it's already closed.

Then, if a form is provided (we'll get to this in a moment), it is added to a form element, along with a **Save** button. The external form is embedded in the element using jQuery's `.load()` function, which also runs any scripts in the external form.

If no form is provided, a message is shown saying that the widget is automatically configured.

Then, a number of links are added to let you remove, disable, or set the pages that the widget is active on.

The only link that works at the moment is the remove link, which simply deletes the widget element, and then updates the panel.

The other links are served by stub functions. We will finish them all before the end of the chapter!

Here's a screenshot showing the widget as it appears now:

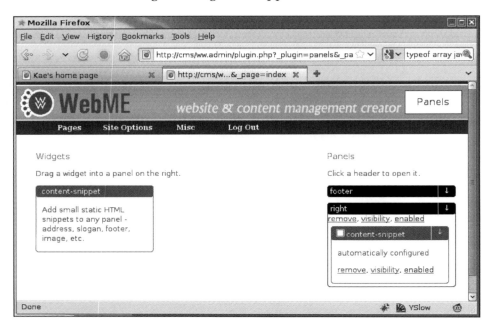

When we were initially creating `/ww.plugins/panels/admin/index.php`, we added a simple "widget forms" comment block. Now, replace that with this:

```
// { widget forms
echo 'ww.widgetForms={';
$ws=array();
foreach($PLUGINS as $n=>$p){
  if(isset($p['admin']['widget'])
      && isset($p['admin']['widget']['form_url']))
    $ws[]='"'.$n.'":"'
      .addslashes($p['admin']['widget']['form_url']).'"';
}
echo join(',',$ws);
echo '};';
// }
```

This builds up a list of panel forms and echoes them to the browser's HTML:

```
ww_widgets=[{type:"content-snippet",description:"Add small static HTML
snippets to any panel - address, slogan, footer, image, etc."}];
ww_widgetForms={"content-snippet":"/ww.plugins/content-snippet/admin/
widget-form.php"};
</script>
```

So let's create the form. Make the `/ww.plugins/content-snippet/admin` **directory** and add a `widget-form.php` file to it:

```php
<?php
require $_SERVER['DOCUMENT_ROOT'].'/ww.admin/admin_libs.php';

// { return content from table if requested
if(isset($_REQUEST['get_content_snippet'])){
  require '../frontend/index.php';
  $o=new stdClass();
  $o->id=(int)$_REQUEST['get_content_snippet'];
  $ret=array('content'=>content_snippet_show($o));
  echo json_encode($ret);
  exit;
}
// }

// { set ID and show link in admin area
if(isset($_REQUEST['id']))$id=(int)$_REQUEST['id'];
else $id=0;
echo '<a href="javascript:content_snippet_edit('.$id.');"
  id="content_snippet_editlink_'.$id.'"
  class="content_snippet_editlink">view or edit snippet</a>';
// }

?>
```

This is not the end of the file—we've only just started. It's a large snippet, so I'll explain just this bit first.

First, we check that the user is an admin and load up the admin libraries, in case they're needed.

Then, we check to see if the browser has asked for the content of the snippet. There'll be more on that in a bit when we talk about the JavaScript part of the file.

Next, we make sure that an ID has been provided or else set it to 0.

Finally, we output a link for the browser to show to the user.

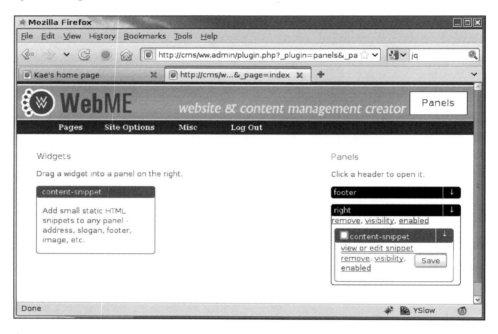

So next, we need to define what happens when the **view or edit snippet** link is clicked.

Add the following code to the same file:

```
<script>
if(!window.ww_content_snippet)window.ww_content_snippet={
  editor_instances:0
};
function content_snippet_edit(id){
  var el=document.getElementById('content_snippet_editlink_'
    +id);
  ww_content_snippet.editor_instances++;
  var rtenum=ww_content_snippet.editor_instances;
  var d=$('<div><textarea style="width:600px;height:300px;" '
    +'id="content_snippet_html'+rtenum+'" '
    +'name="content_snippet_html'+rtenum+'"></textarea>'
    +'</div>');
  $.getJSON(
    '/ww.plugins/content-snippet/admin/widget-form.php',
    {'get_content_snippet':id},
    function(res){
      d.dialog({
```

```
            minWidth:630,
            minHeight:400,
            height:400,
            width:630,
            modal:true,
            beforeclose:function(){
              if(!ww_content_snippet.rte)return;
              ww_content_snippet.rte.destroy();
              ww_content_snippet.rte=null;
            },
            buttons:{
              'Save':function(){
                // leave empty for now
              },
              'Close':function(){
                d.remove();
              }
            }
          });
      ww_content_snippet.rte=CKEDITOR.replace(
        'content_snippet_html'+rtenum,
        {filebrowserBrowseUrl:"/j/kfm/",menu:"WebME"}
      );
      ww_content_snippet.rte.setData(res.content);
    });
  }
</script>
```

What this does is create a dialog, add an instance of the CKeditor rich text editor to it, and then request the snippet content from the server (see the previous PHP section for that).

Note the steps we've taken with CKeditor. At the time of writing, CKeditor 3 is still not complete—the documentation on the main website, for example, has hardly anything in the JavaScript section.

Destroying an instance of CKeditor dynamically is still not absolutely safe, so what we do is that when a dialog is closed, we do what we can using the .destroy() method provided by CKeditor. To be extra sure, we don't reuse a destroyed instance, but we always initiate a new one (see the use of editor_instances in the code).

The previous block of code will render this to the screen when the **view or edit snippet** link is clicked:

You can now insert any HTML you want into that.

Saving the snippet content

The code I've shown doesn't include the **Save** function. Let's add that now.

Edit the JavaScript part of the file, and replace the line `// leave empty for now` with this:

```
var html=ww_content_snippet.rte.getData();
$.post('/ww.plugins/content-snippet/admin/'
    +'widget-form.php',
  {'id':id,'action':'save','html':html},
  function(ret){
    if(ret.id!=ret.was_id){
      el.id='content_snippet_editlink_'+ret.id;
      el.href='javascript:content_snippet_edit('
        +ret.id+')';
```

```
            }
            id=ret.id;
            var w=$(el).closest('.widget-wrapper');
            var wd=w.data('widget');
            wd.id=id;
            w.data('widget',wd);
            updateWidgets(w.closest('.panel-wrapper'));
            d.remove();
          },
          'json'
        );
```

The **Save** functionality sends the RTE contents to the server.

On the server, we will save it to the database. If an ID was provided, it will be an update; otherwise, it will be an insert.

In either case, data including the ID is then returned to the client. If the database entry was an insert, the widget is updated with the new ID.

The panel is then saved to the server in case any of its data (for instance, the widget data in the case where an ID was created) was changed.

In the PHP section, add this to the top of the file, below the require line:

```
// { save data to the database if requested
if(isset($_REQUEST['action']) && $_REQUEST['action']=='save'){
  $id=(int)$_REQUEST['id'];
  $id_was=$id;
  $html=addslashes($_REQUEST['html']);
  $sql="content_snippets set html='$html'";
  if($id){
    $sql="update $sql where id=$id";
    dbQuery($sql);
  }
  else{
    $sql="insert into $sql";
    dbQuery($sql);
    $id=dbOne('select last_insert_id() as id','id');
  }
  $ret=array('id'=>$id,'id_was'=>$id_was);
  echo json_encode($ret);
  exit;
}
// }
```

This simply saves the offered data into the database and returns the original ID as submitted, along with the new one, in case an insert was made and the client-side code needs to update itself.

With this code in place, you can now edit your content snippets, as can be seen in the following screenshot:

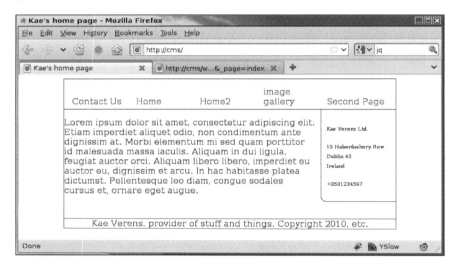

You can see that I've used the panel on the right-hand side to add an address and the bottom panel to add some standard footer-type stuff.

You can add as many widgets to a panel as you want.

We are now finished with the Content Snippet plugin.

Renaming widgets

In a busy website, it is a nuisance if you have a load of widgets in panels and are not sure which one you're looking for. For example, if one of the Content Snippet widgets is an address, it is better that it says **address** in the panel, than **content snippet**.

We've already added the code that calls the function `widget_rename()`, when the widget header is clicked.

Replace the stub `widget_rename()` function in `/ww.plugins/panels/admin/js.js` with this:

```
function widget_rename(ev){
  var h4=$(ev.target);
  var p=h4.closest('.widget-wrapper').data('widget');
  var newName=prompt('What would you like to rename the '
    +'widget to?',p.name||p.type);
  if(!newName)return;
  p.name=newName;
  h4.closest('.widget-wrapper').data('widget',p);
  updateWidgets($(h4).closest('.panel-wrapper'));
  h4.text(newName);
}
```

Very simply put, this sets `p` to the current widget data, asks for a new name for the widget, sets `p.name` equal to that new name, and then saves the widget data again.

In small sites where there're only a few widgets in use, this may seem like overkill, but in more complex sites, this is necessary.

Widget header visibility

On the front-end, you might want to have **Address** written above the address section of the panel on the right.

For Content Snippets, this is simple, as you just need to add it to the HTML that you're already building.

But, if you're using a different widget, then there may not be an editable section of HTML. For example, in an RSS reader widget, which simply displays a list of items from an RSS stream, it would be overkill to add an editor for user-controlled HTML.

So, for these cases, we provide a check-box in the widget's header which lets you tell the server to add a `<h4>` element before the widget is rendered.

Add this code to the `js.js` file, replacing the `widget_header_visibility()` stub function:

```
function widget_header_visibility(ev){
  var el=ev.target,vis=[];
  var w=$(el).closest('.widget-wrapper');
  var p=w.data('widget');
  p.header_visibility=el.checked;
  w.data('widget',p);
  updateWidgets(w.closest('.panel-wrapper'));
}
```

Similar to the widget renaming section, this simply edits the widget data, saves it, and updates the visuals.

For the front-end, edit `/ww.plugins/panels/plugin.php` and add the following highlighted line:

```
foreach($widgets->widgets as $widget){
  if(isset($widget->header_visibility)
      && $widget->header_visibility)
    $h.='<h4 class="panel-widget-header '
      .preg_replace('/[^a-z0-9A-Z\-]/','',$widget->name)
      .'">'.htmlspecialchars($widget->name).'</h4>';
  if(isset($PLUGINS[$widget->type])){
    if(isset($PLUGINS[$widget->type]['frontend']['widget'])){
```

This will add a `<h4>` before any widgets you select:

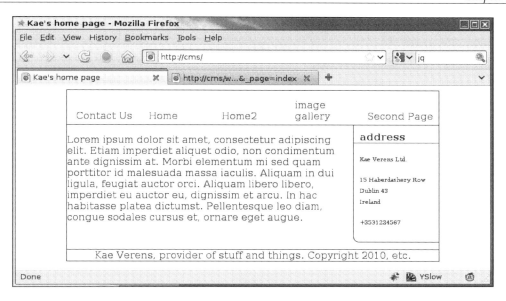

Notice the **address** header. Also, notice that I've not added a header to the footer panel.

Disabling widgets

If you have a number of different widgets that you use for different occasions, it is useful to disable those that you are not currently using, so they don't appear in the front-end and yet are available to re-enable at any point.

An example of this might be a menu for a restaurant, where the "soup of the day" revolves based on the day. If there are seven different soups, it's a simple matter to disable the six that you are not displaying, and each day, enable the next and disable the previous.

As you can imagine, the admin side code of this is easy, based on the most recent examples. Edit the `admin/js.js` file and replace the `widget_toggle_disabled()` stub function with this:

```
function widget_toggle_disabled(ev){
  var el=ev.target,vis=[];
  var w=$(el).closest('.widget-wrapper');
  var p=w.data('widget');
  p.disabled=p.disabled?0:1;
  w.removeClass().addClass('widget-wrapper '
    +(p.disabled?'disabled':'enabled'));
  $('.disabled',w).text(p.disabled?'disabled':'enabled');
  w.data('widget',p);
  updateWidgets(w.closest('.panel-wrapper'));
}
```

In the admin area, after disabling a panel, here's how it looks:

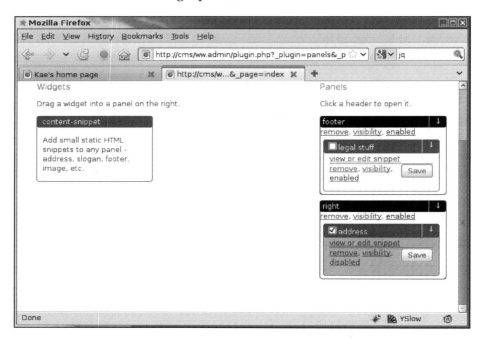

And on the front-end, we simply return a blank string if the panel is disabled.

To do this, edit the `plugin.php` and add the highlighted line:

```
foreach($widgets->widgets as $widget){
    if(isset($widget->disabled) && $widget->disabled)continue;
    if(isset($widget->header_visibility)
        && $widget->header_visibility)
      $h.='<h4 class="panel-widget-header '
        .preg_replace('/[^a-z0-9A-Z\-]/','',$widget->name)
        .'">'.htmlspecialchars($widget->name).'</h4>';
```

If the widget is disabled, you simply ignore that widget and carry onto the next iteration of the loop.

Disabling a panel

Panels are not recorded the same way as widgets, so there's slightly more work needed.

The JavaScript is basically the same. We already have the links for **remove**, **visibility**, and **enable/disable** in there, so it's just a matter of adding the functions they call.

Add this function to /ww.plugins/panels/admin/js.js:

```
function panel_toggle_disabled(i){
  var p=ww_panels[i];
  p.disabled=p.disabled?0:1;
  var panel=$('#panel'+p.id);
  panel
    .removeClass()
    .addClass('panel-wrapper '
      +(p.disabled?'disabled':'enabled'));
  $('.controls .disabled',panel)
    .text(p.disabled?'disabled':'enabled');
  ww_panels[i]=p;
  $.get('/ww.plugins/panels/admin/save-disabled.php?id='
    +p.id+'&disabled='+p.disabled);
}
```

This function switches classes and the visible text in the panel to toggle its mode between enabled and disabled, then calls a server-side file to save the state.

Create the file /ww.plugins/panels/admin/save-disabled.php to handle the saving:

```
<?php
require $_SERVER['DOCUMENT_ROOT'].'/ww.admin/admin_libs.php';
if(isset($_REQUEST['id']) && isset($_REQUEST['disabled'])){
  $id=(int)$_REQUEST['id'];
  $disabled=(int)$_REQUEST['disabled'];
  dbQuery("update panels set disabled='$disabled' where id=$id");
}
echo 'done';
```

After the **enabled** link is clicked (below the panel name), the entire panel is then disabled and is not visible from the front-end.

In the admin area, this is indicated by graying out the entire panel:

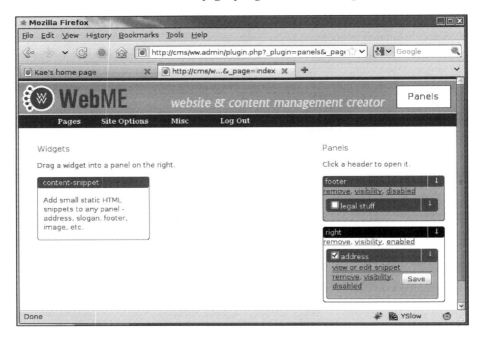

Because the widget statuses are not changed, re-enabling the panel by clicking on **disabled** will bring the panel back to the exact status it had before. For example., if half the widgets contained in it were disabled, then the exact same widgets are disabled and the rest are enabled.

Deleting a panel

Panels are tied in with templates. The panels that appear in the admin area depend on what is visible in the front-end.

Let's say that you were using one theme which had a footer panel and a right panel. And then, you switch to a new theme which has a header, left panel, and footer.

Loading a page in the front-end will register the new header and left panels, but will not remove the obsolete right panel.

Panels don't automatically delete when you switch themes. Because we have not tied a Smarty parser into the panels system, the CMS does not automatically know if a panel is no longer needed because it is not in the new skin.

Add the following function to `admin/js.js`:

```
function panel_remove(i){
  var p=ww_panels[i];
  var id=p.id;
  if(!confirm('Deleting this panel '
    +'will remove the configurations of its contained '
    +'widgets. Are you /sure/ you want to remove this? Note '
    +'that your panel will be recreated (without its '
    +'widgets) if the site theme has it defined.'))return;
  $.get('/ww.plugins/panels/admin/remove-panel.php?id='+id,
    function(){
      $('#panel'+id).remove();
    });
}
```

In this function, we first get the panel ID.

Next, we verify that the admin means to delete the panel—once it is deleted, the widget data will also be deleted, so it's important that the admin realizes this.

Finally, we send to the server to do the deletion, and remove the panel element from the page.

Here is the server-side file, `/ww.plugins/panels/admin/remove-panel.php`:

```
<?php
require $_SERVER['DOCUMENT_ROOT'].'/ww.admin/admin_libs.php';
if(isset($_REQUEST['id'])){
  $id=(int)$_REQUEST['id'];
  dbQuery("delete from panels where id=$id");
}
echo 'ok';
```

Again, a very simple file.

We first check that the requester is an admin, then remove the table row that corresponds to the panel ID.

Panel page visibility—admin area code

Sometimes, you will want a panel to appear on only a few pages.

For example, you may have a vertical side panel that you want to appear on all pages, except for one or two pages which need a lot of space, so you want to hide the panel on those pages.

Instead of creating different templates for these pages, you could simply hide the panels.

To do this, we first need to select what pages the panel is visible on.

Add the following function to admin/js.js:

```
function panel_visibility(id){
  $.get('/ww.plugins/panels/admin/get-visibility.php',
      {'id':id},function(options){
    var d=$('<form><p>This panel will be visible in <select '
      +'name="panel_visibility_pages[]" multiple="multiple">'
      +options+'</select>. If you want it to be visible in '
      +'all pages, please choose <b>none</b> to indicate '
      +'that no filtering should take place.</p></form>');
    d.dialog({
      width:300,
      height:400,
      close:function(){
        $('#panel_visibility_pages').remove();
        d.remove();
      },
      buttons:{
        'Save':function(){
          var arr=[];
          $('input[name="panel_visibility_pages[]"]:checked')
            .each(function(){
              arr.push(this.value);
            });
          $.get('/ww.plugins/panels/admin/save-visibility'
            +'.php?id='+id+'&pages='+arr);
          d.dialog('close');
        },
        'Close':function(){
          d.dialog('close');
        }
      }
    });
  });
}
```

This function is quite large compared to the previous functions, but it is also more complex.

In this case, we first retrieve the list of pages already selected from the server and then show this to the admin.

The admin selects which pages the panel should be visible on. Click on **Save**.

This then gets the page IDs of the selected options and saves this to the server.

There are two server-side files to create. First, the file to retrieve the list of pages is /
ww.plugins/panels/admin/get-visibility.php:

```
<?php
require $_SERVER['DOCUMENT_ROOT'].'/ww.admin/admin_libs.php';

function panel_selectkiddies($i=0,$n=1,$s=array(),$id=0,$prefix=''){
  $q=dbAll('select name,id from pages where parent="'.$i
    .'" and id!="'.$id.'" order by ord,name');
  if(count($q)<1)return;
  $html='';
  foreach($q as $r){
    if($r['id']!=''){
      $html.='<option value="'.$r['id'].'" title="'
        .htmlspecialchars($r['name']).'"';
      $html.=(in_array($r['id'],$s))
        ?' selected="selected">':'>';
      $name=strtolower(str_replace(' ','-',$r['name']));
      $html.= htmlspecialchars($prefix.$name).'</option>';
      $html.=panel_selectkiddies($r['id'],$n+1,$s,$id,
        $name.'/');
    }
  }
  return $html;
}
$s=array();
if(isset($_REQUEST['id'])){
  $id=(int)$_REQUEST['id'];
  $r=dbRow("select visibility from panels where id=$id");
  if(is_array($r) && count($r)){
    if($r['visibility'])$s=json_decode($r['visibility']);
  }
}
if(isset($_REQUEST['visibility']) && $_REQUEST['visibility']){
  $s=explode(',',$_REQUEST['visibility']);
}
echo panel_selectkiddies(0,1,$s,0);
```

First, we make sure (as always) that the request came from an admin.

Next, we define the `panel_selectkiddies()` function that builds up an option list
composed of pages in an hierarchical tree fashion.

Finally, we retrieve the list of pages that are already selected and display the options using that list, to mark some as selected.

This could easily be added as a function of the core engine.

The main reason it is not currently in the core engine is that we have one single use case for it and the core functions should really be functions that are used multiple times.

If you find yourself rewriting functionality that exists in other plugins, then that functionality should be re-factored and added to the core.

When we click **visibility** under the panel, this is what we get:

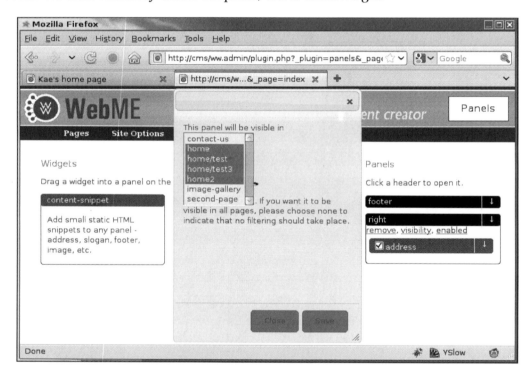

Not very user-friendly, is it?

We can improve this by using the jQuery inlinemultiselect plugin, available from here: `http://code.google.com/p/inlinemultiselect/`.

The inlinemultiselect plugin, by Peter Edwards, is an enhancement of some work I did a few years beforehand to make multi-select elements easier to use.

The version of the file that I'm using is a slight enhancement of the version on the Google repository. I've submitted my changes back and am waiting for the changes to be added to the repository.

In the meantime, you can get my version from Packt, by downloading the code for this chapter.

I place the file as `/ww.plugin/panels/admin/jquery.inlinemultiselect.js` and then edit the file `/ww.plugin/panels/admin/index.php` to link it in (highlighted lines):

```
?>
</script>
<script src="/ww.plugins/panels/admin/js.js"></script>
<script src="/ww.plugins/panels/admin/
    jquery.inlinemultiselect.js"></script>
```

And now, we can amend the `admin/js.js` file to use it. Add these highlighted lines to the end of the `$.get()` section in `panel_visibility()`:

```
      });
      $('select').inlinemultiselect({
        'separator':', ',
        'endSeparator':' and '
      });
   });
}
```

And now, the page selection is much more friendly:

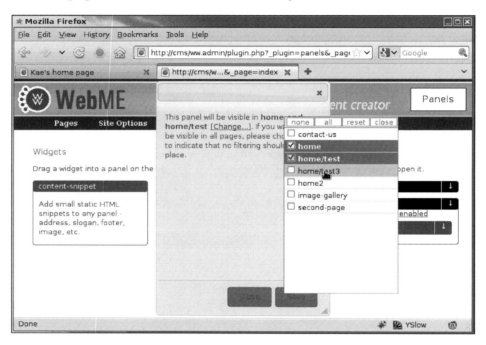

You can see what's happened. When the dialog opens, the list of selected pages is shown inline in the text (you can see the words **home and home/test** are bold. When **[Change...]** is clicked, a pop up appears with the list of pages shown in a check-box version of a multi-select).

Behind the scenes, the original clumsy multi-select box has been removed and converted to this nice check-box version.

When submitted, the check-boxes act exactly the same as the multi-select box, so the server can't tell the difference.

Now, write the save file, /ww.plugins/panels/admin/save-visibility.php:

```php
<?php
require $_SERVER['DOCUMENT_ROOT'].'/ww.admin/admin_libs.php';
if(isset($_REQUEST['id']) && isset($_REQUEST['pages'])){
  $id=(int)$_REQUEST['id'];
  $json='['.addslashes($_REQUEST['pages']).']';
  dbQuery("update panels set visibility='$json'
      where id=$id");
}
```

Again, the server-side code is very simple.

We check that the submitter is an admin, then record what was submitted directly into the panels table.

Panel page visibility—front-end code

The front-end code is very simple.

Edit the `/ww.plugins/panels/plugin.php` file and replace the `"is the panel visible?"` comment block with this code:

```
// { is the panel visible?
if($p['disabled'])return '';
if($p['visibility'] && $p['visibility']!='[]'){
  $visibility=json_decode($p['visibility']);
  if(!in_array($GLOBALS['PAGEDATA']->id,$visibility))
    return '';
}
// }
```

The visibility field in the table is an array of page IDs. If there are any IDs in the array and the ID of the current page is not one of them, then the panel is returned blank.

Widget page visibility

The final piece of the Panels plugin is how to manage widget visibility.

Similar to panels, widgets are not always necessary on every page.

For example, you may have a widget which displays the contents of an online store basket. This widget should not be shown on a page where the online store's checkout shows the same list.

Or maybe you have some widgets that you want to only appear on very specific pages, such as showing an RSS feed from the local cinema on a page which reviews a film.

The script works the same way as the panel visibility code.

Open `/ww.plugins/panels/admin/js.js` and replace the `widget_visibility()` function stub with this:

```
function widget_visibility(ev){
  var el=ev.target,vis=[];
  var w=$(el).closest('.widget-wrapper');
  var wd=w.data('widget');
```

```
    if(wd.visibility)vis=wd.visibility;
    $.get('/ww.plugins/panels/admin/get-visibility.php?'
      +'visibility='+vis,function(options){
      var d=$('<form><p>This panel will be visible in <select '
        +'name="panel_visibility_pages[]" multiple="multiple">'
        +options+'</select>. If you want it to be visible in '
        +'all pages, please choose <b>none</b> to indicate '
        +'that no filtering should take place.</p></form>');
      d.dialog({
        width:300,
        height:400,
        close:function(){
          $('#panel_visibility_pages').remove();
          d.remove();
        },
        buttons:{
          'Save':function(){
            var arr=[];
            $('input[name="panel_visibility_pages[]"]:checked')
              .each(function(){
                arr.push(this.value);
              });
            wd.visibility=arr;
            w.data('widget',wd);
            updateWidgets(w.closest('.panel-wrapper'));
            d.dialog('close');
          },
          'Close':function(){
            d.dialog('close');
          }
        }
      });
      $('select').inlinemultiselect({
        'separator':', ',
        'endSeparator':' and '
      });
    });
  }
```

You can see that this is very similar to the panel visibility code. The main difference is that the panel code calls the server directly in order to save the page IDs, while this code records the page IDs in the widget data contained in the panel and then calls updateWidgets() to record it.

On the front-end, the code is just as simple as the panel code. Add the highlighted lines to `/ww.plugins/panels/plugin.php`:

```
if(isset($widget->disabled) && $widget->disabled)continue;
if(isset($widget->visibility)
    && count($widget->visibility)){
  if(!in_array($GLOBALS['PAGEDATA']->id,
      $widget->visibility))continue;
}
if(isset($widget->header_visibility)
    && $widget->header_visibility)
  $h.='<h4 class="panel-widget-header '
  .preg_replace('/[^a-z0-9A-Z\-]/','',$widget->name)
  .'">'.htmlspecialchars($widget->name).'</h4>';
```

It's the same idea as with panels—we check to see if a list of page IDs is recorded. If there is and the current page is not in the list, then we don't go any further in the loop with this widget.

Summary

In this chapter, we enhanced and completed the panels and widgets system such that you could disable them, choose which pages they were visible on, and customize the widgets.

In the final chapter, we will build an installer for the CMS.

12
Building an Installer

Throughout the book, we have built up a CMS. This CMS works on your machine. The next step is to make sure that it works on other machines as well.

This chapter will cover topics such as:

- Creating a virtual machine using VirtualBox
- Creating the installer application
- Checking for missing features on the server

At the end of this chapter, you will be able to package and release your CMS for others to use, whether in-house or the general public.

This chapter shows how to detect various settings on the host machine. It is not a 100% complete installer, but it details how the tests can be done. As an example, I have not added a test to see that MySQL has been installed. You can add your own detection script for that.

Although it is possible to create and test the installer on your own machine, it's not ideal—you've already had the CMS installed and running, which means that your web server is already set up and compatible with the CMS's needs.

Ideally, you should create and test the installer on a machine which has not been carefully adjusted to match those needs. This way you can alert the eventual admin who installs the program of any missing requirements.

Because it is unrealistic to have a separate computer for testing each possible web server configuration, it is best to test using virtual machines.

Installing a virtual machine

A **Virtual Machine (VM)** is an emulation of an entire computer, which runs in a "host" machine, whether it is your laptop, a desktop, or even your company server.

There are many different VM engines out there. Examples include VMWare, QEMU, VirtualBox, Virtuozzo, Xen—and the list goes on.

In this chapter, we will use VirtualBox, because it's free, and it works on the four most popular server operating systems: Linux, Windows, Solaris, and OS X.

Installing VirtualBox

You can download a VirtualBox binary for your operating system from this place:

http://www.virtualbox.org/wiki/Downloads.

I will describe installation using Fedora (a Linux brand). If you are not using this brand or operating system, use the online material to properly install your program.

First, create a Yum repository configuration file. Yum is a downloader which automatically installs programs and their dependencies.

Create the file /etc/yum.repos.d/virtualbox.repo (from the root of your machine):

```
[virtualbox]
name=Fedora $releasever - $basearch - VirtualBox
baseurl=http://download.virtualbox.org/virtualbox/rpm/fedora/\
    $releasever/$basearch
enabled=1
gpgcheck=1
gpgkey=http://download.virtualbox.org/virtualbox/debian/\
    sun_vbox.asc
```

Next, install the program with this command:

```
[root@ryuk ~]# yum install VirtualBox
```

Note that if you are using a bleeding edge distribution, you may need to change $releasever to an older version number of Fedora. At the time of writing, the current release of Fedora is 13, and Sun (the makers of VirtualBox) has not updated their servers to include this, so I needed to change $releasever to 12 to get the installation to work:

```
baseurl=http://download.virtualbox.org/virtualbox/rpm/fedora/\
    12/$basearch
```

After installation, you may need to configure a kernel module to allow VirtualBox to run at a reasonable speed. Enter the following command:

```
[root@ryuk ~]# /etc/init.d/vboxdrv setup
```

This may require further dependencies, but any error message that shows up will tell you what those dependencies are.

After these steps, you will have a fully installed VirtualBox application. You can now start installing a guest operating system.

Installing the virtual machine

The operating system (OS) which runs inside the VM is called a **guest**. The main operating system of the machine is called the **host**.

Installing a guest OS is straightforward. It's almost the same as doing it on the real machine itself.

First, download an ISO image of the operating system you want to install. ISO is an archive format which is used to store DVDs and CDs as single files. When you download any OS from an online repository, it's usually in ISO format.

If you don't have fast bandwidth, you can also get installation DVDs from Linux magazines.

The choice of operating system is up to you, but you should keep the following in mind:

1. Don't choose an operating system that you are certain will never need to be supported. With my own CMS, I never expect it to be run on Windows. It may be run on any variety of Linux, though. And so, I won't try to run it on Windows but would choose a variant of Linux (including Unix variants such as perhaps OS X or Solaris, but with no great effort to make it work for those).

2. Don't choose a totally up-to-date operating system—the installer should work on older systems as well—such as systems that have older PHP installations, or missing Pear dependencies, or older versions of console applications such as ImageMagick.

3. Try to choose operating systems that are popular. Debian, CentOS, Fedora and, Ubuntu, are all very popular Linux variants for hosting. Don't focus all your energy on a variant that you are not likely to come across in professional life.

CentOS 5.2 fits the bill almost perfectly—it's a well-known variant of RedHat Enterprise Linux, is free to download, and has a very conservative upgrade history. While Ubuntu and Fedora push the limits of what can be done with Linux, CentOS is about stability.

You could also use Debian for exactly the same reason. I'm more comfortable with CentOS.

Go to `http://mirror.centos.org/centos/5/isos/` and download the appropriate ISO for your machine.

The files online at the time of writing are actually for Centos 5.5, but I have a copy of 5.2 here from a previous installation I did, and the process is identical in both cases (5.5 is more stable than 5.2, but apart from that, there are not many visible changes).

The file I have is called `CentOS-5.2-i386-bin-DVD.iso`, and the 5.5 equivalent is `CentOS-5.5-i386-bin-DVD.iso`.

Note that this is for installation on your own machine for testing purposes. If you were to use a production server, you should naturally use the latest version available, 5.5.

Okay—start up the program. In my machine, it's under **Applications | System Tools | Sun VirtualBox**:

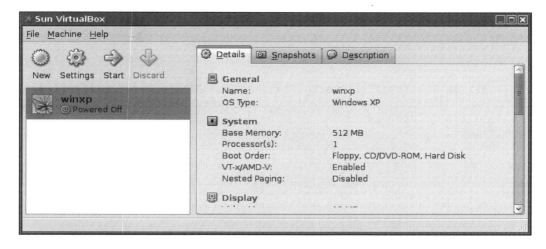

You can see from the screenshot that I already had one virtual machine installed from earlier testing. This also illustrates that virtual machines can be used to install totally different guest operating systems than the host. The screenshot shows an installation of Windows XP which is inside a Fedora Linux host.

Click on **New**, and follow the setup wizard. Here are some suggested answers to the questions:

Name	Centos5.2
Operating System	Linux
Version	RedHat
Base Memory	256 MB

Boot Hard Disk should be checked, as well as **Create new Hard Disk**. Click on **Next** until the next question appears.

Dynamically expanding storage lets the fake hard disk of the VM expand if it's near full, so tick that.

Accept the defaults for the rest of the wizard.

On completion, the screen should now appear similar to the next screenshot:

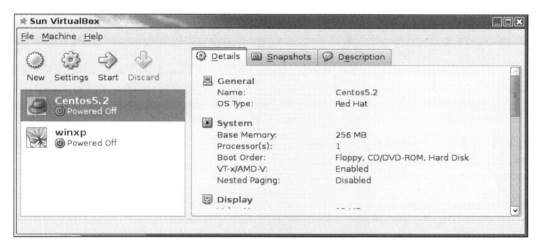

Now, make sure that **Centos5.2** is selected, then click on **Settings**.

Click on **CD/DVD-ROM**, tick **Mount CD/DVD Drive**, tick the **ISO Image file** box, and select the ISO file that you downloaded, as seen in the next screenshot:

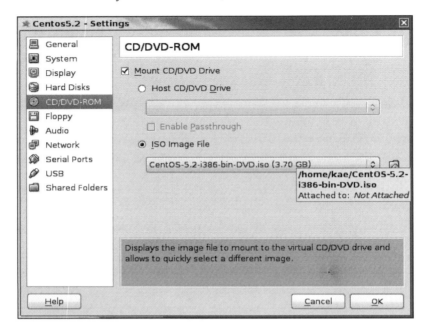

Then click on **OK**.

Now click on **Start**.

The Centos5.2 machine will boot up, acting like the ISO file you selected was a disk sitting in the virtual machine's DVD drive.

After a few moments, the installation will begin. Follow the wizard and install your guest operating system.

In most cases, the default selected option is the correct one, so if you're not sure about something, just click on OK—it's only a virtual image anyway, so if something goes wrong, you can always reinstall it.

When the wizard asks you which packages to install, accept the pre-selected packages and click on **Next**—we want a default installation which is not tailored to work with the CMS.

When the wizard is completed, the installation will take place. This can take anywhere from a few minutes up to half an hour or so:

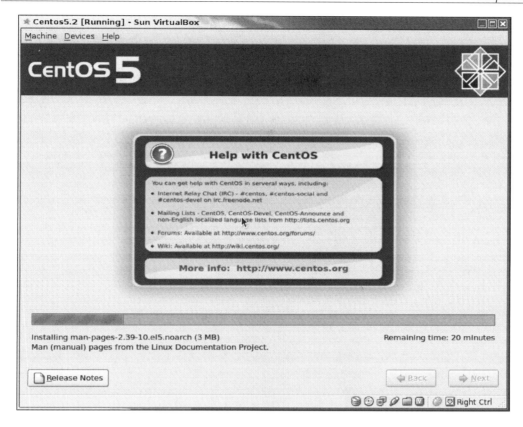

Notice the **Right Ctrl** message in the bottom-right-hand side of the screen — when you click into the VM's window, your mouse and keyboard are trapped by the VM. To escape from it, so you can select other applications on the host, and use the *Right Ctrl* button on your keyboard to release the trap.

Another useful key combination is *Right Ctrl + F*, which will show the window in full screen, as if you had booted the laptop or desktop from the guest OS instead of your main OS.

When the installation is complete, click on the **Reboot** button in the guest screen. The virtual machine will reboot.

You will be asked a number of config questions — user setup and so on. Accept the defaults where possible. Create a user account when asked.

Okay — all done!

One final thing before we get to the CMS installation: When you log in, the machine will check for upgrades. Don't bother upgrading. Remember that we want the installer to work on older machines as well, and upgrading will therefore be pointless.

Installing the CMS in the VM

Now, log in to the guest OS. Open a console (**Applications** | **Accessories** | **Terminal**), su to root (use su - root, so we have access to root's environment variables) and install the absolute minimum you would expect to find on a hosting platform — web server, MySQL database, and PHP:

```
[root@localhost: ~]# yum install httpd php-mysql php mysql\
    mysql-server
```

Note that the PHP version installed with the default CentOS installation will be out-of-date. In the case of 5.2, the version installed is 5.1.6. This is not recent enough for our CMS to run (it's missing json_encode(), for example), but is a good test for the installer.

When that's done, we can install the CMS code.

By default, an installation of Apache in CentOS (and most other Linux variants) will have its default webroot set to /var/www/html, so copy your CMS to that location using FTP, or HTTP, and so on.

> Oh — before we go any further, open up the VirtualBox application again, go into settings for the CentOS 5.2 machine, and uncheck the box next to **Mount CD/DVD Drive**.
>
> Otherwise, your VM may try to reinstall itself next time you turn it on.

Transferring the file from your laptop or desktop to the virtual machine can be done in many different ways, including setting up an FTP server on the guest or host or creating a shared directory where files are visible in both systems.

Personally, I chose to zip up the latest copy of the CMS, upload it to a file server I control, and download it through HTTP on the virtual machine. As a PHP developer, you no doubt also have a file server or web server somewhere where you can temporarily place a file while transferring it. This is probably the easiest way to transfer files without any prior preparation.

After unzipping, move all of the contents of your zipped file to /var/www/html, such that in that directory, you have the following files:

Note that this is from directly zipping up a working copy of the CMS.

Delete the .private, f, and ww.cache directories—they are specific to an installed copy of the CMS, and should not be there before the installer places them there:

```
[root@localhost html]# cd /var/www/html && rm -rf .private \
    f ww.cache
```

Your files are in place. Now we need to start up the web server and database server:

```
[root@localhost html]# /etc/init.d/httpd start && \
    /etc/init.d/mysqld start
```

And finally, let's make sure those two load up automatically the next time the virtual machine is turned on:

```
[root@localhost html]# chkconfig --add httpd && \
    chkconfig --add mysqld
```

Now that your files are in place and the web server is running, you can load up a browser (**Applications | Internet | Firefox Web Browser**), and point it at localhost:

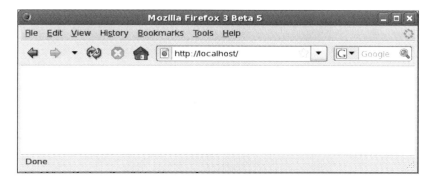

The screen is blank because the server expects the .private directory to be there, and crashes because it's not found.

This is the point at which we can begin writing the installer.

Firstly though, make sure that your normal user account can edit the web files—you should not stay logged in as `root` while working:

```
[root@localhost html]# chown kae.kae /var/www/html -Rf
```

Change `kae` in the the command to whatever your user account is.

Creating the installer application

You can either edit the files within the VM, or edit them on the host machine and upload them to the VM after each change.

Personally, I prefer to edit things in-place, so all work in the rest of the chapter will happen within the virtual machine itself.

If you are comfortable with Vim (the console-based editor), then you're ready to go.

If not, then either install an editor you are comfortable with, or use gedit (**Applications | Accessories | Text Editor**), which is installed by default in most Linux systems.

Core system changes

The first thing we need to do is to intercept the failed loading of `/.private/config.php`, and redirect the browser to the installer.

Create the directory `/ww.installer` within `/var/www/html` (all directory references will be relative to `/var/www/html` in the rest of the chapter), and edit `/ww.incs/basics.php`. Add the following highlighted new lines around the existing un-highlighted line:

```
if(file_exists(SCRIPTBASE . '.private/config.php')){
  require SCRIPTBASE . '.private/config.php';
}
else{
  header('Location: /ww.installer');
  exit;
}
```

This checks to see if the `.private/config.php` file exists, and if not, it is assumed that this is a fresh system, so the server redirects the browser into the `/ww.installer` directory.

And that's all we need to do to the core scripts. Now we can concentrate solely on the `/ww.installer` directory.

The installer

We need to first decide exactly what the job of the installer is.

In most systems, an installer handles three things:

1. Checking the environment to see if it is suitable for the application.
2. Choosing and entering starter configuration options.
3. Installation of the database.

Based on this, we can extend the installation process to this:

1. Check the environment, including:
    - PHP version. We need the `json_encode()` and `json_decode()` functions, so the version needs to be at least 5.2.
    - SQLite support, for KFM.
    - Writable `/f`, `/ww.cache`, and `/.private` directories.
2. Ask for any admin-entered configuration options needed for the system, including:
    - MySQL database access codes.
    - Details for the first administrator's user account.
3. Install the database, then save the configuration file to `/.private/config.php`.

You can see that the `config.php` file is created absolutely last. It is also obvious that if a `config.php` file already exists, then the installer has already been run, and should not be run again.

Therefore, the first thing we need to do is to create the `/ww.installer/index.php` file and tell it to exit if the installer has already been run:

```php
<?php
if(file_exists('../.private/config.php'))exit;
?>
<html>
  <head>
    <script src="http://ajax.googleapis.com/ajax/libs/
        jquery/1.4.2/jquery.min.js"></script>
    <script src="http://ajax.googleapis.com/ajax/libs/
        jqueryui/1.8.0/jquery-ui.min.js"></script>
    <script src="/ww.installer/js.js"></script>
    <link rel="stylesheet" href="/ww.installer/css.css"
```

```
            type="text/css" />
    </head>
    <body>
      <div id="header"></div>
      <div id="content">please wait...</div>
    </body>
</html>
```

We will handle the configuration through jQuery.

Checking for missing features

First, we need to check for missing features. To do this, we will first show the list of required features, then use jQuery to ask the server about each of those features one at a time.

The reason we use jQuery here is purely visual—it looks better to have things appear to be checked and then removed from the screen, than to just have a PHP-generated page list the problems.

If all of those feature requirements are resolved, we automatically go forward to the next step, configuration. Installation on the ideal server will not display the first step at all, as there will be nothing to resolve.

Create the file /ww.installer/js.js:

```
function step1(){
  var tests=[
    ['php-version','PHP version 5.2 or higher'],
    ['sqlite','PDO SQLite version 3+'],
    ['f','Write permissions for user-files directory'],
    ['ww-cache','Write permissions for cache directory'],
    ['private','Write permissions for config directory']
  ]
  var html='';
  for(var i=0;i<tests.length;++i){
    html+='<div id="'+tests[i][0]+'" class="checking">'
      +'Checking: '+tests[i][1]
      +'</div>';
  }
  $('#content').html(html);
  $('.checking').each(function(){
    $.post('/ww.installer/check-'+this.id+'.php',
        step1_verify,'json');
  });
```

```
}
function step1_verify(res){
}
$(step1);
```

The last line is what starts everything off—when the page has loaded enough for JavaScript to safely run, the function `step1()` is called.

This function then draws out a list of points to the screen, as seen in the following screenshot:

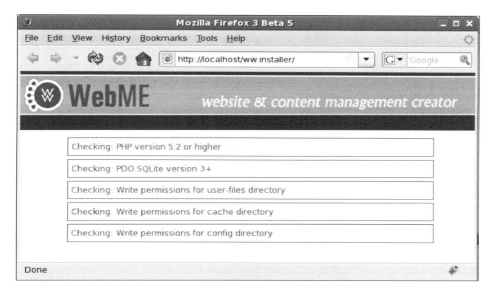

After drawing the points to the screen, a separate HTTP request is called depending on the check.

For example, for the first item, where the array is `['php-version','PHP version 5.2 or higher']`, the file `/ww.installer/check-php-version.php` is called on the server.

The result is then passed to the stub function `step1_verify()`.

Let's write the first of the checking files, `/ww.installer/check-php-version.php`:

```
<?php
if(file_exists('../.private/config.php'))exit;
$vs=explode('.',phpversion());
if($vs[0]>5
   || ($vs[0]==5 && $vs[1]>=2)){
```

```
    echo '{"status":1,"test":"php-version"}';
    exit;
}

echo '{"status":0,"error":"'
    .'The PHP version must be at least 5.2. '
    .'It is currently '.phpversion().'",'
    .'"test":"php-version"}';
```

First, we check that the `config.php` file does not exist—we do not want people snooping on the capabilities of the server, so these checks should only be available while you're installing.

Next, we check that the version number is greater than 5.2. The version string returned by `phpversion()` is of the form "x.y.z", so the string needs to be separated into distinct numbers before it can be compared.

If the version number is higher, then a JSON object is returned containing a status variable which is true. Basically, it returns a "this is OK" message.

Otherwise, we return an error message.

Now, on the client-side, we want error messages to be highlighted to point out to the admin that something needs to be done. Edit `js.js` and replace the stub `step1_verify()` function with this:

```
function step1_verify(res){
    if(res.status==1){
        $('#'+res.test).slideUp(function(){
            $('#'+res.test).remove();
        });
        return;
    }
    $('#'+res.test)
        .addClass('error')
        .append('<p>'+res.error+'</p>');
}
```

This simple function first sees if the check was successful, in which case the displayed text for the check is removed in a sliding motion.

Otherwise, the element is highlighted as being in error. We add the class `"error"` to the displayed `<div>` and add some text explaining what went wrong. The explanation is sent by the server, allowing it to be tailored specifically to that server if you want.

The other tests are similarly done.

Here is the SQLite one, `check-sqlite.php`:

```php
<?php
if(file_exists('../.private/config.php'))exit;

if(extension_loaded('pdo_sqlite')){
  echo '{"status":1,"test":"sqlite"}';
  exit;
}

echo '{"status":0,"error":"'
  .'You must have the PDO SQLite library installed. '
  .'"test":"sqlite"}';
```

The same process is followed. First, verify that the script is allowed to be run, then check to see if the requested feature can be verified, and finally, give an error message if it fails.

The default CentOS 5.2 installation we've installed does have SQLite installed as a PDO library, but doesn't have the required PHP version, as we can see here:

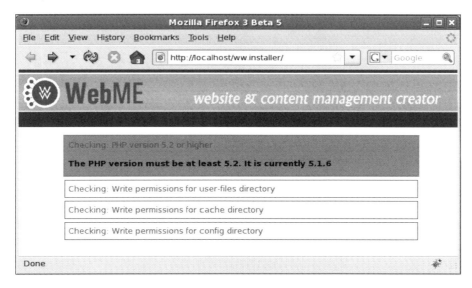

In this image, you can see that the PHP version has returned an error message with a clear description of the problem, and the SQLite test succeeded, so has been removed from the screen.

There are three remaining tests. They are all basically the same. Here's the first, /ww.installer/check-f.php:

```php
<?php
if(file_exists('../.private/config.php'))exit;

$dname='f';
@mkdir('../'.$dname);
@file_put_contents('../'.$dname.'/test-permissions','test');
if(file_exists('../'.$dname.'/test-permissions')){
  echo '{"status":1,"test":"f"}';
  unlink('../'.$dname.'/test-permissions');
  exit;
}
$dir=preg_replace('/ww.installer$/',$dname,dirname(__FILE__));
if(!is_dir($dir))$error=$dir.' does not exist. '
    .'Please create it.';
else $error=$dir.' is not writable by the web server.';
echo '{"status":0,'
  .'"error":"'.$error.'",'
  .'"test":"f"}';
```

The other two are basically the same, but for ww.cache and .private respectively. Simply copy the above file to check-ww-cache.php and check-private.php, then replace the $dname value in both with ww.cache and .private respectively, and then change the returned test variable in the JSON to ww-cache and private respectively.

The next step is for you to resolve the pointed out problems for yourself.

In my case, that's done by upgrading the PHP version, then creating the user directories and making them writable by the server.

When the page is then reloaded, you end up with a blank content area.

We need to add a piece of code to watch for this and then move to step 2.

So, add this to the bottom of the step1() function (highlighted line):

```javascript
    });
    setTimeout(step1_finished,500);
}
```

And then we need to add the step1_finished() function:

```javascript
function step1_finished(){
  if($('.checking').length){
```

```
        setTimeout(step1_finished,500);
    }
    else step2();
}
function step2(){
}
```

This function loops every half-second until the checkpoints are gone. This should only loop once on any reasonable server and connection, but with slow bandwidth or a slow server, it will take a few seconds, and you'll see the valid points gradually vanish as they're checked and verified.

Adding the configuration details

Step two is to ask for information such as database and user details.

So, first, let's display the form. Replace the step2() stub function with this:

```
function step2(){
    $('#content').html('<table>'
      +'<tr><th id="db" colspan="2">Database name</th></tr>'
      +'<tr><th>Name</th><td><input id="dbname" /></td>'
          +'</tr>'
      +'<tr><th>Host</th><td>'
          +'<input id="dbhost" value="localhost" /></td></tr>'
      +'<tr><th>User</th><td><input id="dbuser" /></td></tr>'
      +'<tr><th>Password</th><td><input id="dbpass" /></td>'
          +'</tr>'
      +'<tr><th id="ad" colspan="2">Administrator</th></tr>'
      +'<tr><th>Email address</th><td><input id="admin" /></td>'
          +'</tr>'
      +'<tr><th>Password</th><td><input id="adpass" /></td>'
          +'</tr>'
      +'<tr><th>(and again)</th><td><input id="adpass2" /></td>'
          +'</tr>'
      +'</table><div class="error" id="errors"></div>');
    $('#content input').change(step2_verify);
}
function step2_verify(){
}
```

This will display a form with the most commonly needed configuration items. It can be expanded at a later date if you want it to include rarely changed things such as the database port and so on.

We print out the form to the page, and set a watch on the inputs such that any change to them will cause step2_verify() to call.

The form looks like this:

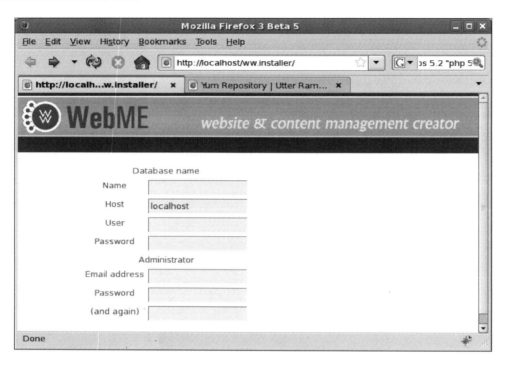

Now let's replace the step2_verify() stub form:

```
function step2_verify(){
  var opts={
    dbname:$('#dbname').val(),
    dbhost:$('#dbhost').val(),
    dbuser:$('#dbuser').val(),
    dbpass:$('#dbpass').val(),
    admin:$('#admin').val(),
    adpass:$('#adpass').val(),
    adpass2:$('#adpass2').val(),
  }
  $.post('/ww.installer/check-config.php',
    opts,step2_verify2,'json');
}
function step2_verify2(res){
}
```

This function just grabs all the input values and sends them to the server to be verified, which then returns its result to the `step2_verify2()` stub function.

Let's start with the verification file. Create `/ww.installer/check-config.php`:

```php
<?php
if(file_exists('../.private/config.php'))exit;

$errors=array();

$dbname=@$_REQUEST['dbname'];
$dbhost=@$_REQUEST['dbhost'];
$dbuser=@$_REQUEST['dbuser'];
$dbpass=@$_REQUEST['dbpass'];
$admin=@$_REQUEST['admin'];
$adpass=@$_REQUEST['adpass'];
$adpass2=@$_REQUEST['adpass2'];

if($dbname=='' || $dbhost=='' || $dbuser==''){
  $errors[]='db requires name, hostname and username';
}
else{
  $db=mysql_connect($dbhost,$dbuser,$dbpass);
  if(!$db)$errors[]='db: could not connect - incorrect '
      .'details';
  else if(!mysql_select_db($dbname,$db)){
    $errors[]='db: could not select database "'
        .addslashes($dbname).'"';
  }
}
if(!filter_var($admin,FILTER_VALIDATE_EMAIL)){
  $errors[]='admin account must be an email address';
}
if(!$adpass && !$adpass2)$errors[]='admin password must not '
    .'be empty';
else if($adpass!=$adpass2)$errors[]='admin passwords must '
    .'both be equal';

echo json_encode($errors);
```

This checks the various submitted values, and builds up an array of error strings.

The error strings are then returned.

On the client-side, we then need to display the errors on the screen so the admin knows what to correct. Edit the js.js file again and replace the step2_verify2() stub function with this:

```
function step2_verify2(res){
  if(!res.length)return step3();
  var html='<ul>';
  for(var i=0;i<res.length;++i){
    html+='<li>'+res[i]+'</li>';
  }
  html+='</ul>';
  $('#errors').html(html);
}
function step3(){
}
```

So, if there are no errors returned, then step3() is called.

Otherwise, the errors are displayed in a <ul> list:

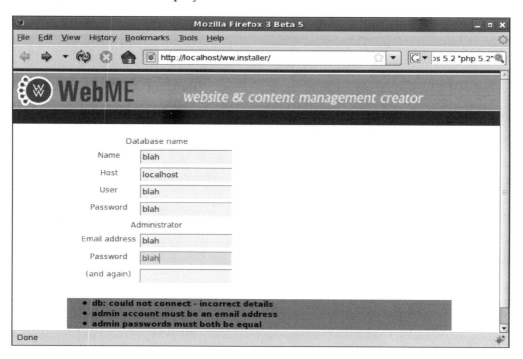

So what do we do when the values are finally correct?

We need to save the values to file, and then display a message explaining that we're done.

On the server-side, we know exactly when `step3` will be called, because that's where we're doing the checking, so all we need to do is to do the `step3` process (saving the values to the config file) if we find nothing wrong with the submitted values.

To do that, place the following code before the final line of `check-config.php` (highlighted):

```
if(!count($errors)){
  mysql_query('create table user_accounts(id int
      auto_increment not null primary key, email text,
      password char(32), active smallint default 0, groups
      text, activation_key char(32), extras text)default
      charset=utf8');
  mysql_query('insert into user_accounts values(1,"'
      .addslashes($admin).'", "'.md5($adpass).'",
      1, \'["_superadministrators"]\',"","")');
  mysql_query('create table groups(id int auto_increment not
      null primary key,name text)default charset=utf8');
  mysql_query('insert into groups values
      (1,"_superadministrators"),(2,"_administrators")');
  mysql_query('create table pages(id int auto_increment not
      null primary key,name text, body text, parent int, ord
      int, cdate datetime, special int, edate datetime, title
      text, template text, type varchar(64), keywords text,
      description text, associated_date date, vars text)
      default charset=utf8');
  $config='<?php $DBVARS=array('
    .'"username"=>"'.addslashes($dbuser).'",'
    .'"password"=>"'.addslashes($dbpass).'",'
    .'"hostname"=>"'.addslashes($dbhost).'",'
    .'"db_name"=>"'.addslashes($dbname).'");';
  file_put_contents('../.private/config.php',$config);
}
echo json_encode($errors);
```

Because there are no errors, we know the configuration is complete and ready for installation, so we carry on with the installation, installing the core database tables and then recording the values to the config file `/.private/config.php`.

Finally, the result is returned to the client-side.

On the client-side, the result contains no errors, so we display a simple message saying it's all done. Replace the `step3()` stub function with this:

```
function step3(){
  $('#content').html(
    '<p>Installation is complete. Your CMS is ready for '
    +'population.</p>'
    +'<p>Please <a href="/ww.admin/">log in</a> to the '
    +'administration area to create your first page.</p>'
  );
}
```

And with that in place, the CMS is installed:

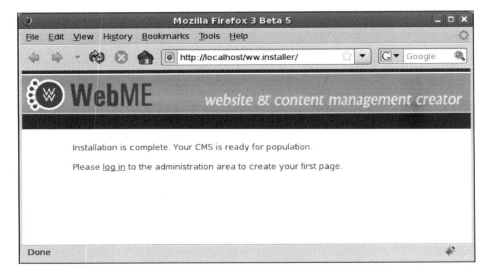

Note that this does not mean the installer is absolutely finished.

Other problems may arise later, due to unforeseen incompatibilities between the system and the CMS, which allowed the installation to complete, but don't allow some unspecified function to work.

When these things happen, all you can do is to find out what the problem is—maybe you are missing a certain PHP extension or Pear library—add a test for that problem to the installer, and re-run the installation to make sure that fixes it.

But, for the most part, this is it.

Summary

In this chapter, we completed the CMS by adding an installer.

You now have a completed CMS, including administration area, plugins, and all the extensibility that you could possibly need.

From this point forward, doing anything you want with the CMS is up to you—add new plugins to give new features, or redesign the administration area to suit your own company. You are free to do as you wish with it.

Have fun!

Index

Symbols

$custom_tabs array 180
$custom_type_func 195
$DBVARS array 144, 163
$menus array 167
$pagecontent variable 175
$PAGEDATA 158
$PAGEDATA object 158
$page table data 181
$plugin 156
$plugin array 159, 163
$PLUGINS array 159, 174, 180
$PLUGINS_TRIGGERS array 174
$PLUGIN_TRIGGERS array 174
$plugin version 163
$posopts variable 139
__autoload function
  installing 113
.click() events 135
.destroy() method 273
.htaccess 14
_link 168
.load() function 269
{{MENU}} template function 139
#menu-top element 166
.mouseover() events 135
.outerHeight() function 135
#page-comments-submit anchor 175
.sortable() even 204
.sortable() plugin 204
/ww.admin 13

A

action parameter 94
ad-gallery plugin 234
admin area, CMS 10
admin area login page
  about 38
  forgotten password section 55-60
  logging in 47-52
  logging out 53, 55
  working 38-46
administration area
  theme, selecting 141-143
admin sections 155

B

bit field 96
buildRightWidget() function 260

C

CentOS 5.2
  about 296
  settings 298
CKeditor
  about 104, 221, 273
  displaying 104
  downloading 104
  URL 104
CMS
  about 7
  admin area 8
  admin area login page 38-42
  advantages 10
  configuration details, adding 309-314
  configuration file 15

database structure 14
database tables 36-38
directory structure 12, 13
event, adding to 173-177
front-end 8
installing, in CMS 300, 301
missing features, checking 304-308
page management 69
pages, working 69
roles 34
user management 33
user, types 33
CMS core 7
CMS events 154, 155
CMS files 12
config_rewrite() function 159, 173
configuration details
  adding 309-314
configuration file
  about 15
  executable format 15
  parse-able format 15
Content Delivery Network (CDN) 42
content snippet plugin
  creating 255, 256
contentsnippet_show() function 265
core 154
custom content forms
  adding, to page admin form 194-200

D

database structure, CMS 14
datepicker plugin 92
dates
  about 91
  formats 91, 92
dbAll() function 61
DBVARS['plugins'] variable 160
design templates 115
directory structure, CMS 12, 13

E

event
  about 12
  adding, to CMS 173-177

F

FastTemplate 117
FCKeditor
  about 104
fg_menu_show() function 138
filament group menu (fg-menu)
  preparing 134-136
file management
  KFM used 107-112
finish trigger 155
form
  displaying, on front-end 206-211
form_display() function 207
form fields
  defining 200-205
formfieldsAddRow() function 203, 204
form_send_as_email() 213
Forms plugin
  about 187
  form fields, defining 200-205
  page admin section 190-193
  plugin config 188-190
  saved data, exporting 217-219
  working 187, 188
form submission
  handling 211
  saving, in database 215, 216
  via e-mail 214, 215
form_submit() 211
form_template_generate() function 207
form_url parameter 256
front-end, CMS
  about 8, 9
  form, displaying 206-211
front-end gallery
  displaying 232-235
front-end navigation menu
  creating 126-132

G

gather plugin data 195
getInstanceByName method 29
getInstanceBySpecial method 29
getInstance method 29
getRelativeUrl() method 128
getURLSafeName() method 128

grid-based gallery
creating 239-243
guest 295

H

Hello World example
building 16
front controller 20-22
page data, reading from database 23-31
setting up 16-19
host 295
hot-linking 107
HTMLarea 104

I

Image Gallery plugin
creating 221
front-end gallery display 232-235
grid-based gallery 239
images, uploading 226
initial settings 224, 225
page admin tabs 223, 224
plugin configuration 222
settings tab 235
images
deleting 230, 231
kfmget mod_rewrite rule, adding 229, 230
uploading 226, 227
uploads, handling 228, 229
image uploads
handling 228, 229
index.php 14
initial settings, Image Gallery plugin 224
inline linking 107
installer 303
installer application
core system changes 302
creating 302
installer 303
is_spam field 177

J

jQuery
adding, to menu 133, 134
jstree plugin 100

K

KFM
about 107
downloading 107
installing 109
working 108
kfm_dir_openNode() function 227
kfmget mod_rewrite rule
adding, to images 229, 230

L

leeching 107

M

MD5 37
menu
filament group menu (fg-menu), preparing 134-136
integrating 137-141
jQuery, adding 133, 134
menu_build_fg() function 127
missing features, CMS
checking 304-308
mod_rewrite 12
mouseenter event 136

O

outerWidth() function 135

P

page admin
tabs, adding to 179-185
page admin form additions 155, 156
page admin, Forms plugin
custom content forms, adding 194-200
page admin section, Forms plugin 190-193
page admin tabs, Image Gallery plugin
creating 223, 224
page_comments_ 158
page_comments_comment table 178
Page Comments menu item 169
page_comments_show() 174
page content
running, on Smarty 150-152

page-content-created event 155
page management 69
page management system
  about 91
  dates 91
  file management, KFM used 107-112
  page, saving 94
  pages, deleting 101-103
  rich-text editing, CKeditor used 103, 104
  top-level pages, creating 98
pages
  administrating 78-87
  deleting 101-103
  hierarchical viewing 73-77
  listing, in admin area 70-73
  moving 77
  parent select-box, filling 87, 89
  rearranging 78
  saving 94-97
  working 69
pages_delete function 102
pages_new() function 191
page_tab array 157
page template
  selecting, in administration area 147, 149
page_type function 195
page types 155
page variable, Image Gallery plugin
  autostart 225
  captionlength 225
  directory 225
  slidedelay 225
  thumbsize 225
  type 225
  x 225
  y 225
panel
  deleting 282, 283
  disabling 280, 282
panel admin area 251
panel-body element 259
panel plugin
  creating 245-247
panels
  about 245
  displaying 252-255
  displaying, on front-end 264-266
  registering 248-250

panels_init() function 254
panels_show() function 246, 250, 264
panels table, fields
  body 247
  disabled 247
  id 247
  name 247
  visibility 247
PHAML 117
plugin config, Forms plugin 188-190
plugin.php file, Image Gallery plugin
  creating 222, 223
plugins
  about 11, 153, 154
  admin sections 155
  CMS events 154, 155
  configuration 156-158
  custom admin area menu 166-172
  database tables, handling 163
  enabling 158-161
  page admin form additions 155
  page comments plugin 164
  page types 155
  upgrades, handling 163

Q

QEMU 294

R

reCAPTCHA library
  URL 44
recaptcha-php script
  downloading 45
RemoteSelectOptions plugin 191
render() call 155
rich-text editing
  CKeditor, used 103-106
Rich-text Editors (RTEs) 103
role 34, 35
RPC API 10

S

saved data, Forms plugin
  exporting 217

settings tab code, Image Gallery plugin
  writing 235-239
SHA1 37
showWidgetForm() stub function 268
Site Options menu 169
Smarty
  running, on page content 150-152
smarty_setup() function 121, 249
Smarty templating engine
  setting up 120-126
src parameter 107
start trigger 155
status field 177
step1_finished() function 308
step1() function 308
step1_verify() function 306
step2() stub function 309
step2_verify2() stub function 311
step2_verify() unction 310
step3() stub function 314

T

tabs
  adding, to page admin 179-185
template
  about 116
  example 116, 117
  working 116
template_functions array 246
templating engines
  about 117
  FastTemplate 117
  issue 117
  PHAML 117
  PHP 116
  Smarty 116
  Twig 117
  working 115-117
theme
  about 115
  file layout 118, 119
  selecting, in administration area 141-147
  working 115
theme field 144
this.chooseItem() function 135

top-level pages
  creating 98, 99
  sub-pages, creating 100, 101
trigger
  about 12
Twig 117
typeOf() function 263

U

updateWidgets() function 262, 290
upgrade.php script 165
user_accounts table
  activation_key 36
  active 36
  creating 36-38
  email 36
  extras 36
  groups 36
  id 36
  password 36
user management
  about 33, 60, 61
  user, creating 64-67
  user, deleting 63, 64
  user, editing 64-67

V

VirtualBox
  downloading 294
  installing 294, 295
Virtual Machine (VM)
  about 294
  CMS, installing 300, 301
  guest OS, installing 295
  installing 295-300
Virtuozzo 294
VM engines
  QEMU 294
  VirtualBox 294
  Virtuozzo 294
  VMWare 294
  Xen 294
VMWare 294

W

WebME (Website Management Engine) 7
widget forms
  creating 267-270
  panel, deleting 282, 283
  panel, disabling 280, 282
  panel page visibility, admin area
      code 283-288
  panel page visibility, front-end code 289
  snippet content, saving 274-276
  widget header visibility 277
  widget page visibility 289-291
  widgets, disabling 279, 280
  widgets, renaming 276, 277
widget header visibility() function 277, 279
widget_rename() function 277

widgets
  about 245
  disabling 279, 280
  renaming 276, 277
  adding, to panel 256
  displaying 257, 258
  dragging, into panels 258-261
  panel contents, saving 261-264
widgets_init() function 257
widget_toggle_disabled() function 279
widget_visibility() function 289
ww_widgets array 258

X

Xen 294
x_kfm_loadFiles() function 227

Thank you for buying
CMS Design Using PHP and jQuery

About Packt Publishing

Packt, pronounced 'packed', published its first book "*Mastering phpMyAdmin for Effective MySQL Management*" in April 2004 and subsequently continued to specialize in publishing highly focused books on specific technologies and solutions.

Our books and publications share the experiences of your fellow IT professionals in adapting and customizing today's systems, applications, and frameworks. Our solution based books give you the knowledge and power to customize the software and technologies you're using to get the job done. Packt books are more specific and less general than the IT books you have seen in the past. Our unique business model allows us to bring you more focused information, giving you more of what you need to know, and less of what you don't.

Packt is a modern, yet unique publishing company, which focuses on producing quality, cutting-edge books for communities of developers, administrators, and newbies alike. For more information, please visit our website: www.packtpub.com.

About Packt Open Source

In 2010, Packt launched two new brands, Packt Open Source and Packt Enterprise, in order to continue its focus on specialization. This book is part of the Packt Open Source brand, home to books published on software built around Open Source licences, and offering information to anybody from advanced developers to budding web designers. The Open Source brand also runs Packt's Open Source Royalty Scheme, by which Packt gives a royalty to each Open Source project about whose software a book is sold.

Writing for Packt

We welcome all inquiries from people who are interested in authoring. Book proposals should be sent to author@packtpub.com. If your book idea is still at an early stage and you would like to discuss it first before writing a formal book proposal, contact us; one of our commissioning editors will get in touch with you.

We're not just looking for published authors; if you have strong technical skills but no writing experience, our experienced editors can help you develop a writing career, or simply get some additional reward for your expertise.

jQuery 1.3 with PHP

ISBN: 978-1-847196-98-9   Paperback: 248 pages

Enhance your PHP applications by increasing their
responsiveness through jQuery and its plugins.

1. Combine client-side jQuery with your server-
   side PHP to make your applications more
   efficient and exciting for the client

2. Learn about some of the most popular jQuery
   plugins and methods

3. Create powerful and responsive user interfaces
   for your PHP applications

PHP 5 CMS Framework
Development - 2nd Edition

ISBN: 978-1-849511-34-6   Paperback: 416 pages

This book takes you through the creation of a
working architecture for a PHP 5-based framework
for web applications, stepping you through the
design and major implementation issues, right
through to explanations of working code examples

1. Learn about the design choices involved in
   the creation of advanced web oriented PHP
   systems

2. Build an infrastructure for web applications
   that provides high functionality while avoiding
   pre-empting styling choices

Please check **www.PacktPub.com** for information on our titles

3867924R00188

Printed in Great Britain
by Amazon.co.uk, Ltd.,
Marston Gate.